CUSTOM
GUNSMITHING
for Self-Defense Firearms

Steve Sieberts

Published by

Gun Digest® Books, an imprint of F+W Media, Inc.
Krause Publications • 700 East State Street • Iola, WI 54990-0001
715-445-2214 • 888-457-2873
www.krausebooks.com

To order books or other products call toll-free 1-800-258-0929
or visit us online at www.gundigeststore.com

Cover photography by Steve Sieberts
All photos by author except where noted.

ISBN-13: 978-1-4402-4731-6
ISBN-10: 1-4402-4731-5

Designed by Dane Royer
Edited by Corey Graff

Printed in The United States of America

10 9 8 7 6 5 4 3 2 1

DEDICATION

Anyone who writes a book, never does so in a vacuum, and this one is no exception. I've had many friends and mentors over the years who've influenced me in my career in professional gunsmithing. I've always been interested in firearms — not only shooting them, but how they worked — and I knew at a young age that I wanted to make a career of it. One of the first major influences in my career was "Doc" Krekle at the Colorado School of Trades Gunsmithing School. Doc taught the Design and Function portion of the course and the wealth of knowledge he brought to the program was immeasurable. Other influencers in my profession were the pistolsmiths on the Army Marksmanship Unit's pistol team: Sgt. Snow, Sgt. Heilman, and Dalton Graham, who worked on our guns to make sure we had firearms that could deliver National Championship-winning scores, if we could do our part. Make no mistake. Those custom gunsmiths instilled much confidence in the shooters to win every time they stepped up to the line. That is no small contribution, and goes way beyond simply customizing and maintaining the guns.

Another person that heavily influenced me was Bruce Woodford, who taught the Army's National Match Armorer's Course at Rock Island Arsenal. Bruce held two Distinguished Badges, one as a rifle competitor, the other in pistol. He also repaired and customized the guns at Camp Perry's National Championships each year. I attended his month-long school, and experienced what building custom match-grade firearms for high-level competitive shooting was all about. Finally, I would also like to dedicate this book to my wife Lori, who has stuck with me through the thick and the thin, and knew early on that my chosen career would not bring fabulous fame nor riches in monetary means, but other treasures like life experiences and great memories. And, last but not least, I dedicate this book to my two children, Kyle and Kelly, who have taught me what is most important in life.

ABOUT THE AUTHOR

Steve Sieberts has been a competitive shooter, gunsmith, firearms writer and editor for over 40 years. He was a member of the original Southwest Pistol League in the mid-70s, shot Bullseye with the U.S. Army Marksmanship Unit summer team in 1981 and 1984, and was a permanent member of the U.S. Army Marksmanship Training Unit (USAMU) #1 at Ft. Meade, Maryland, for the 1982-83 shooting seasons. While competing with USAMU, Sieberts achieved the NRA 2600 award in 1983 and his Distinguished Pistol Shot Badge that same year, then the President's Hundred Tab in 1984. He was a Paratrooper and Small Arms Technician with the 82nd Airborne Division's Small Arms Repair facility for 3 ½ years and NCOIC of the Small Arms Shop for the 8th Infantry Division, (FRG) for 18 months. He has attended five gunsmithing schools, including the Colorado School of Trades, Army National Match Gunsmithing course at Rock Island Arsenal, NRA Riflesmithing Course, and two 1911 pistolsmithing courses sponsored by the NRA and taught by Fred Wardell, of Wardell Custom, and Dalton Graham, former pistolsmith for USAMU. Sieberts has attended numerous factory armorer's courses, including Glock, Remington, Sig, Beretta, HK, Smith & Wesson and Ruger. He's also attended two Army sniper schools, and the Oehler Ballistics Course.

Formerly the Chief Gunsmith for a classified Department of Defense contractor responsible for the building, testing, evaluation and prototype development of small arms systems for U.S. Special Operations forces for over ten years, Sieberts specializes in building and testing tactical 1911 handguns and precision bolt-action rifles, as well as testing and evaluation and building of various classified prototype small arms systems. He has been an IPSC competitor on and off since the 1970s, and currently shoots IDPA at his local range. Sieberts is a regular contributor for many publications, including *Shooter's Bible*, *SWAT*, *American Handgunner*, *Guns and Weapons for Law Enforcement*, and was the Contributing Editor for *The Varmint Hunter*. He is a former writer and editor for *Concealed Carry Handguns*, and *Pocket Guns* and was editor of the 2015 and 2016 *Gun World Buyer's Guide*, *2017 Knives Illustrated*, and the Gunsmithing Editor at *Gun World*, where he wrote a monthly column on gunsmithing tips and projects. This is Steve's second book for *Gun Digest* Books, his first being the *Gun Digest Guide to Competitive Pistol Shooting*. He lives in the South with his wonderful wife of 27 years, his two beautiful and amazing children, and three dopey dogs. In his spare time, he enjoys the three B's of life: barbeque, bourbon and baseball, not necessarily in that order.

FOREWORD

BY FRANK BROWNELL, CEO, BROWNELLS, INC.

Bob Brownell, my dad, was a gunsmith. There are family stories about him moving my crib around — with me in it — to make more room for the gunsmithing tools and supplies that shipped to his house in Montezuma, Iowa. As he built the business that would someday become Brownells, he constantly worked on guns, first for his friends and neighbors, and then for people around the country. He particularly loved bluing, and considered it an art form. Even though he closed his own gunsmith shop in 1951 to focus on growing Brownells, he considered himself a gunsmith for the remainder of his life.

Needless to say, I've always had a soft spot in my heart for gunsmiths. Steve Sieberts is a highly-skilled, knowledgeable gunsmith who graduated from the Colorado School of Trades and worked for the Department of Defense on firearms projects for U.S. Special Operations, and even shot with the Army Pistol Team. He knows a thing or two about guns and gunsmithing, and certainly knows his way around a bench and a lathe.

Anyone involved in gunsmithing — the tinkerer or hobbyist, the beginner or the experienced 'smith, even the competition shooter looking to give himself an extra edge — will learn something from this book. There are chapters about general projects any gunsmith must know how to accomplish, as well as more high-level sections about building a truly custom 1911 pistol or Remington 700 rifle. There's also information about Steve's personal story, his "journey" if you will, in becoming the expert gunsmith he is today.

That's one of the things I like the most about guns and gunsmithing — the stories. Every gun has stories connected to it. Maybe it was the shotgun your grandfather shot his first deer with when he was only a young boy. Perhaps it's a rifle that used to belong to a good friend, and you remember the day he watched you make that amazing shot on game. I myself love the memories of squirrel hunting with Dad, me with my .22 and him with the flintlock squirrel rifle he built.

That's one of the amazing things about gunsmiths. With their knowledge and skill, they keep the guns of yesteryear working just like they did when new. A good gunsmith can equip you to hunt deer with the very same shotgun your grandpa carried. Even better, a good gunsmith can help you pass down that gun to your own child or grandchildren, in fine working order, shooting just as straight and true as it did all those years ago.

And gunsmiths themselves become characters in our stories — the smith who cut down the stock to fit your son for his very first trap shoot, or who somehow miraculously fixed your rifle during your once-in-a-lifetime sheep hunt out West, or whose shop became one of your favorite places to visit in the whole world, and who became a good friend, too.

All these things make gunsmiths just a little bit different, maybe even a little more special than other knowledgeable professionals whose services we seek. Gunsmiths work on guns. And while guns certainly are tools, they are so much more than that. Guns are history, both national and family. Guns are fun days spent in the field and at the range. Guns are venison steaks seared perfectly on the grill and shared with friends. Guns might have even saved your life or the life of somebody you love, of which is the primary focus of this book. And finally, guns are the physical proof of the unique freedoms we enjoy here in the United States.

For those of us who count ourselves members of the "gun culture," or who might even label ourselves as "gun nuts," a gunsmith is the person who keeps our guns running, who makes them fit us well and shoot better. A gunsmith is the person we turn to for knowledge and advice. And a visit to our favorite gunsmith's shop feels more like going to a friend's house than patronizing a business. Steve Sieberts is a gunsmith, and a good one at that. – Frank Brownell

INTRODUCTION

One of the greatest, most enjoyable aspects in the field of gunsmithing is its history as a profession. Firearms, as we know them today, go back to 13th-Century China. Gunpowder was invented in the 9th Century, and it took 400 years to figure out how to make a tube, fill it with explosive gunpowder and launch the projectile. Rockets had been around since the invention of gunpowder and these were used to scare one's enemies, but the firearm didn't come about until much later. One of the drawbacks of these early firearms was that they tended to explode. This isn't bad if you're firing off rockets with long fuses at your enemy, but if you're holding onto a pipe filled with explosive powder and it goes off in your face, it tended to ruin the day of those early gunmakers. This early Chinese contraption was called the "fire lance" and was the forerunner to all modern firearms. Also used in those early days were variations of "hand cannons," which actually looked like miniature cannons and were held in the hand, hence the name. These hand cannons go back to the Yuan Dynasty in the 13th and 14th Centuries. By the 13th Century, blackpowder and cannons had spread to Europe, most likely over the Silk Road or by invading Mongol warriors. The earliest known example of a firearm in Europe was found in Estonia and dates back to the 1390s.

In the early Modern Age of firearms, around the 15 and 1600s, these hand cannons evolved into modern matchlocks and wheelocks, and then ultimately flintlocks. The firearm had spread throughout Europe, and the early craftsmen gravitated toward these new implements. All of these early firearms needed skilled craftsman to build and maintain them, since the early guns were hand built one at a time, and when parts wore out or broke, they needed to be handmade and then hand-fitted to each individual firearm. Mass production and the concept of interchangeable parts would not be introduced to the firearms field until much later.

The professional gunsmithing trade had its start in Medieval Europe with the rise of guilds, which were professional organizations for tradesmen who were not allowed to work their crafts without such membership. There were guilds for most of the trades, including blacksmiths, weavers, and various other professions. A person would join the guild, and then work their way up from Apprentice, Journeyman, and finally Master. Attaining the title of Master in any trade meant that the Journeyman had completed a work, or piece, that was worthy of the person being elevated to the next level, hence the term Masterpiece. Also, because of the custom nature of the work, many gunsmiths were specialized in one area or another. Many were carpenters that worked exclusively on wood stocks, and the blacksmiths would work on the metal lockwork and barrels. The first true gunsmithing guild in Suhl, Germany was formed in 1463.

German, Belgian, and Swiss gunsmiths immigrated to the newly formed United States in the 17th Century, settling into the Pennsylvania area, bringing their extensive gunsmithing skills with them. The Kentucky rifle was developed from the experiences of these Master German gunsmiths and it was these rifles — and the men who built and maintained them — that opened up the American frontier. Gunsmiths are no longer required to belong to guilds in order to practice the art, although there are professional gunsmithing guilds today that will be covered in this book.

No book about gunsmithing would be complete without an overview of the man that could be described as arguably the greatest gunsmith and firearms inventor that has ever lived: John Moses Browning. His brilliant mind and genius in firearms design carries through to firearms that are still very much in use today. What many people don't know about Browning, is that his father and son were excellent gunsmiths and firearms designers in their own right. In fact, John Browning first learned about firearms manufacturing and design at his father's gun shop in Utah in the 1870s. John M. Browning was the holder of 128 patents in firearms design. His father encouraged him to think about ways to improve existing designs as well as to come up with new ones. When Browning died of heart failure on November 26, 1926, he was at the work-

bench in his son Val's gunshop, working on a new self-loading pistol that would later become the excellent P-35 Browning Hi-Power.

Modern custom gunsmithing today has evolved from simple repairs and maintenance of firearms to producing modern works of art. Competitive shooting today, whether it's with handguns, rifles or shotguns, has become more sophisticated and specialized. The craftsmanship and artistry of the modern custom gunmaker has elevated the custom firearm to a high art form.

This book will discuss and demonstrate procedures that are used by many professional working gunsmiths today. These procedures are a reflection of my experience and expertise, and do not represent the only way to perform a certain procedure, only what has worked for me and the professional gunsmiths that I've learned from over a 40-year span. I once heard a good say-

ing, that there is more than one way to train a dog or catch a fish, and this is true of gunsmithing; there are more ways to get similar results than the ones I show in this book. If you use different tools or procedures to get the same results in the same amount of time, then those techniques and/or procedures are fine. Some of the procedures that I show in the book could be accomplished much easier with heavy machinery like lathes and milling machines. However, this book is geared toward the beginning to intermediate gunsmith or hobbyist, and assumes you do not have machine tools in your garage or basement workshop. For example, I show how to rebarrel rifles with pre-threaded and short-chambered barrels, when in fact, if I had the use of an appropriate-sized lathe, I would not use a pre-chambered barrel, instead opting to thread and chamber the barrel myself, even though the end result may or may not be any better.

Finally, working on firearms is a great hobby, and very rewarding and personally satisfying, but remember, we are working with firearms, and safety is paramount. In my workshop, I also have a reloading bench, so at any time there is loaded ammunition and gunpowder in close proximity to firearms. Additionally, I also use dummy cartridges for function testing and, while these are easy to spot, a live round could possibly work its way from my reloading bench to my workbench, so I always make sure there is no ammunition anywhere near the workbench before I start a project, and I always identify the dummy cartridges for the caliber on which I'm working. Lastly, eye protection is mandatory when working on firearms. Virtually all firearms use some type of spring to perform a variety of functions, and these springs are under high compression. Releasing these compressed springs can result in the spring and possibly other parts being launch at high speed. ALWAYS wear eye protection when working on firearms. You will also be working with compressed air and solvents, so the risk of getting foreign objects in your eyes is high. I have had a foreign object embedded in my eye and it's not fun. Here's my story and I hope you can learn a lesson from what happened to me.

I was a young, 45B Small Arms Technician and paratrooper assigned to the 82nd Airborne Division's Headquarters and Main Support Shop's 782nd Maintenance Battalion, working in the DS/GS (Direct Support/ General Support) Small Arms Repair Shop. We were the highest level of military small arms support for the entire 82nd Airborne Division, and would provide support to other units at Fort Bragg, such as the 5th and 7th Special Forces, when asked. In other words, if we could not fix the weapon, that usually meant the receiver was unserviceable and had to be sent up to the civilian shop to be demilled, or cut up with a blowtorch. There were four of us working in the shop at the time, and we had a tank repair shop next door where they maintained the Division's Sheridan tanks. One of the tank repairmen was in our shop, because they didn't have much to work on that day. I was walking through the shop when, as he was sitting at a bench, he took a ball peen steel hammer and hit the jaws of the bench vise with it. He was bored, I think. I turned my head just as he did this, to tell him not to do that as it was dangerous to hit steel with steel. When the hammer struck the vise, it seemed like a bit of dust went into my eye, though I didn't think much of it. Later that night, every time I blinked, the inside of my eyelid felt like it was being scratched. I went on sick call the next morning when I could barely open my eye. In medical, I explained what had happened the day before, and they immediately ran a quick test and confirmed I had a very small flake of steel embedded in my cornea. I was not wearing safety glasses at the time of the accident, because I wasn't actually working at my bench. They laid me on my back, turned out the lights, squirted some type of gel into my eye and turned on a blue fluorescent light to make the steel glow. They then placed the tip of a hypodermic needle onto the steel fragment and, using the suction of the syringe, popped the steel fragment out of my eyeball. Not fun. They then patched me up and sent me on my way. The downside was that now, anytime I get an MRI, the first question asked is if I have ever had any metal foreign objects in my body, and I have to say yes. MRI's work like a giant magnet, so any magnetic part in your body will be pulled out of your body at very high speed when the MRI machine is turned on. So, I always answer yes, and then I have to get my eyes examined to ensure there are absolutely no foreign objects or fragments remaining.

Also, not as traumatic, but just as dangerous, I cannot tell you how many times my co-workers or I have accidently let spring-loaded parts fly across the shop. Work in a gunshop long enough and you will experience this many, many times. Take this lesson and always wear eye protection when working on firearms.

TABLE OF CONTENTS

Chapter 1

WHY CUSTOM GUNSMITHING?

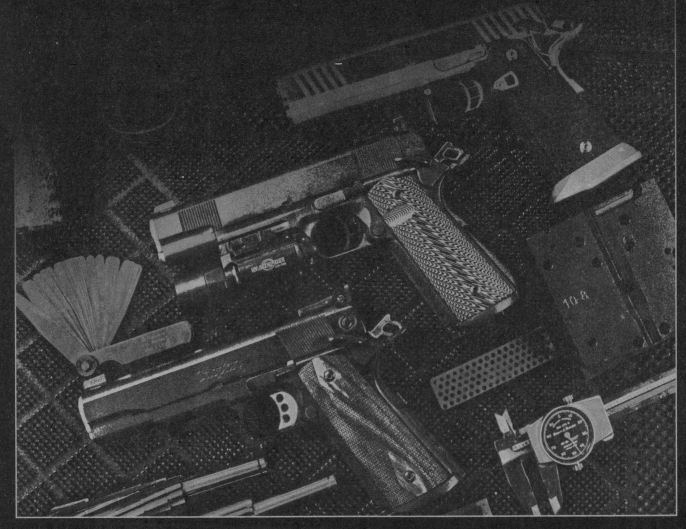

This book is about a specific aspect of gunsmithing, and that is custom gunsmithing firearms that are used for self-defense. Gunsmithing, by definition, is the repair and maintenance of firearms, but custom gunsmithing, or modifying the specific firearm for a specific purpose, or simply to enhance the factory gun in a way that makes it more accurate, reliable, valuable or simply easier to shoot takes a very specific set of skills. Firearm repair means the gun is malfunctioning in some fashion because of a worn or broken part, and the repair usually involves simply replacing the problematic part. Whereas, custom gunsmithing involves replacing a perfectly good part with one that performs the function better than the original.

A good example of this is installing a match barrel on the 1911 handgun. This is a common enhancement for competitive shooters. The original factory barrel may be brand new, and may not have ever had more than just a few live rounds fired through it. The barrel is capable of delivering an acceptable level of accuracy for many hundreds of thousands of rounds, but is not capable of delivering the level of accuracy desired by the owner, or demanded by the type of competitive shooting for which it's being used. So, an enhanced part — in this case a match-grade barrel — is installed to improve the gun's performance. This is what differentiates custom gunsmithing from general gunsmithing. In the latter, you are enhancing the base level of performance the gun is capable of delivering.

Sometimes, those enhancements may not be tangible, the performance of which can be measured with tools like micrometers and Ransom Rests. These enhancements may be more of a functional nature, like installing a better recoil pad on a rifle, a set of hi-vis sights on a shotgun, a beavertail grip safety on a 1911, or a red dot sight on your revolver. The recoil pad may not improve the accuracy in a measurable way, but if it allows you more comfort, or helps you use the gun in a more effective manner, then that custom product or modification has done its job. Sometimes, such enhancements may or may not actually improve the gun in any quantifiable way, but if you feel that the modification performed is helping, then your perception of the enhancement has accomplished its mission. Some of the modifications outlined in this book fall into that category. The custom enhancement is designed to allow you to more effectively use the firearm for its intended use in either a tangible or perceived way. So, where the general gunsmith needs to be able to troubleshoot, disassemble, repair and reassemble a seemingly endless

GUNSMITHING LEGALITIES: DO YOU NEED A FEDERAL FIREARMS LICENSE?

One question that always comes up when discussing firearms repair, and gunsmithing in general, is: Does a gunsmith need to be licensed to engage in the business? The licensing agency for the firearms business, the Bureau of Alcohol, Tobacco, Firearms and Explosives, (ATFE) uses the phrase "engaged in the business" to define people that are differentiated from the home "hobbyist" gunsmith. If a gunsmith is "engaged in the business," it means that the person is deriving some type of income from the work of gunsmithing. Also, the IRS will get involved if you are exchanging gunsmithing services for cash or other tangible items, e.g., bartering — then you are engaged in the business for tax purposes.

So, if you install a match barrel in your buddy's 1911, and in exchange for your services, he fixes your transmission, you are effectively "engaged in the business" in the eyes of the ATFE and the IRS. In both instances, either for cash or tangible assets, you will need to apply to become a licensed dealer, since the ATFE does not have a separate license for a gunsmith, the dealer license covers you.

Also, remember, that if you decide to go this route, you will need to comply with all other applicable city, county, state and federal zoning, business and tax laws specific to your area. For example, if you want to start a simple gunsmithing business out of your home, one of the first things to do is apply for a zoning variance to open a home-based business. You'll need to comply with city zoning laws by getting a business license, and may even need to get written approval for your business from every household that resides within a 300-yard radius of your house. If anyone objects to the gunsmithing business — and you know someone will — you cannot go forward. Also, remember that you cannot have people ship you firearms for repair or modification, either through the U.S. Postal Service, or by any other means, without being a licensed dealer.

The ATFE does not typically allow a firearms dealer to operate from his or her place of residence. So, yes, you can perform gunsmithing for your shooting buddies and their friends and their friends' friends, but if tangible assets or services exchange hands, then you will be "engaged in the business," and will need to be licensed.

---

variety of firearms, the custom gunsmith may focus his or her skills on one specific firearm, and often, one specific firearm for a specific use. Good examples of this would be the riflesmith that only works on National Match Hi-power rifles for competition. Ask that 'smith to repair a worn hammer on a Winchester Model 12 shotgun, and they would most likely be lost, but in their world of NRA Hi-power rifle competition, they can take a box stock M1A or AR-15 rifle and, using their specific skills, make them into tack-driving shooting machines capable of winning National Championships.

Another example is the custom pistolsmith who only customizes the ever-popular Glock, or tricks out the timeless 1911A1. This is what separates this book from books on general gunsmithing. I'll guide you through the steps needed to perform custom gunsmithing on

several of the most popular firearms, including handguns, rifles and shotguns. Depending on your level of experience, you may or may not want to jump right into the more complex projects of custom gunsmithing, though most of the projects can be performed by someone with just a basic knowledge of gunsmithing tools and procedures. I'll outline some basic bench techniques, and walk you through the various operations step by step. If, at any time you feel like the technique or procedure is over your head, stop, take a step back, and try not to just plow through as hastiness can lead to negative results. If you have some experience in general gunsmithing and want to step up your game, this book will help you do that. If you are just starting out, stick to some of the simpler projects and techniques first, and then work your way up.

Chapter 2

SETTING UP THE
WORKSPACE

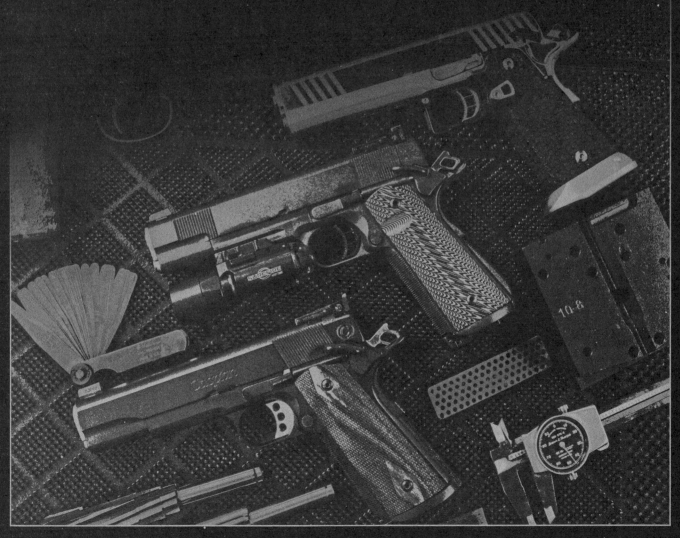

In order to set up a place to start gunsmithing, you have to start with a good foundation, and that means a sturdy bench. A quick Internet search will turn up many plans for various types of benches, and depending on your wallet and carpentry skills, can either be affordable and simple or expensive and extremely complex. Since I like to keep things simple and inexpensive, I have a bench design that I've used for not only gunsmithing, but reloading as well. In my shop, I'll be doing the work throughout this book in a space no larger than a two-car garage, but you can also do good work in much smaller spaces. Assuming you have at least this much space to work with, these bench plans will serve you well, and if you are working in larger or smaller spaces, you can scale these plans up or down to fit your needs and space. These benches are sturdy, inexpensive, easy to build with basic tools, don't require Master carpenter skills and can be put together in an afternoon, including time to gather up the materials.

The bench should be about 36 inches high, with solid legs on the corners. Make the bench 8-ft. long, with a bottom shelf for storage. Use 4x4s on the legs. A single 12 ft. 4x4 will make four legs. Or if you don't own a truck, two 6-ft. 4x4s or four 3-ft. 4x4 posts will do. Purchase outdoor-rated and treated lumber, to keep humidity from warping the legs. You will need 2x4s for the rails and connector pieces, and a single 4x8-ft. sheet of plywood or OSB (Oriented Strand Board) wood for the benchtop. The bench is 2 ft. wide, so have the lumber yard cut the 4x8 ft. sheet (that will become the top and bottom shelf) into two, 2x8 sheets. As a bonus, it's easier to transport home that way.

Thickness of the benchtop will depend on your budget, but I would not use anything thinner than 1/2 inch, while 5/8ths to 3/4-inch thickness is even better. Like I said, you want a sturdy workbench and if you use this space for reloading, you will likely be mounting reloading presses and doing bullet swaging. You may even need to reload large caliber ammunition like .50 BMG, or do case forming, operations that use heavy camming power and will put a lot of torque on the benchtop. For these heavy operations a sturdy bench is a must. Thicker benchtops are better.

Start by laying out two of the 4x4s and connect them with the 8-ft. 2x4s. These will become the sides of the workbench. Use wood screws and a good cordless drill to drive them. Build the bench with a bottom shelf with two 2x4s used to connect the 4x4s. Measure across the corners to make sure everything is square. Stand up the two sides of the bench and connect them on the ends with 2x4s. At this point, you can cut your shelf corner notches so the shelf fits around the legs of the bench. Now, you can secure the benchtop to the frame, and check to make sure everything is square. Finish by stapling or gluing a single piece of inexpensive indoor/outdoor carpeting to the top of the bench. Here's the link to the plans: http://www.hammerzone.com/archives/workshop/bench/below20xl.html

This is a basic bench that can be used for gunsmithing, reloading, or many shop duties. When I built mine, the entire workbench took about three hours, including the one-hour drive to my local home improvement store to purchase the materials, and about two hours to build. Total cost for materials was about $75.00. Once you have the bench constructed, cover it with inexpensive indoor/outdoor carpeting, and finally, a rubber mat on which you will be actually performing the work.

LEFT: The bench is laid out and legs are cut to length. RIGHT: The bench is starting to take shape.

The finished bench.

The rubber mat will protect the fragile finishes of your firearms, and covering with carpeting keeps splinters out of your skin.

Once you have the workbench set up, next is lighting, one of the most overlooked part of most shops. You cannot have too much lighting. Remember, you will be working on small, intricate gun parts, and making measurements down to .001 of an inch. Setting up fluorescent shop lights is pretty straightforward, but make sure to run the power cords where they won't get kinked or stepped on. Electrical fires are a real danger, especially when dirty, oily shop rags are combined with electricity. I have six banks of 4-ft. shop lights, and could use more. Once the shop lights are installed, you also need localized lighting at the spot you are working, to highlight small areas and procedures. I have an inexpensive bench mounted light that has a small magnifying glass incorporated into it. It is invaluable when working with small parts and performing detailed, intricate operations like wood or metal checkering.

Once the workbench and lighting are in place, the next step is to get some shop machinery and basic hand tools. When setting up a home gunsmithing shop, install a good cleaning station. This includes a quality air compressor and a solvent tank. Air compressors come in many sizes and price points, but mine cost about $100 from Sears and works really well. It does double duty filling up my kid's footballs, bicycle tires, etc. Note when selecting an air compressor the size of its tank and motor. More expensive compressors have larger tanks and bigger motors, and as such, have greater volume and put out more pounds per square inch of air volume.

The larger tanks require less running to fill, but mine can last several hours of use before refill. Remember, the larger compressors are typically used in automotive shops to drive air tools and you won't need that level of power. The smaller air compressors also take up less space and cost less, too. Mine is a 1 HP, 3-gallon tank that puts out 125 PSI, and I can pick it up and move it around the shop with one hand. It's served me very well for years. For a solvent tank, I like to keep it simple, and a metal coffee can half filled with paint thinner works really well and is about as simple as it gets. Paint thinner is cheap and works perfectly as a gun cleaning solvent. The downside to using a coffee can is that it's more difficult to clean large parts like rifle and shotgun receivers. There are solvent tanks available from machinery supply houses that have filters and lids, which cycle the solvent through a pump. These can be very useful and can be had from local resellers for about $100. The solvent used in these types of tanks is environmentally friendly and biodegradable. They do take up more space than a coffee can, so it may or may not be appropriate for your available shop space.

Other items for your cleaning station include an assortment of cleaning brushes and shop rags. Beware: When shop rags get dirty, especially oily, they become flammable. Always keep oily shop rags in some type of fire-retardant metal container until they can be properly disposed of. I like to use old GI ammo cans for this purpose, they seal up really well, and keep sparks and other fire hazards away from the rags. Keeping oily shop rags laying around the shop, with electrical cords, sparks and other fire hazards, is a recipe for disaster. Always keep a good fire extinguisher handy in the garage, just in case.

For cleaning, use a stiff bristle brush to loosen packed-in carbon fouling from corners of firearms like pistol slides and frames. Get a GI double-ended firearms brush, and a long bristle brush to scrub into holes and tubes. Finally, good quality lint-free shop rags can be purchased at your local home improvement store. Always get the lint-free rags, otherwise the lint will get into the firearm you have just cleaned, negating the point of cleaning the gun of debris in the first place.

The author's cleaning/drilling/air compressor station. It works very well for working on small parts, and is very economical to set up in a corner of the garage.

MACHINE TOOLS

You now need what accountants refer to as capital equipment. This means power tools and machinery. The types of equipment fall into two categories: bench mounted and handheld. The first is a good, quality drill press. This tool can be used for a variety of uses besides simply drilling holes. There are two types — bench mounted and floor standing — the size and capability determined by price, with the floor-mounted units capable of drilling larger and deeper holes more precisely. I have a small, bench-mounted drill press that has worked well for years. Drill presses do what they do very well, as long as the tool is used for its intended purpose. DO NOT use a drill press as a makeshift milling machine. The first milling machines were actually derived from early drill presses many, many years ago during the Industrial Revolution, but if you put an end

mill into a drill press today and try to remove metal from a part you will most assuredly shatter the end mill and the part you are working on will get chewed up as well. For example, do not put a dovetail cutter into a drill press thinking you can use the drill press to cut a dovetail into a 1911 slide to mount a sight. The drill press is not robust or precise enough, and the spindle does not rotate true enough for that type of work. The tool is not held precisely and will push with side pressure through the work, until it chatters and then breaks, shattering the tool and severely damaging the work. Drill presses are used to provide force to drill through material in a downward motion, thus using it to cut through material sideways will result in disaster.

Two other good pieces of capital equipment to have are a sturdy bench grinder and a belt sander. The bench grinder can be set up with various wheels to suit a specific purpose. There are wire wheels for burnishing and removing rust. Acquire grinding wheels of various grits to remove metal, sharpen tools like chisels, as well as shape tooling to fit specific uses — for example, grinding a screwdriver bit to precisely fit a screw slot. I have two wheels installed on my bench grinder; one a fine grinding wheel for metal shaping and removal, the other a medium grit deburring wheel like those used in machine shops for taking the sharp edges off of machined parts, which I use to "melt" the sharp edges of handguns edges, specifically on 1911 custom handguns.

The belt sander is required to perform procedures like installing a recoil pad, and the belts can be changed with different grits for specific purposes and to achieve various finishes. Note that the bench grinder and belt sander create a lot of dust, which is not good when working on firearms. So, when setting up these types of tools, always put them into the farthest corner of the shop, keeping the dust as far away from the workspace as possible. In professional gun shops, factory firearm manufacturing plants, and in gunsmithing schools, so-called "dirty rooms" are set up where all of the sanding, grinding and polishing are performed in closed off areas, specifically to keep the fine dust particles confined. Such rooms are fitted with filters to remove the dust from the room. When I was working in and running a DoD gunsmithing facility, we set up a "dirty room," which included a belt sander, floor-mounted bench grinder with a diamond wheel, and four large industrial buffing wheels equipped with varying grits for polishing barrels and other gun parts. This room had a separate air exchanger with filters to collect the dust and grit. Prior to setting up this room, every time someone

LEFT: The bench set up and ready to start working. RIGHT: This workbench is set up for sanding/grinding operations like recoil pad fitting, dehorning and deburring parts.

would do any amount of sanding or grinding, the dust would float about, settling on and in everything. You especially want to isolate this dust if you are doing any type of refinishing, such as painting fiberglass stocks and Parkerizing, as the dust will contaminate the wet finish.

The last item on your list of bench-mounted capital shop equipment should be a good, sturdy, bench mounted vise. Make no mistake; a bench vise will probably be your most used tool in the shop, and it pays to invest in the best you can get. I've always had good luck with Yost bench vises, although Wilton also makes good products. Try to avoid hobby grade, and stick with industrial grade or machinists' vises. The vise should have a swivel base, and jaw width should be no less than 4 inches. Yost brand vises have been around since 1908. Their industrial-grade machinist vise with a 4-inch jaw and swivel base is priced at $557.00, but you will hand it down to your grandkids, it's made that well. Just apply a little bit of axle grease to the main screw, and it will last forever. One item you will need to complement the bench vise is a good set of padded vise jaws, and Brownells sells a wide variety of both pads and inserts, so talk to them and they can help you pick out a set based on what type of work you are doing.

HAND TOOLS

That covers bench-mounted capital equipment, but what about handheld tools? There are three hand tools that are critical to the custom gunsmith. The first is a good, quality hand grinder. The most popular of which is the Dremel tool. This is an invaluable piece of tooling that can get into small spaces, and be fitted with a wide variety of bits designed for specific functions, including

sanding, grinding and polishing. As good as the Dremel tool is, and I've had several of them over my career, for my money the king of handheld gunsmithing grinding tools is the Foredom tool. The difference in the tools is that, while the Dremel is indeed a handheld tool, its motor and the polishing/grinding end are held in the hand, while the Foredom's motor is isolated, and the tool is mounted in a handpiece separated from the motor by a flexible shaft. The result is that the Foredom motor is larger and can generate more torque and horsepower, which translates into quicker results and longer life. The Foredom motor is much more robust. In the ten years I worked as a Gunsmith for the DoD, I had exactly one Foredom burn out on me and I used the tool virtually every day; whereas, when I was in gunsmithing school for a single year, I went through two Dremel tools. That may be anecdotal evidence, but that was my experience and was also the experience of other people at the Colorado School of Trades, as well as 'smiths who worked for and with me at the DoD facility. We all had Foredom tools at the facility, and they

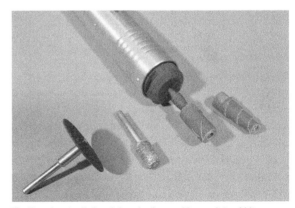

The Foredom tool's handpiece is shown with a variety of bits.

would usually last about 8-10 years or more. The Foredom is more expensive than the Dremel, so you will need to balance the price of each tool with the amount of usage you will get from each. Also, remember that the shank diameter used for the Foredom and the Dremel are the same, so if you want to start out with the less expensive Dremel tool, and later upgrade to the Foredom, you won't have to invest in new tooling — they both use 1/8th-inch shank diameter tools. If you can afford it, the 1/3rd HP Foredom tool is the Mac Daddy of handheld grinders, but the 1/8th HP tool is also great. There are two types of handpieces available for the Foredom, and you will want the hanging motor version of the tool, not the bench mounted, although either will work well and last for a good long time. If you get the Foredom, I recommend the model with the foot pedal, as you can use both hands on the handpiece to apply pressure and direction with the tool.

The second handheld tool you should get is an orbital palm sander. This tool is not gunsmith-specific, so if you like a particular brand of palm sanders, go with it. I've always had good luck with Makita brand, but any orbital palm sander that uses the 4x4-inch square sanding inserts will work. This will be invaluable for a variety of both wood and fiberglass stock work and finishing. The orbital motion of the sanding pad will result in better finishes.

Another hand tool that's useful is a cordless drill, and again, this is not a gunsmith-specific tool, so any decent brand will work. I actually have two — a 3/8ths cordless, the other a heavy duty ½-inch drill with a cord. Finally, to round out your shop, a good wet-dry shop vac will be invaluable to vacuum up wood, metal and fiberglass dust and shavings that will quickly fill the shop floor and workbenches.

MEASURING & MISCELLANEOUS TOOLS

Now that you have your shop set up, you need to fill it with measurement tools. Some of the tools that are needed are gunsmithing-specific, while others are generic. One important tool is a set of calipers. Calipers are used for making precise measurements of parts, and also measure how far you are progressing when filing or otherwise removing metal from a piece of work. These can be either digital or analog, but since this is a precision piece of equipment, buy the best you can afford. You don't want to be making wrong measurements. I use an analog Brown & Sharpe dial caliper, but Mitu-

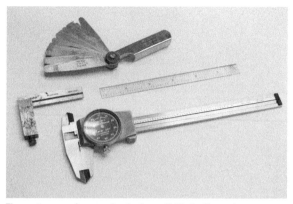

The vast array of measuring tools available to the custom gunsmith are only limited by the type of work he or she does. Standard tools are available for a wide range of uses. Clockwise from bottom: Dial calipers, machinists' square, machinists' scale, feeler gauges.

toyo and Starrett also make excellent ones, in both dial and digital form. Also needed will be a machinist scale. This is a small, metal 6-inch steel scale. I use this tool constantly when working on 1911s and other handguns. A micrometer is handy, but not necessary, unless you have a small lathe or milling machine in the workshop. Normally, the calipers will be quicker than — and nearly as precise as — a micrometer. I like to use my calipers since it gives me a rough measurement of both inside and outside diameters and has a rod for measuring depth, something a micrometer cannot do. Again, the micrometer can be had from several manufacturers, such as Starrett and Mitutoyo, and comes in either digital or analog versions.

WOOD AND METAL FILES

Probably no tool is used more by the gunsmith than the file in its various forms. Metalworking files come in many types, sizes, shapes and uses. Some of them are for general metal removal, others have very specific uses and a couple I have modified to suit a specific need. As you gain more experience, the number of tools, especially files, will grow.

Regardless of the type of file, the basic use is the same: to remove material in order to either shape or dimension the metal being worked on, or both. When I went through the Colorado School of Trades in the mid-80s, one of the first points our instructors made was that we had to take care of our tools, especially files. One way we did this was to make protective covers for all of our files. We got manila folders and cut out sleeves into which the files would slip. Most of us didn't see a

Here is a small sample of files used by the custom gunsmith. From left to right, flat #2 Swiss double-cut file, round file, dovetail file, flat bastard file, 20 LPI checkering file.

need for this, because those of us with files in our toolboxes in our garages at home were made for working on cars or whatever, and we were used to just throwing the files into the toolbox drawer. Our Instructors, however, would remind us that when unprotected files come into contact with others in the toolbox drawer, the constant contact would break and dull the teeth of the files, greatly diminishing their effectiveness. Files are expensive, and you want them to last.

Brownells ships all of their files with plastic sleeves, and I always keep them on until I'm ready to use them, then use it as a protective case until the file is worn out. I then simply throw out the file and sleeve.

Another useful tool to keep your files in good shape is a file card. File cards work like your toothbrush, keeping metal from getting stuck in the teeth. Aluminum is especially nasty when it gets clogged in the file, something it's very prone to as it's such a soft metal. If you keep filing when the teeth get clogged, it will cause "pinning," meaning clogged material in the files' teeth will dig deep grooves into the work as you file. Chalking the file's teeth will help keep it from clogging. This pinning condition means that you have to file more to remove these deep grooves, and you may not be able to remove them if it means taking off more material than what is available. So, you end up with deep scratches in the work that can't be removed. If you have filed down to where you need to be dimensionally, and the file starts pinning, you'll need to take off more material or leave the deep grooves in the metal. If the scratches and grooves are on the outside of the firearm it's very unsightly and unprofessional.

The solution is to file a few strokes with the file, clean the teeth with the file card, and keep filing. It will take longer, but you will achieve much better results.

You should also check your work as you go, which is always a good technique. Remember, when removing material, whether metal, wood or fiberglass, it's always easier to remove material than it is to put it back on. Go slow and check your work. After you gain experience, you will be able to judge how much material is being removed using a specific file, on a certain type of material, with a given technique.

For general metal work focus on four main file types: the flat file, in #0, #2, and #4 cut; the half-round file in #0 and #2 cut; round files in both parallel and tapered; and needle files. Specialty options include triangular files with safe edges for sight work, slide rail files, and metal checkering files that are listed in the lines per inch (LPI) that they cut. The range for these types of files is 20LPI, 30LPI, 40LPI, 50LPI, and 75LPI. I'll cover metal checkering with the 1911 project gun in a later chapter. The #0 files are very aggressive and will take off metal quickly. The upside is they make quick work of steel and aluminum and don't get clogged easily. The downside is, it's easy to take off too much material, too quickly. On the flip side, #4 files clog and pin the work easily and have to be cleaned often. Both files come in single and double cut. Single cut have one row of cutting teeth, while double cut have two rows of teeth in a cross-hatch pattern. My go-to file was always a #2 double-cut file. It takes off material at a pretty good clip and doesn't clog easily. The same goes for the half-round file. The #2, or possibly the #0 half round, is essential for fitting a beavertail grip safety.

One technique to know is draw filing. It's a technique that works by holding the file perpendicular to the work, and drawing the file toward or away from you. Remember, the file only cuts in one direction as the teeth are angled away from your body, so if you draw file using pressure in both directions you will

The 30 LPI checkering file laying out the vertical lines on a Caspian Officer's Model frame.

The author draw filing the top of a 1911 frame to prep it for slide fitting.

wear out the teeth prematurely. Get yourself some bar stock in steel and aluminum and practice filing, rather than working on actual firearms. It's definitely a skill that needs repetition to do well.

I always keep a large, flat file for this technique, although you can draw with any file. Since the file won't bend, surfaces remain flat and true. The trick is to keep pressure equal while you're filing, otherwise you can end up with angled surfaces when you wanted to keep things true. Use these files to act as a flat backer for sandpaper, a trick I use after I've gone as far as I can with the file and need to switch to something that will provide a smoother finish. I'll usually transition from the #4 file to something like #120-grit sandpaper strips, then #180 grit and then I'm done. Always remove file marks with progressively finer grits of sandpaper.

Needle files are handy for getting into tight places. It's a good idea to have a wide assortment of them. There are other specialty files the gunsmith will use. I've already talked a little about checkering files. Next are sight base files. These are triangular files that have safe edges, or no cutting teeth on two sides. This allows you to file a dovetail to fit a sight, removing material from one side of the dovetail. Remember to always look to see what the sight base requires. Sight base files come in either 60 or 65 degrees.

Different sights bases use different sight base angles. There isn't much difference visually between the 60- and 65-degree file, so be sure to make sure you have the right one before you start filing. Use the wrong file and you will have a sight that will never fit tight, one with large, ugly gaps between the sight base and the dovetail. When fitting a sight into a dovetail, you are trying to

get it "light tight." In other words, you want maximum contact between the sight and the dovetail with no light being visible through the joint when you hold it up to the light. At most gunsmithing schools, there is a practical exercise in which the student has to fit a piece of work into a dovetail "light tight" in order for the project to pass.

The other specialty tools are slide rail files, which are handy for fitting the 1911 slide to its frame, and a custom-made barrel-fitting file. This is a small, narrow single-cut file ground on a surface grinder to exactly .175 inches wide. The top barrel lug grooves on a match 1911 barrel are .180 inches wide, so you can fit the top lugs easily with this custom-made file.

The last point about files: always put a handle on them, no matter if they're a large flat file, or a small needle file. Brownells sells simple wooden handles that can be glued on easily. When the file is worn out, simply throw out the file and get a new one with a new handle.

POLISHING STONES

There are few tools in the gunsmith's toolbox more essential than polishing stones. Gunsmiths have been using polishing stones of various types and grits for over a hundred years to achieve a desired finish on metal, or to arrive at a final dimension in a manufacturing or prototyping facility.

The first Arkansas polishing stones were manufactured by the Norton Company, in 1823, and gunsmiths were probably using them the next day to work on the famous Hawken rifles that debuted that same year. Each of those rifles were handmade one at a time. Gunsmiths in that era were probably very interested to hear about a new tool that would help them achieve the final fit and finish of their famous rifles. There are many types and grits of stones, the grit being the porousness of the stone's material. The more porous the stone, the courser the grit and the lower the number assigned to it. Conversely, the finer the pores, the smoother the finish that can be achieved and the higher the number that is assigned. For example, a Hard Arkansas stone of 220 grit will be more aggressive and take off more material than a soft Washita stone of 1000 grit, which will take off less material, but leave a glass-like finish.

It can be a little confusing, and the choices available can be daunting, so for this book I'm going to simplify things for the person who's not a professional gunsmith

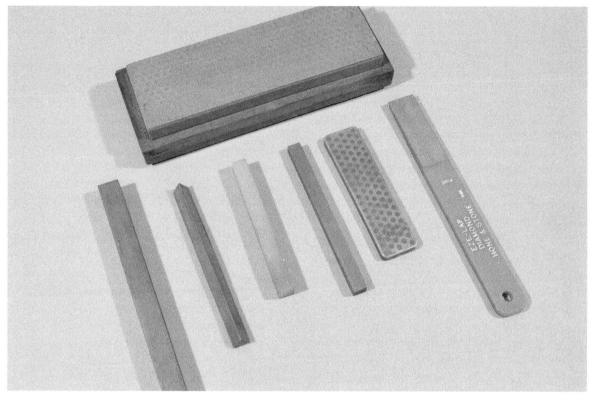

A small selection of polishing stones available to the custom gunsmith.

and doesn't need a wide array of stones, but still wants to have a good assortment to be able to tackle most of the common gunsmithing duties.

DIAMOND STONE

The first stone in this review is the hardest material out there, and is really indispensable. They are a little expensive, but once you purchase them, they will never wear out, won't break and do a really good job very quickly. The finish they produce is not mirror smooth, but for the majority of the work you'll do there are very few situations in which you'll need to get a mirror finish. I'm talking about diamond stones. They are available in a wide variety of grits, shapes and sizes. One of my most-used stones is a large diamond bench block. It runs about $90, but like I said earlier, it will never wear out. It's coarse, about 60 grit, so it's a very aggressive polishing stone, yet provides a large, flat surface to get a part very smooth and flat in a quick hurry. I use it often on the sides of parts that have friction surfaces, machining marks, burrs or tool marks that need to be removed, while keeping the surface flat. 1911 hammers and sears are a good example. Diamond stones come in several grits and configurations. They are available from

industrial tool supply companies. The smaller diamond stones and laps are available from Brownells.

INDIA, RUBY AND ARKANSAS STONE

The second most-used type of stone in my toolbox is a good, India stone. The India stone is a porous, soft stone made from aluminum oxide, available in various grits. It does a great job. It's aggressive, but not excessively. Being porous, it needs to be kept clean, otherwise it will load up and not cut as well. As with all stones, the India stone comes in various grits and shapes.

Another good stone to have in your toolbox is the ruby stone. This stone is very hard and non-porous, so it produces an exceptionally good finish. I like to use a ruby stone to go over the nose of the 1911 sear where the primary and secondary angles meet, when the shooter wants a trigger with a little softer roll off. Like the other stones, it comes in a variety of shapes, but being a synthetic ruby impregnated onto a hard plastic surface, only one grit is available.

The Hard Arkansas stone was actually one of the first stones ever made for sharpening tools and for gun work. First made in the early 1800s, it still does a fantastic job on firearm parts where a smooth finish and good material removal is desired. The Norton Company has been making Hard Arkansas stones since the 1820s and theirs still set the standard. Made from actual stone — not a synthetic silicon carbide or aluminum oxide — the Norton Arkansas stone produces excellent results when doing trigger work and most any other gunsmithing job. It really is the gold standard in polishing stones.

Another type of material popular for polishing stones is ceramic, which provides some distinct advantages to other types. For one, ceramic is not as prone to breakage. Anyone who has polishing stones in their toolbox also has pieces of polishing stones in their toolbox. This is usually the result of dropping them on the shop floor, plopping heavy parts on top of them, or just general use. Edges on stones are sharp and, after time, will chip and break. Ceramic stones are not unbreakable, but are less fragile than either Arkansas or India stones. They also cut very fast and leave a great finish. They don't cut as fast as an India stone, though, so you will have to experiment with various stones and judge each one for speed and finish. Go for the one that gives you the results you are looking for.

The last element to consider when talking about stones is lubricant. All stones need lubrication, the type determined by and depending on the type of use for which the stone is used. Lubes are essential to keep the material being worked on from clogging the stone and decreasing its cutting ability; it also contributes to a better finish. The synthetic stones, such as diamond, ruby and ceramics use water as a lube. In fact, with my large diamond bench stone, I simply put a few drops of water on it, and rinse it off under the sink when done. I run mine under the faucet with an old sponge to clean it when it needs it. Just a little water is needed to do a great job. Pro tip: Don't use a new sponge from the sink that your wife uses to clean the kitchen with if you want to keep the peace.

With the India and Arkansas stone, a good cutting lubricant is called for. Brownells and Norton both carry excellent cutting oils. As with most oils, a little bit goes a long way, so just use a drop or two for each job. The key is to use enough to keep the stone from loading up, but not so much that it makes a mess.

Polishing stones serve a significant role on the gunsmith's bench. If you are just starting out and don't want to make a big investment, get a large, 6x1/2-inch India or coarse ceramic stone, and a large diamond bench stone to start out, and build from there as your needs arise. With the large bench stone, you can polish big surfaces quickly, while still maintaining a flat surface. The 6-inch India stone will be invaluable with trigger work using various jigs and fixtures. Go slow when working with polishing stones, check your work, and get some practice material. (Keep old, broken or worn out parts to practice on. Just make sure they are kept in a bin marked as such so they don't get mixed in with new parts, and you will be producing excellent results in no time.)

PUNCHES

As a custom gunsmith you will need a wide variety of punches in order to disassemble various firearms. You'll need drift punches to remove retaining pins and the like, and center punches to make spots for drilling. Also needed will be nylon and brass punches to tap pins and other parts back into place without marring the finish of the firearm.

GUNSMITHS' SCREWDRIVER SET

Screwdrivers are a critical tool for any gun owner and the custom gunsmith is no exception. Small screws hold together many parts on guns, and you will need a wide variety of types of screwdrivers to be effective. They need to be hollow ground, meaning that the tip is ground parallel. Regular screwdriver blades are not hollow ground and are actually in a wedge shape. This will damage the screw head. Always make sure you are using gunsmithing screwdriver bits, not just general blades when working on firearms. Brownells sells a great screwdriver set that includes 58 bits that fit into a magnetized screwdriver handle. When paired with a short LE screwdriver handle, this allows you to comfortably work on virtually any firearm. There are many specialized bits that work with the same screwdriver handle that are critical for getting the job done. Remember, always have the right tool for the job.

HAMMERS

Finally, the last items that you will need are quality gunsmithing hammers. The main hammer I use is medium-sized with two replaceable heads — one side is nylon, while the other is a brass insert. You should also have a dead blow hammer, which is used for moving parts into place. Throw in a couple of good bench blocks for driving pins in and out, and your gunsmiths' workbench is tooled up for a good start.

Chapter 3

GUNSMITHING PROJECTS & USE OF TOOLS

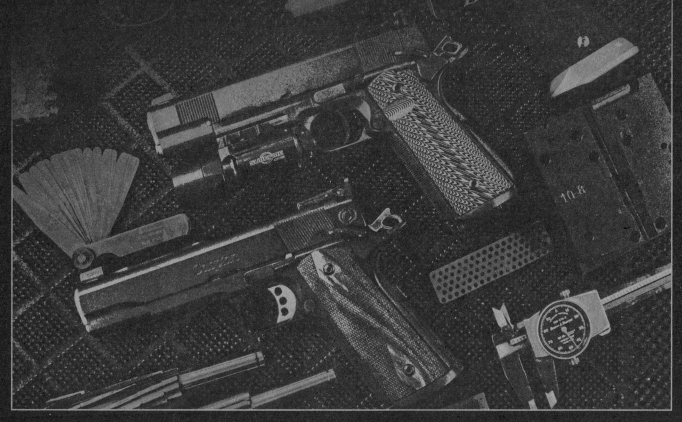

For this chapter, I'm going to cover three very important skills that the custom gunsmith must know how to perform: filing, metal checkering and drilling and tapping.

DRAW FILING

If you want to get into custom work, you have to master the draw filing technique. If you are a hobbyist, you may know how to use a file properly, and may even know how to use other types of files like chainsaw files and big, flat bastard files and the like. But for the custom gunsmith, draw filing is what separates the men from the boys. The draw filing technique is also useful when polishing metal, since the file can be used as a backing with sandpaper to achieve great finishes.

Draw filing is pretty easy to explain, but difficult to execute. Basically, the file is held at right angles to the work and is drawn either into, or away from the work, depending on the direction the teeth of the file are facing, then slightly raised off the work on the return stroke, and repeated. I like to push the file through the work, as opposed to pulling it toward me. This technique is normally used with a single-cut file and produces a very smooth and true surface. In regular filing, the file is held at the tang and at the tip, and is pushed into and through the workpiece. You can actually file in either direction as long as the teeth of the file are oriented into the direction of the filing stroke. In other words, make sure the angle of the teeth are facing the same way you are filing into the work. So, if the teeth are facing away from you, you should be applying pressure to the file as you draw it away from you and vice versa. Most gunsmiths push into the work to remove material and lift off the work on the return stroke. Make sure you keep the file true and flat, and have the file card handy to keep the teeth clean. As mentioned earlier, chalk applied to the teeth of the file will help keep them from getting clogged.

METAL CHECKERING

Metal checkering, as it pertains to custom gunsmithing, usually means custom hand checkering on the 1911 platform. One of the most important points about metal checkering on the 1911, or any firearm for that matter, is to get the initial lines straight and parallel to the sides of the frame. I can't emphasize this enough; keeping the lines straight in the beginning of the checkering process is paramount to obtaining a straight and true end product.

Use the bench vise as a guide to lay out the vertical lines first. Start with a new, sharp checkering file (I replace the file after checkering about four to five 1911 frames). My vise jaws have been ground smooth. I took them to a machine shop and had those surfaces ground flat. With the frame held in the vise, the vise jaws act as guides for the sides of the checkering file, and as long as you keep pressure on the file and its sides against those of the smooth vise jaws, you will cut straight, vertical lines. Slide the frame out, and again, using the ends of the vise jaws, keep the file perpendicular or square to the frame. In this way, you can start cutting square, horizontal lines. Once the initial horizontal and vertical lines are laid out, it's simply a matter of deepening those lines, all the while keeping them straight and true. Good checkering can go south when the vertical lines are being deepened by pushing with the heel of the hand in order to drive the file into the work. This technique will cause the tang of the file to be pushed to the left, (if you are checkering with the right hand). That'll cause the vertical lines, or grooves, to be slanted from left to right. The way to avoid this is by keeping pressure on the file with the fingertip or the right hand at the top of the file to prevent it from drifting, and watching that the sides of the file are kept parallel with the sides of the frame. I'll explain metal checkering in more detail in the 1911 chapter.

DRILLING AND TAPPING

Drilling and tapping holes goes back to the early 1800s, and there is both art and science to the technique. Drilling and tapping holes in a variety of materials is a common practice for a custom gunsmith. Drilling holes in wood calls for different tooling and technique than steel. That's because there is a wide variety of metal materials you will drill into, such as aluminum, stainless steel, carbon steel, and the like. For woodwork, the custom gunsmith will need spade drills and tools like Forstner bits to drill straight holes in wood. In the rifle section I outline and discuss these tools. For drilling and tapping into metal, you will need a variety of tooling to accomplish the job. Drills for working with metal should be HSS, or High Speed Steel. Some gunsmiths like carbon steel drills, which are harder but more brittle than HSS. I use HSS drills and taps for most of my work, although carbide drills and reamers do come in handy.

When drilling holes in metal, you can use a drill press

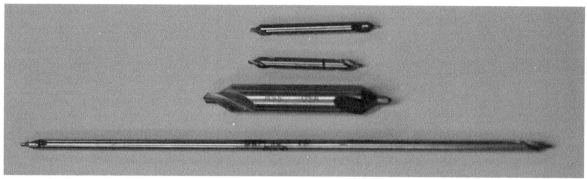

An assortment of center drills can really help out the custom gunsmith.

or a milling machine. I like a milling machine whenever possible because I know it will give me a precisely located hole, and when I do drill into the work, the drill is more likely to run straight and much less likely to "walk" or drift when plunging into the work. If this happens, the hole will either be oversized or not located where it's supposed to be. One type of drill that will help keep the drill bit centered on the work is a center drill. This is a short, stubby drill that is used to start the initial hole at a precise location, and then switched out for the regular drill for the remainder of the drilling operation. If a milling machine is not available, then the next best piece of machinery to have is a floor-mounted drill press. These are heavier duty than the bench-mounted variety, and will drill straighter, truer holes.

At its most basic level, you have to layout and mark the spot where you want to drill your hole. If you are drilling a spot through another piece of work, such as the rear elevation screw for the Bomar rear sight on the 1911 pistol, you can use a transfer punch to get the spot marked properly. Transfer punches come in a set and are fairly expensive, but really come in handy. Alternatively, you can run a proper-sized drill down through

the sight and give it a light tap with a small hammer to mark the spot where you want to drill. Then remove the sight, and install the proper-sized center drill into the chuck, and spot drill the slide. Next follow up with the correct-sized drill for the 6-48 thread you'll be tapping. When drilling holes in metal, always use a good cutting fluid, and clear the chips as you go.

Other drills used are carbide drills, which are very hard and can break easily, but will absolutely bore a hole though very tough, hardened steel. Finally, TiN-coated drills (titanium nitride) are very useful as such coating adds life to the tool.

Once the hole is drilled, it needs to be tapped to form the threads. There are two basic types of taps you will use: tapered and plug. Tapered taps are used for through holes, or holes that go all the way through the part, while plug taps, also called bottoming taps are used for blind holes. When tapping holes use the milling machine or a good drill press. However, if neither is available, it can be done by hand. Actually, while holes can be tapped by hand, it's easy to get a tap started crooked using this method. If the hole is deep, then it's usually not a problem since the tap will self-center itself, but if

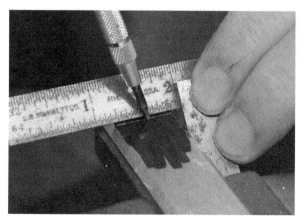

LEFT: Laying out guidelines ensures the drill starts at the correct spot. RIGHT: The drill press drops the center drill right on the spot marked by the gunsmith.

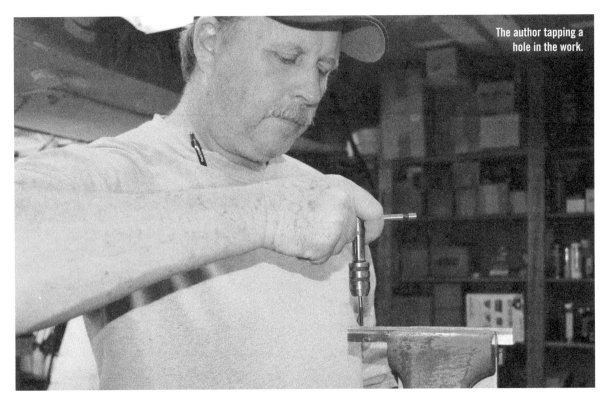

The author tapping a hole in the work.

LEFT: The spring-loaded tap guide is an excellent way to achieve true, straight holes with the drill press. It keeps constant pressure of the tap. RIGHT: The spring-loaded tap guide in action.

it's a shallow hole, then the tap should be started into the work as straight as possible.

The best way to do this is by using a spring-loaded tap follower or tap guide. I made one when attended gunsmithing school, but they can be purchased through any machine supply house for less than $30 and are a handy item to have. To tap a hole, place the tap into a tap handle. For smaller taps this is usually a T-handle. Then place the tap guide into the drill press and lower it down to the tap. Turn the tap and drill chuck by hand so the tap guide places downward pressure on the tap

as it goes into the work. Use cutting fluid and compressed air to blow out the chips. Turn the tap a quarter turn, then reverse the tap slightly to "break" the chip, and then continue tapping. (With large taps, like those you'll use when tapping out shotgun barrels for choke tubes, this technique of reversing the tap doesn't apply.)

TOOLS FOR THE 1911

The scope of custom work typically performed on the 1911 revolves around tightening the slide to frame

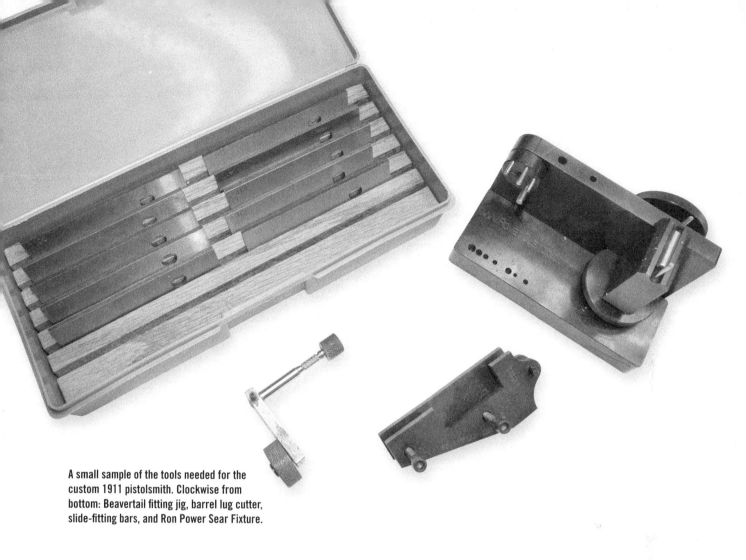

A small sample of the tools needed for the custom 1911 pistolsmith. Clockwise from bottom: Beavertail fitting jig, barrel lug cutter, slide-fitting bars, and Ron Power Sear Fixture.

fit, installing match-grade barrels and bushings, trigger work, metal checkering, installing safeties and sights.

Tightening the slide to frame fit on the 1911 is something that was initially performed on bullseye pistols used by the Air Force pistolsmiths in the 1950s and 60s. Those custom pistolsmiths and the shooters they supported were some of the finest marksman on the planet and set many records, some of which still stand today. As with many techniques in this book, there are often multiple ways to achieve the same result. Tightening the slide to frame fit on the 1911 is one example. The technique I learned to build the 1911 at the National Match Armorers Course at Rock Island is similar, but not the same technique I use today. I'll discuss this more in the 1911 section of the book. For now, let's focus our attention on the tools needed for tightening the slide to frame fit, because it's really not a custom 1911 unless the slop between the slide and frame is eliminated.

Three items you will need are slide-fitting bars, rail micrometer and a ball peen hammer. You will also need a good sear jig. I like the Ron Power Series I or II sear fixture. I've used the Series I for decades and it always

gives consistent results, but other 'smiths swear by the Marvel and Ed Brown. Also needed for working on the 1911 are a beavertail fitting jig, disconnector scraper, and a lug cutter with a barrel alignment block and a barrel bushing reamer.

For other guns such as the Glock, Sig, Smith & Wesson and Springfield XD series, Brownells sells specialized tools that make working on these guns go smoothly. Mostly, they fall into the category of sight pushers and assembly/disassembly tools. These guns are mostly service or duty-type pistols, and are not as customizable as the 1911, so the number of tools needed to work on them are fewer. Nevertheless, I'll cover the tools needed for them in subsequent chapters.

For revolvers, the Power Sear Jig, both the Series I and II, come with adapters that allow you to perform trigger jobs on a variety of handguns, both pistols and revolvers. If you get into rebarreling revolvers, especially the Smith & Wesson wheelguns for NRA Action Pistol and similar events, you will need an action wrench and other tooling.

Chapter 4

BUILDING THE CUSTOM 1911

Once you have mastered the fundamentals of 1911 pistolsmithing, it's a simple matter to apply those skills to other forms of the gun. Here is a custom 1911 the author built using the Caspian slide and frame, with a Kart barrel, a forward-mounted Kensight, Sniper Grey Cerakote finish, again applied by Accurate Plating, 20 and 30 LPI checkering on the frontstrap and under the trigger guard, respectively, and a Surefire X300a tactical light.

I n this section, I'm going to cover how to set up and build three different types of 1911s. Since the 1911 platform is so versatile, it has tremendous crossover potential — from survival and self-defense to competition. You can build one that would be a great daily carry gun, but also a fantastic competition pistol. A good example would be the Government Model 1911. You can set up this timeless handgun for defensive use, daily carry, as well as IDPA or IPSC competition. The same can be said of the 1911 Officer's Model. It makes an ideal daily carry and defensive pistol, but I would not be averse to entering into any IDPA match with it — in fact, it would make a great choice for performing double duty. So the small frame version of the 1911 could be used for daily carry, defensive and competitive use. That's why, for this chapter, I'll set up three different 1911 pistols, and by changing a few items, you can decide which version of the gun would best suit your needs.

FITTING THE SLIDE

To begin, I'm starting this build with new carbon steel slide and frame components. Namely, parts from Caspian Arms Ltd. These are, in my opinion, the finest parts to use when building a custom 1911 from the ground up. For this book, I'll demonstrate how to fit the slide and frame using the oversized parts from Caspian. Start this job by measuring the slide and frame rails, though the Caspian parts are normally so boringly consistent dimension-wise that this step is almost superfluous. Measure the width of the frame rails, and the width of the corresponding groove in the slide. The frame rails should be a few thousandths oversize. File the top and sides of the frame rails until the top of the frame has clearance and the slide will start to go on the frame. Use the Magic Marker to check for high spots, filing them down as needed. Once the slide will fit onto the frame about three-quarters of the way, you can start lapping in the slide to frame fit. In slide

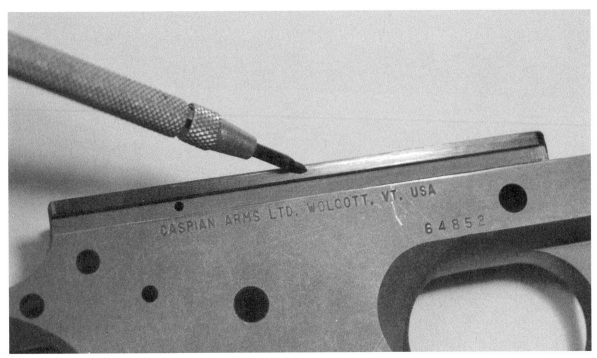
Using a Magic Marker will show you where the high and low spots are and where to file.

fitting, there are a few trouble spots to look out for: You want to make sure that the slide's recoil spring plug housing is not making contact with the frame's dust cover. This will give you a false reading when fitting the slide to frame. Also, if you are working with used parts, the slide rails should not be thinner than .114. Any thinner and you will run the risk of taking down the frame rails too much during the tightening process. Fitting the slide to frame on the Caspian involves filing the top and sides of the frame, only removing the amount of material needed for the slide to go halfway onto the frame. At this point, you can start using lapping compound and lap the slide onto the frame. When done, the slide should move freely from the battery position, to the fully rearward position and back. I like to have a little bit of snugness when the slide goes into battery when I'm fitting the slide, as this will leave a little material for final fitting.

BARREL SELECTION AND FITTING

Normally, the Caspian slide rail measures in at .118 inches, so you will not run into a situation in which the slide rails are too thin. Now that you have the slide to frame lapped in and properly fitted, it's time to fit the barrel. There are two types of aftermarket barrels that come in two styles. A match target barrel must be fitted by a professional 1911 pistolsmith, whereas a "drop-in" type barrel can be installed with little to no fitting. Also, either type of barrel can be had in either carbon or stainless steel. I've used both and have not seen a difference accuracy-wise between the two. The barrels I've installed most frequently are the excellent Match Target stainless version from Bar-Sto Precision Machine, the carbon steel Match Target version from Kart Precision Barrel Corp., and the stainless barrels from Wilson Combat. I've installed about 100 Wilson barrels, 200 Bar-Sto MT Barrels, and 200 Kart barrels. All delivered excellent accuracy when properly fitted. The accuracy standard of the pistols I built during my time as Chief Gunsmith for the DoD was 10-shot groups of 2 inches or less, delivered from a Ransom Rest at 25 yards using Federal 230 Match hardball ammunition. I never had a barrel from any of those manufacturers that wouldn't consistently deliver that level of accuracy. Drop-in barrels can deliver excellent accuracy, but this is a book on custom gunsmithing, so, for our purposes, we will only discuss the Match Target or gunsmith-fit barrels.

Once you've decided on the type and brand of barrel, there are a few specialized parts and tools that you need to get the job done. You will need a barrel alignment tool and block, lug cutter, loose-fitting 1911 barrel bushing, headspace gauge, chamber reamer, and a barrel alignment rod. For this book, I'll outline how to install

ABOVE: The author using the Brownells slide lapping tool and lapping compound to achieve final slide to frame fit.

RIGHT: Measuring the slide rail thickness with the slide rail micrometer.

the Bar-Sto stainless Match Target (MT) barrel. Start prepping the slide by lightly polishing the breechface, making sure the firing pin hole is deburred. If you take too much off the breechface, it will affect the headspace of the gun. Use an 8-inch center drill to deburr the firing pin hole. Just make sure you don't overdo this procedure. Taking too much off the firing pin hole will cause primer material to flow into the hole when the pistol is fired, causing all sorts of problems.

To fit the barrel, first measure the width of the hood, and the slide recess into which the hood fits. Now, the hood will be oversized, so you'll need to subtract the difference between the barrel width and the slide width, and divide by two. This is the amount that needs to be removed from each side of the hood. File the sides of the hood equally, fitting the barrel into the slide, using the loose barrel bushing as a guide. There should be a few thousandths of an inch clearance between the sides of the hood and the slide itself. At this point, you need to fit the length of the hood. File the end of the hood, trying barrel fit into the slide after a few file strokes and using a factory bushing. You don't want to use the match bushing at this point, just a loose-fitting factory bushing for this stage of the barrel fitting process. EGW makes a good hood-length gauge that you can use to determine the amount of material that needs to be re-

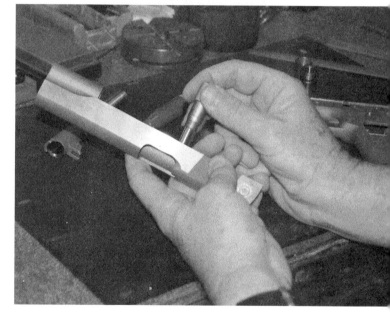

moved, or you can simply file and check.

Once the barrel starts to fit into battery the fun starts. Use the barrel alignment block and the alignment rod to see how far the barrel is moving up into battery, and if the barrel is going into battery on center. You want the barrel to be as centered on the firing pin hole as possible. Ideally, you will fit the barrel up into battery perfectly when the tip of the barrel alignment rod drops into the firing pin hole. The reason you want this condition is so the firing pin strikes as close to center as possible so the primer will detonate consistently — giving the pistol the best accuracy. I like to fit the barrel to the point where it

IPSC AND IDPA: THE CASE FOR COMPETITIVE PISTOL SHOOTING

In the mid-1970s, I was living in Los Angeles and was visiting a local gunshop looking at the latest and greatest firearms on the racks. They had a flyer posted for a new form of competitive pistol shooting that combined the practical use of the handgun with a physically demanding course through which you moved while shooting. I attended that match and several more, competing with my trusty Colt Trooper MkIII .357 Magnum revolver, and have competed in USPSA/ IPSC matches ever since. The match was held at the Southwest Pistol League, which later became one of the founding clubs of the new United States Practical Shooting Association, (USPSA). This organization came about because shooters at the time wanted more realistic courses of fire than just standard paper Bullseye-type target shooting. In 1984, the USPSA was incorporated into the International Practical Shooting Confederation (IPSC). USPSA/IPSC began with the intent to foster the realistic uses of the defensive handgun, and attempted to simulate real-world examples of how the handgun might be used to defend a person's life. Eventually, though, the game became more and more of an equipment race, and the shooter who could "game" the system would usually win.

The guns and equipment became more and more impractical from a defensive point of view, so Bill Wilson, of Wilson Combat, designed a new form of practical pistol shooting that would use basic, mostly non-modified handguns in short range, real-world defensive applications. In 1996, the International Defensive Pistol Association (IDPA) was born. Being a competitor in either USPSA or IDPA is a great way to improve your practical handgun skills in well-designed, real-world scenarios. Shooting on the move, reloading, shooting around and through obstacles and barricades, malfunction drills, and thinking through a realistic, self-defense situation is the focus of these two organizations.

goes up into battery, and will stay up into battery when pushed into place. It should only drop out of battery with slight finger pressure. Also, if you push the barrel up into battery above or below this point, you will need to use either a long- or short-barrel link, and this will cause more problems with feeding and functioning than you can imagine. If you fit the barrel so it centers the bore axis to the firing pin hole, you will use a #3 or factory standard link, which is the condition you want.

So, you may or may not have to remove some material from the first locking lug at its top. Wilson barrels needed to be fitted in this area, and the Kart EZ Fit barrels have pads placed on both sides at the locking lug recess to provide a fitting surface. The Bar-Sto barrel may need to have some material removed, and I have a fine cut Swiss file that was narrowed to fit the width of the rear locking lug recess. Remove material as needed until the barrel is centered on the firing pin hole and the alignment rod tip drops down the barrel and into the firing pin hole.

At this point, you can cut the lower barrel lugs. To start, make sure the barrel is installed into the slide, the barrel alignment rod is placed into the barrel and the tip is inserted into or, at the very least close to the firing pin hole. Make sure the barrel is aligned by using the alignment tool and double check the alignment with the barrel alignment block. Once all three tools are installed into the barrel, be sure that the barrel is properly located into the slide. Use the loose barrel bushing at this point. Fitting the barrel bushing will come last. For this step, you'll need a factory thumb safety. Install the slide, with the alignment gauge and alignment tool installed, onto the frame. With the frame located in the padded vise, take the lug cutter and place a couple drops of cutting oil on the teeth. Use the factory thumb safety to install the slide pusher and lug cutter into place. Push the slide forward while rotating the lug cutter clockwise.

Stop cutting when the thumb safety goes up into the cutout in the slide. Remove the slide and measure the

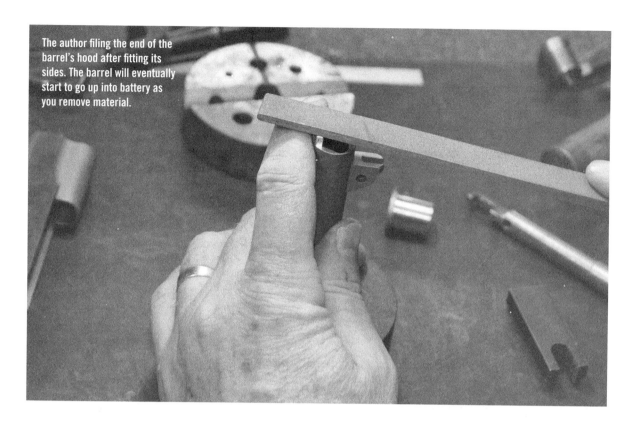

The author filing the end of the barrel's hood after fitting its sides. The barrel will eventually start to go up into battery as you remove material.

thickness of the lower feet of the lugs. DO NOT cut the barrel feet less than .100 of an inch thick. Any thinner and you will risk having the feet crack and break off, allowing the slide to go flying off the frame. Trust me, I've seen it happen. One of my builders cut the feet too thin, and after a couple of shots, they sheared off sending the slide flying down range — not a fun day of testing. Also, do not make the mistake of using the rear of the slide as a guide for how much to cut. Some beginning builders keep cutting until the back of the slide is flush with the back of the frame. This is incorrect, and may lead to

cutting the feet too thin as well. Remember, do not cut the feet thinner than .100 of an inch. Simply keep cutting until the thumb safety goes fully up into the cutout of the slide and stop. If the back of the slide is not flush with the back of the frame at this point, you will blend it in later when you fit the beavertail grip safety.

You've cut the bottom lugs, and now have to fit and time them. The handheld rotary lug cutter you used will leave the bottom lugs a few thousandths of an inch oversized, so you have a little more to fit. I use a small cobalt grinding bit on the Foredom tool, as it removes a very small amount and leaves a good finish. Use the Magic Marker to see where the high spots are, and remove material from these spots. Gradually, it will be easier for the barrel and slide to go into battery. Leave it a little sticky at lockup at this point, do a final fit after fitting the barrel bushing later. Install the barrel link. You should only use a #3 link, which is .278 inches center to center. Anything longer or shorter will cause serious issues. Remember, the barrel link's only function is to yank the barrel down and out of battery, that's all. Make sure the link pin does not extend beyond the side of the lower lugs. Running a reamer designed for this hole

Barrel alignment rod installed, ensuring its tip falls into, or very close to, the firing pin hole. Also installed is the barrel alignment tool to double check alignment with the black barrel alignment block.

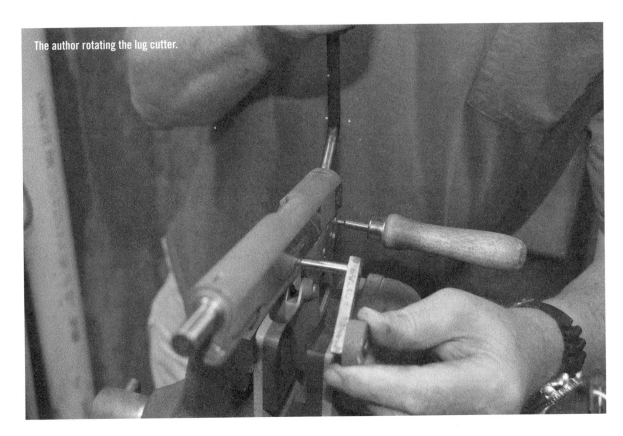

will make it easier and more consistent to install and fit the link pin. Also, you want to make sure the barrel sits properly on the frame bed when it drops out of battery. With the link installed, and the barrel and slide stop pin in place (but without the slide), push the barrel out and down onto the frame bed, and apply rearward pressure to the barrel. The slide stop should not be trapped or bind on the link. If it's binding, you can open up the bottom of the lower link pin hole slightly with a round file. Conversely, if you push the barrel rearward, and it stops on the frame and drops down slightly, then the barrel is hitting the frame too soon. This condition can shear the lower lugs off the barrel during firing.

The fix is to set the frame's spot face back a little. You want the barrel to hit the frame's spot face at the same time it sits on the frame bed with a #3 barrel link installed. You also want to make sure the barrel's feed ramp has a slight gap with the frame's feed ramp. Typically this gap is about .025-030. If the barrel ramp is up against the frame, it will actually be overhanging a little when the barrel starts to come off the frame bed during cycling, causing feeding malfunctions. Also, once the barrel hood is fitted, check the chamber with the headspace gauge to make sure the chamber isn't too short. The rear of the GO gauge should sit flush with the barrel hood, and the NO-GO gauge should

sit slightly above flush. If the chamber is too short, the pistol will fail to fully chamber a loaded round. If short, use the chambering reamer on a tap handle to very carefully cut the chamber so the GO gauge sits flush with the barrel hood. This will also do double duty as sometimes chambers can be a little tight, which causes feeding malfunctions. Running the chambering reamer into the chamber will eliminate this condition.

Now that you have the barrel fitted, the barrel bushing is the last step. National Match 1911 barrel bushings are made oversized on the OD (outside diameter) of the bushing where it bears against the slide, and on the ID (inside diameter) of the bushing hole where the barrel reciprocates during firing. You can use a bushing mandrel and your drill press to turn down the OD of the bushing to achieve a finger tight fit. You want the bushing to fit tightly but not too snugly in the slide. Use the Brownells bushing reamer to cut the barrel ID to the proper size. You also want a good fit with the barrel on the ID, but remember that the barrel has to tilt up and down during the firing cycle, so make sure there is clearance in the top and bottom of the ID of the bushing hole. Check the bushing ID for this clearance. Take the slide off the frame with the barrel and barrel bushing in place, and hold it upside down. Push the barrel down into the slide and, if it springs back,

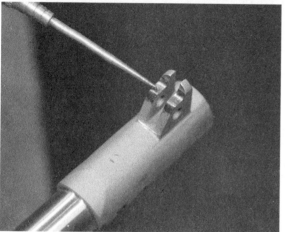

TOP: Measure the barrel lug feet to ensure the thickness does not go below .100 inches. BOTTOM: There is a small flat at this area of the bottom lugs that needs to be fitted to the slide stop pin.

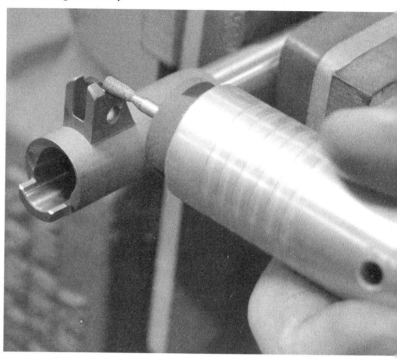

BELOW: The author using the cobalt bit in the Foredom tool to fit the bottom lugs to the slide stop pin. You need to remove a little material, then use the Magic Marker, and install the barrel, trying to get the barrel to go into lockup.

you do not have enough clearance in the ID of the bushing for the barrel to properly tilt during lockup. This is where the Foredom and the 120 grit sanding drum can be used to put an internal bevel in the bushing to provide this clearance. If the barrel is "springing" it can cause the shots to string vertically on the target. An adjustable bushing reamer will correct the hole ID, then you can use the Foredom and a sanding drum to gently machine the upper and lower bevel on the bushing ID for proper clearance.

BEAVERTAIL SAFETY

Once the barrel and bushing are fitted, installing the beavertail is next. With the slide off the gun, and the plunger tube removed, place the beavertail jig onto the frame and use the belt sander to grind the frame ears down close to, but not touching, the frame jig. With the jig still in place, file down to the jig with a #2 file until you make contact with the jig. Take a tapered pin punch and, with a Magic Marker, mark the frame and install

the beavertail onto it with the thumb safety, and pivot it up and down. The marker will show the high spots and the Foredom with a sanding drum can be used to take the high spots down until the beavertail moves freely. At this point, the upper assembly is finished, and you can blend in the slide, frame and beavertail. Install the firing pin, extractor, and ejector in the gun. Use a half round #0 file to get the rear of the slide down to flush with the frame, blending in the bottom portion of the frame ears around the beavertail. Once the material is filed close, switch to the #2 half round file until everything is blended nicely. Then switch to the trusty Foredom and a #120-grit sanding drum to blend everything together — including the rear of the slide and the frame. The #120 drum will remove most of the file marks, but you have to make sure that all of the file marks are actually removed. Look at the parts with a strong light and magnifying glass. Once the file marks are removed, go over the back of the slide, the beavertail safety and frame with a sandpaper-backed file. File the sides of the frame where it meets the beavertail, which can be wider than the frame, or vice versa. Also, the sanding drum will create ripples in the metal that are difficult to see. Strips of 120-grit sandpaper will remove the ripples and make a nice, even finish, ready for the bead blaster.

Use a small beavertail fitting jig to file the rear ears of the frame. Remove material until the file hits the buttons, then use a tapered punch and Magic Markers for a final fit.

SIGHT INSTALLATION

Depending on the use of the gun, you can install two types of sights, either fixed or adjustable. For a strictly competition pistol, many shooters opt for the adjustable rear sight, especially Bullseye shooters like myself. The trend today in practical shooting circles is to go with one load, and a good set of high visibility fixed sights for the practical shooting games. Bullseye-style shooting has transitioned to electronic sights, a trend established now for many, many years.

So, for this section, I'll show how to install a dovetail and tenon-style front sight, along with a fixed and adjustable rear sight.

To install the dovetail front sight, I'm going to assume that your dovetail cut is already machined into the slide. This is a book for the home hobby gunsmith, so this job will need to be farmed out if the slide isn't purchased with the dovetail cut already provided. Caspian offers dovetail cuts as an option. If the slide does not have a dovetail, send the sight and slide to any competent gunsmith with a milling machine, who can cut it for you. Assuming this is done, secure the slide in the vise and, with the correct dovetail file, work the dovetail striving

to put a slight taper on it from right to left, as this is the direction all parts should enter any dovetail. The Rule of Thumb is, "In from the right, out from the left."

File the dovetail until the sight starts to go into the slot, then tap it into place. Here experience comes into play. You want it tight; but, if it's too tight it will be difficult for the refinishers to remove it later. Too loose, and it may come out, although dovetail front sights, like the Novak-style, regardless of whether or not they are tight or loose, when pinned in place and secured with a drop of red Loctite are not likely to come out. It should be firm and go into place with four to five solid taps with the nylon punch. Once in place, drill the front retaining pin hole using the drill press with a 1/16th-inch drill and a little cutting oil. Do not pin in place at this time. Use the 75 LPI checkering file to cut the horizontal serration on the sight before installing it. You can also use the same checkering file to either give the sight a slight ramp style, or more of a target undercut, depending on how you apply pressure. Cut the sight down to an overall height of .180 inch with a slight downward taper of the top of the blade. Finish up the final height at the range, rather than the many formulas you can use

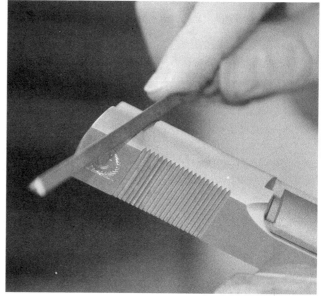

LEFT: The dovetail cutter in the milling machine is cut by Accurate Plating, so the author can install the Novak front dovetail sight.
RIGHT: Using the triangular sight base file, open up the dovetail until the sight starts to enter the dovetail from right to left.

to calculate sight height and the pistol's zero.

Always break the sharp edges. If you do not want a dovetail sight, and some people don't like them, you can get a very solid sight installation with the tenon-style sight when properly installed. The tenon-style is very easy. Remove the old sight. You can do this by twisting off the blade, and using a center punch to punch out the old tenon. Be careful you don't mar the finish when twisting off the old sight. Also, you may have to use a ball end bit on the Foredom to remove the bottom of the tenon inside the slide. Degrease all of the parts. Use a small needle file to open up the tenon hole until the new tenon sight will press down into the hole. Look for a flush fit between the sight and the slide. This caveat is true for all parts that fit into a dovetail. Look for a condition of 'light tight,' again meaning no light visible between the two parts. Now that you have the sight fitted to the slide, there is a special sight fitting tool that will swage the tenon into the cutout in the slide. Mount the swaging tool with the sight in place onto the slide. Place some anti-seize compound on the swaging tool, and drive it into the slide. Swaging is cold forming steel, and this is what the tool does. It will compress the tenon up into the cavity and effectively lock the sight into place. Use a dab of red Loctite to make sure, but the act of swaging alone is normally sufficient to secure the sight in place for a very long time.

Turning your attention to the rear sight, again, there are two types, fixed and adjustable. For the fixed sight, the style is typically some form of low-mount like the excellent Novak. The slide should be already milled for this sight, and if it is, it's simply a matter of filing the dovetail slot, favoring the right side and creating a slight taper in the slot on that side until the sight starts to enter the dovetail. Tap it into place and secure with the set screw. If the slide is going to be fitted with the adjustable BoMar-style sight, then it's a little more complicated. The slide should be already milled for this sight, you just need to fit it in the traditional manner by filing the dovetail until the sight starts to go into the slide. The 6-48 threads per inch (TPI) hole for the elevation screw should already be in place, so fit the sight until it slides into place over the hole. Install the dual spring system and the elevation screw, and you're done.

SMITH & ALEXANDER MAG WELL

You now have the slide, barrel, and beavertail grip safety roughed in, and the sights installed. Now I'm going to demonstrate how to install, fit and blend a Smith and Alexander (S&A) style magazine well to the gun. There are several types of mag wells, but I think the S&A is both attractive and functional, especially when fitted and blended into the slide. When I was building guns for U. S. Special Operations, we installed hundreds of them on 1911s. They were a solid accessory. In order to do this correctly, make sure the tips at the front of the mag well are up against the bottom of the frame when the mainspring housing pin is installed. Mount the frame with the mainspring housing

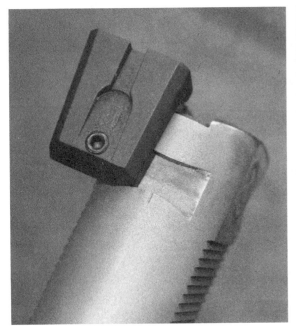 

LEFT: Fitting the rear sight body to the existing dovetail cut into the slide by Caspian. RIGHT: The front sight swage tool installed and ready to tap the swage into place.

installed into the vise, upside down, and file the opening of the mag well at a 45-degree angle to blend it into the frame. Do this to the rear of the mag well. Use a round parallel file and a needle file to get into the corners and blend those areas, and file the tips of the mag well flush with the frame. Use a combination of sanding drums and sandpaper-backed files to blend and smooth everything together.

The checkering on the mag well is 20 LPI, but is not very sharp, so put the mag well into your holding fixture and, with the 20LPI checkering file, go over the checkering in both directions. Then, using a needle file, point up the checkering in both directions. Use a strong light and an OptiVisor at this point to make sure the checkering is straight and full depth in both directions. You should end up with checkering that will really stick to the hand when you're done.

At this point, the only things left are checkering the front strap, and if you're in the mood, checkering under the trigger guard, performing the trigger job, installing and fitting the safeties, fitting the extractor and ejector, dehorning the gun, and a final inspection and fit test. I recommend doing the checkering of the frontstrap now, just to get it out of the way.

CHECKERING THE FRONTSTRAP

To start, place the stripped frame into the vise with the padded jaws removed. Have the vise jaws ground parallel by a machine shop, which will keep your lines straight right off the bat. Hold the 20 LPI checkering file up against the right side of the vise and apply pressure to the left side of the file — this will start the lines near the center of the frame's

The S&A magazine well is installed and blended with the frame.

LEFT: The tapered #120-grit sanding drum on the Foredom tool is a great way to get the file marks out of the magazine well once it's been fitted. This is followed up with small, sandpaper-backed files. RIGHT: The magazine well has been initially blended, and still needs some final sanding and finishing.

frontstrap. Keep applying pressure and move the file front to back, striving to keep the teeth in the grooves you are cutting the entire time. Keep cutting until you have three or four fairly deep grooves in the frontstrap of the frame. Remove the frame from the vise and mount it into the frame holding fixture. Place the checkering file's left teeth into the center grooves and continue to cut, working your way over to the right side of the frontstrap one groove at a time. Don't try to jump over three or four grooves as this will cause the file to slip out. File and move over one groove at a time. Once you've reached the flat of the frame on the right side, rotate the frame over and, starting from the center grooves, work your way over one groove at a time toward the left side of the frame. Once the vertical grooves are in place, clamp the frame in the vise and, using the edge of the vise, place the checkering file horizontally onto the frame, and slowly file the horizontal grooves near the top of the frontstrap by the trigger guard. Always keep the file horizontal and perpendicular to the side of the frame by continuously looking at its orientation, with the frame sides as a reference. If they are not perpendicular, the horizontal lines won't be straight, square or aesthetically pleasing. Work your way down the front of the frontstrap one or two grooves at a time until you reach the bottom of the frame.

Go back and redo the vertical lines, then the horizontal until you've reached full depth with the checkering file. At this point, you're halfway done. With a new, sharp triangular needle file, start to "point up" the checkering. You will definitely need the OptiVisor even if you have perfect vision, as it's very easy to cut the peaks of the checkering leaning one way or the other, which is very visible when the job is complete.

Remember, what you are striving for at this point are peaks that look like rows and rows of tiny pyramids. Assuming everything has gone well, the final part of the job is to clean up the overruns — where the checkering file has gone past a certain point near the top of the frame. This is where it gets a little tricky. You need to remove the file marks without damaging the checkering at a certain stop point. Use a small half round needle file to take the last row of points down to the bottom of the groove, and then follow it up with small strips of sandpaper backed needle files. Eventually, you'll get it down to where the file marks are removed, and the finish is ready for bead blasting.

Once the frontstrap is checkered, you can also checker other areas of the pistol. I like to checker underneath the trigger guard, since when I shoot, the index finger of my weak hand has a tendency to shift a little right there, so the added grip is a welcome addition. Also on the plus side, it looks really good and shows

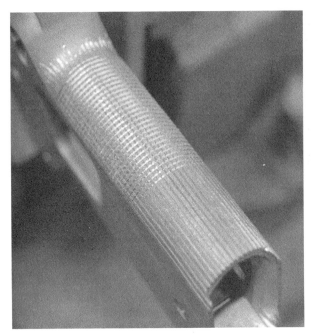

LEFT: The checkering is coming along nicely. ABOVE: The author starting to cut the vertical lines into the Caspian frame, using the 20 LPI checkering file. Hold the file up against the vise in order to keep the lines straight.

off your metalworking skills. Checkering this area can be easier than the frontstrap in one sense, and harder in another. It's easier since you are only checkering a small area, but it's also more difficult because you use a 30 or 40 LPI checkering file, and the smaller teeth have more of a tendency to jump out of the grooves as you are checkering, which can be a disaster. To checker the trigger guard, remove the vise jaw pads, and set the frame upside down into the vise and secure it. Start with the right side of the file up against the vise jaw, similar to the technique used when starting the checkering on the frontstrap. Use the left set of teeth to cut the grooves starting in the center of the trigger guard. Cut them fairly deep, and then move the file to the center, then to the left of the guard. At this point, you should have a set of grooves the full width of the trigger guard that are parallel with the sides of the guard itself.

Move the frame out of the vise so you can use the edge of the file up against the vise jaw, like you did when checkering the frontstrap. File the trigger guard, keeping the file perpendicular to the frame. Run the grooves the length of the trigger guard. At this point, you should have horizontal and vertical grooves covering the full surface of the trigger guard. Continue using the checkering file to deepen the grooves until they are almost full depth, then switch to the three square needle file to "point up" the checkering points. Clean up the overruns like you did on the frontstrap and you're done. The technique of using the sides of the vise to get the checkering lines started, and then switching to the

edge of the vise for the horizontal lines can also be used to checker the rear of the slide as well. This is a common technique that custom pistolsmiths use, ostensibly to cut the glare from the rear of the slide, but really it's to show off the pistolsmiths' checkering skills.

Your 1911 pistol is coming together, and is actually starting to look like a handgun and not just a box of assorted parts. Since you have been working on the checkering, and barrel to slide fit, you should now scrub the pistol of all dust, dirt, and metal filings. Clean the pistol's interior and degrease prior to the trigger work.

THE TRIGGER ASSEMBLY

Trigger work and fitting of the safeties is the most critical aspect to the build process. If you make a mistake here, it will affect the safety and function of the pistol, and therefore the safety of the shooter and bystanders at the range.

If you gunsmith or tinker with guns for long enough and work on trigger systems, you will experience a semi-automatic firearm that doubles, or even worse, goes full-auto. This is very disconcerting when it happens, not to mention it can be disastrous if you let a weapon with a full magazine go full-auto. Every semi-auto firearm that I work on that I have modified or replaced any part of the fire control system will get test fired with only two rounds in the magazine until I'm sure the gun is safe to fire with a full magazine. Let me repeat that. If you have performed any trigger work to the firearm, never fire

any semi-automatic weapon with a full magazine until you have tested it with two rounds repeatedly and are absolutely sure the firearm is safe.

I cannot stress this enough. Proceed carefully anytime you are working on, replacing or modifying any part of the fire control system of any firearm. Having said that, the steps to fit and install the trigger parts to the 1911 are fairly straightforward. Fortunately, we are working

with brand new, high-quality aftermarket parts. Working with used parts has its own set of challenges and techniques, so for this build, we'll focus on the tools and techniques needed to fit new, aftermarket trigger and safety parts into your 1911 pistol in a safe manner.

The first thing is to inspect the parts to make sure there are no obvious flaws in the manufacturing. This rarely happens. Companies are very cognizant of the

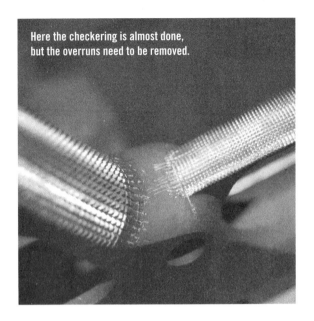
Here the checkering is almost done, but the overruns need to be removed.

Next prep the parts by polishing the sides of the sear and hammer to remove machining marks. You want to keep flat surfaces flat, so use a large diamond stone. Break any sharp edges with a soft India stone.

For this gun I've chosen the popular Videki three-hole aluminum trigger, but the technique is the same for the synthetic triggers that are popular as well. This trigger is oversized in height, so take a little bit off at a time using your trusty #2 flat file, checking for fit as you go. It should freely slide into the slot and operate without vertical movement. Using a deburring wheel lightly go over the sides and rear of the stirrup, as well as the edges so it slides in the trigger track smoothly. Use a Magic Marker to look for high spots on the upper part of the trigger as this will help the fit.

Now is the time to install the hammer strut to the hammer, and to make sure the retaining pin is flush. Stake the pin with a center punch, then stone the sides so the pin doesn't protrude and drag on the frame. Make sure the hammer and sear pins are a good fit in the frame, as well as the hammer and sear. If they are a sloppy fit, get the oversized hammer and sear pins and

fact that these parts need to be made as safe as possible, and stick to very close manufacturing tolerances. They tend to have very ambitious QA/QC people checking before parts go out the door, but things can happen.

The checkering of the frontstrap and trigger guard is complete and the overruns are cleaned up.

their respective reamers from Brownells and ream the hammer, sear and frame holes. This ensures the trigger pull will be consistent. One critical measurement is to the disconnector. This part must be kept at the factory dimension, not below. Too short and it could be unsafe. Next, stone the hammer and sear surfaces on the Power Sear Fixture. Always use some type of fixture to do this work, never do it freehand.

There are several types of fixtures for trigger work, and different pistolsmiths will use various types of tools and techniques to achieve the same result. The sear nose gets stoned at a 60/40 ratio, where the primary angle surface is 60 percent of the total, and the escape angle, or backside of the sear nose is cut at 40 percent of the total surface. The Power sear fixture is set to 20 clicks up from the bottom as a starting point, then raised or lowered to set the trigger weight of pull.

The hammer hooks get lowered using the fixture and a feeler gauge to no lower than .015. Some pistolsmiths will go higher or lower, depending on personal preferences. I use the hammer as a lever to hold the sear in place. The Power instructions recommend a C-

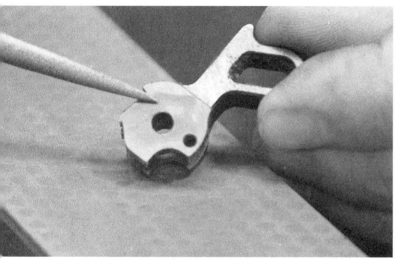
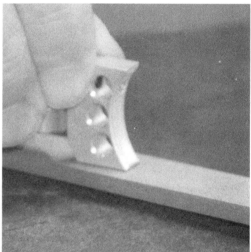

LEFT: The large diamond stone is an expensive tool, but it works fast to clean up and polish flat surfaces. RIGHT: Run the trigger over the file to remove material. This technique works with small or irregular parts.

The trigger is installed and the hammer and sear can now be fitted.

clamp for this, but I find this takes too long to set up and remove, so I use the hammer to hold the sear, and the sear to hold the hammer. Check the sear spring and polish to the top of the left and center leaf. The left leaf of the sear spring bears on the sear, the center leaf bears on the disconnector. The sear spring can be used to make slight ¼-lb. adjustments, up or down, to the weight of the trigger pull, but if the weight is too heavy or light, look at the hammer and sear engagement surfaces. Avoid bending the sear spring excessively to get the trigger pull adjusted up or down 1-2 lbs., trying to get it really light, as the sear spring will end up flattened, or worse, bent back, and the hammer will follow when the pistol is fired because there won't be enough spring pressure to keep the sear engaged.

The .015 hammer hook height and the 60/40 sear nose relationship should result in a crisp, clean, safe trigger pull of about 3 ½ - 4 lbs. Next install the hammer and sear shims per the manufacturer's instructions to remove the side to side movement of those parts. Always check trigger pull with a set of NRA weights. These are the most accurate way to test trigger pull of rifles and handguns, and never wear out or go out of calibration.

Install all of the trigger parts but leave out the grip safety. Try the trigger pull. If you hear two clicks when cycling the action, releasing and then pulling the trigger, the first one is disconnector click, which is where the disconnector is too long and is dragging on the disconnector timing slot. The fix is to scrape the disconnector timing slot with the disconnector scraping tool, not by shortening the disconnector. Never shorten a disconnector for any reason, and never polish the top of a disconnector. The second click is the disconnector resetting, and is normal. Scraping the timing slot will allow more room for the disconnector and will remove the annoying click.

THUMB AND GRIP SAFETIES

Once the trigger pull is set, fit the thumb and grip safeties. The stud on the thumb safety bears against the shelf on the left side of the sear when the thumb safety is engaged. You can look at the thumb safety stud and see where it bears on the shelf of the safety when the grip safety is removed and all of the trigger parts are in place. With the thumb safety in the UP position, it should block all movement of the sear rearward. Carefully file the stud of the thumb safety where it bears on the sear until the thumb safety goes fully into the up position and totally blocks the sear. To fit the grip

TOP: The Power Sear Fixture is used for setting the correct angles on the hammer and sear. In this photo, the hammer is mounted on the lower pin, the sear on the upper pin, with the hammer applying pressure to the sear to keep it in place, while the sear nose is stoned for the proper angle. BOTTOM: The hammer holds the sear in place on the fixture, while stoning the sear nose.

safety, file away the lower grip safety arm to give the trigger stirrup clearance. Then give it a slight angle upward to let the grip safety reset when the shooter releases the safety from his/her grip, and check it with the mainspring housing tool in place. Go slowly and check your work as you go. To check both safeties for proper functioning, engage the thumb safety and depress the trigger; release the trigger, then lower the safety, and the hammer should not move at all. Using your thumb, pull back slightly on the hammer. If you hear a click, you've removed too much from the stud of the thumb safety, making it too short. This needs to be fixed immediately. There are a couple of solutions, but the goal is to not take off too much material in the first place. This is why custom gunsmiths always check their work as they go. If you have access to a person who is a good

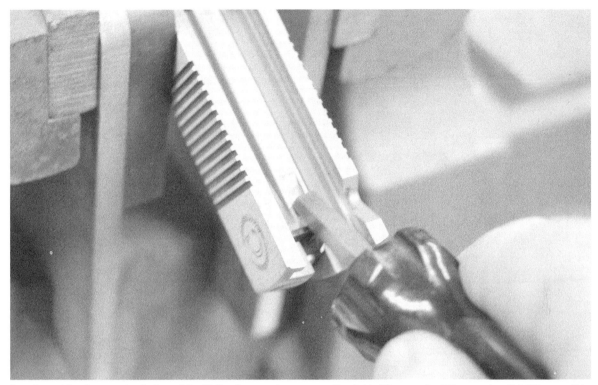

Scraping out the disconnector timing notch with the disconnector scraper will get rid of the annoying "disconnector click." Never polish or shorten the disconnector.

TIG welder, you can have them build up the area on the stud of the thumb safety where it blocks the movement of the sear, and then refit the safety. Alternatively, you can use your ball peen hammer to stretch the stud out slightly so it makes contact again with the shelf of the sear. Either way, the goal is to have the stud of the thumb safety make contact with the flat of the sear when the thumb safety is in the full up position.

The grip safety is checked by pressing the trigger without actually gripping the pistol; the hammer should not move or fall. Pull back on the hammer like you did with the thumb safety check and listen for a click. If you hear a click, the grip safety arm is too short. If the hammer moves during the test, the arm is really short, and the nose of the grip safety arm is not blocking the rear of the trigger stirrup, allowing it to move too far and pushing the sear out of the hammer notch. Again, the fix is to stretch this arm out with light taps using a ball peen hammer. You should not run into this condition, however, as usually the arm of the grip safety is made with extra material to fit against the trigger. But if you take too much off you will cause the condition described. Fitting these parts is always time-consuming but hand-fitting parts is the definition of a custom pistol. Craftsmanship is the name of the game.

DEHORNING

The next step is to dehorn the gun, install and fit the extractor, ejector, and magazine catch, making sure the parts function correctly. You are also going to install the grip screw bushings, and perform a final overall QC check and function test with dummy ammunition. Make sure the barrel is throated and the feed ramp properly, but not excessively, polished.

Dehorning, or breaking all of the external sharp edges of the pistol, is a technique that has been around for a very long time, and is one of the more simple procedures to do to the 1911. Disassemble the gun, and take the frame and slide over to the bench grinder. My grinder has what's called a deburring wheel mounted to one side, and this is what I use to round off the edges of any part. Deburring wheels are available from machine shop supply houses like MSC Industrial, and McMaster & Carr. I usually use a medium grit, 1-inch wide deburring wheel, which is a little more aggressive than a fine grit wheel. Dehorn the front of the dust cover, back of the slide, around the back of the beavertail safeties tail, and around the trigger guard. Then take your Foredom tool with a 120-grit sanding drum and touch up the edges that the deburring wheel can't reach — around the ejection port and inside the trigger guard. Speaking of the ejection port, this area is already lowered by Caspian, so no need to do anything with it, just make sure there are no sharp edges and leave it alone. Some 1911s need their ejection ports lowered and this is best done with a milling machine, so it's not covered in this book. But it can be done by hand if you lay out the lines on the slide and don't go any lower than about .475 from the bottom of the ejection port to the bottom of the slide.

EXTRACTOR AND EJECTOR FIT

Fitting the extractor and ejector is a pretty straightforward process, but it's critical to the proper feeding and functioning of the gun. With the extractor, firing pin, firing pin spring and firing pin stop installed, and the slide off the frame and the barrel removed, slide a dummy cartridge under the extractor hook to the position it would be if the pistol had just chambered a cartridge. Hold the slide in the horizontal position and rotate it around its horizontal axis, ensuring that the dummy cartridge stays in place throughout the

entire test. It should flop around a little while you're rotating it. If it doesn't, it might be too tight and can cause malfunctions. Another check for the extractor is to make sure its nose is not crashing into the extractor groove on the cartridge case. If it is, use a #2 file to take down the extractor nose. At the same time, make sure the tip of the extractor hook is not burying into the sides of the case. The edge of the base of the cartridge case should be grabbed by the groove in the extractor, and should not be touching anywhere else. To adjust the extractor tension, simply pull the extractor out of the extractor hole about halfway, and bend it in the direction you need; for more tension, bend it toward the center of the slide, and for less, bend it away.

The ejector is a simple fit, and I know some pistolsmiths who don't even fit it at all. They leave the nose of the extended ejector full length, and don't install the crosspin. Their thinking is that the ejector will still function even if it's not pinned in place, and it's easier to remove if needed if not pinned. I use extended ejectors, but cut the nose back until it clears the rear of a cartridge case when a magazine is inserted, as I want to be able to eject a loaded round if needed. I also put a

The author's son is taking his newly built 1911 out to the range to give it some exercise. Giving him some great shooting tips is USPSA president and professional Wilson Combat sponsored competitor Mike Foley.

bevel into the right side of the nose to help kick out the case up and to the right.

Lastly, pin the ejector in place. Many pistolsmiths simply install the ejector, and run a 1/16th-inch drill bit through the ejector pin retaining hole, install the pin and call it a day. There are a couple of problems with this approach. The ejector pin may not be bearing on the ejector stud, and while this will retain the ejector, it won't keep it from moving around during the firing cycle. Also, use a solid retaining pin, not a roll type. Solid pins hold the ejector much more securely. If the ejector is not retained properly, it can cause the gun to eject the spent shells in a random pattern. My technique is to install the ejector, and use a 1/16th-inch pin punch through the short side of the retaining pin hole, and tap it with a hammer. This will make an elliptical mark on the front ejector mounting stud. Use a flat needle file that has rounded edges on the sides and only cuts on the edges to file a scallop where the punch made its mark. Try driving the solid pin into place, and file as needed until the pin is driven into and holds the ejector in place. Check to make sure the ejector pin does not extend past either side of the frame since

this will cause it to drag on the slide during cycling. This technique will hold the ejector solidly in place and provide more consistent ejection. The next step is to secure the grip screw bushings. Use a long punch and a bushing staking tool, with a dab of blue Loctite on the threads, as you don't want the bushings coming out with the screw when the grips are removed. Once the bushings are staked in place, check that the inside of the bushing didn't raise up in the staking process, protruding into the magazine well, as this can cause the magazine to stick when the mag release button is pushed. Not a good situation. In a match, this can cost you points. In a defensive situation, it could cost a life. Also needing to be installed is the plunger tube, and there is a special staking tool for this operation. Always use the staking tool with red Loctite to be sure it's flush with the sides of the frame.

OVERTRAVEL STOP

Set the overtravel stop with the set screw. Don't set the stop too close, especially with a defensive pistol, as a little dirt or grit can get between the trigger stop and

The Ransom Rest is invaluable for testing and evaluating both handguns and handgun ammunition. Once the pistol has been function tested, test it in the Ransom Rest for accuracy with proven ammunition.

It's a good idea to test with proven accurate ammunition. The author likes both Federal Match 230-grain .45 ACP ball, and Hornady 230-grain XTP hollow point. Both are very accurate rounds, and give excellent results. The Federal consistently prints five-shot groups under an inch at 25 yards. The Hornady XTP is a defensive round capable of this level of accuracy.

the magazine catch it bears against and, if this happens, the gun will not fire. To set the trigger stop, screw it in until the pistol won't fire. Then, holding the hammer back with the weak hand thumb, try to pull the trigger, backing out the screw, until the hammer drops and goes past the sear as you let it down. Don't set it too close.

FIT CHECKS

Another check to perform is to run the magazine up into the frame. It should fall free. Install the magazine release button and repeat. The magazine should fall free when the release button is depressed. Make sure you run this test with the slide off the gun or the slide to the rear so that nothing is pushing the magazine down from the top. You want to test to see if gravity alone will allow the magazine to fall free. Do this test with a new frame before starting work just to make sure the magazine will fall free from the frame and that the frame's magazine well is not too narrow. If it is, you have to go in with a file and clear out the magazine well interior until the magazine falls free.

Completely disassemble the pistol and clean it thoroughly. Reassemble it with a small amount of oil on the slide rails, barrel end and hammer hooks, and cycle

the gun a few times, then perform a complete function check. Check for proper function of the grip safety, thumb safety, disconnector, and weight of pull. DO NOT cycle the gun by letting the slide slam down on an empty chamber. This is one of the worst things you can do to a custom 1911. What happens is, when the slide slams shut the forward momentum causes the hammer to shove forward, bouncing slightly on the hammer hooks, ruining the carefully polished sear and angles and that crisp 4-lb. trigger pull you worked so hard on. Install the grips, and ensure that there is clearance for the thumb safety, especially if you've installed an ambi safety. Once you are satisfied the pistol is finished, and have cycled it with dummy ammo, take it to the range and function test the gun with at least 100 rounds of various types of ammunition.

Remember to only load two rounds into the pistol at first, until you are sure it is safe. Once you're satisfied the gun functions properly, you can test it in the Ransom Rest for accuracy, or send it off to the finishers and have the finish of your choice applied.

This is how to build a 1911 that will serve many purposes — competition, concealed carry, and general range duties.

Setting up a 1911 for specific functions is easy, de-

TOP: The pistol, once built, can be placed into a fitted presentation case, like the author did for this handgun, a gift for his son's 21st birthday. The finish is a black Cerakote applied by Accurate Plating and Weaponry. BOTTOM: The fit and finish of the pistol is vital. All of the edges have been dehorned using the debriding wheel. The rosewood grips and Allen head grip screws give it a subdued, classic look.

The forward-mounted Tritium adjustable night sight. This gun also has a fiber optic front sight for very high visibility. Note the serrations on the palm pad of the lower portion of the beavertail safety. This helps keep the hand in place when gripping the pistol. On some guns, the author checkers this area at 50 LPI.

Another shot of the 1911 built for the author's son, this time with Goncalo Alves grips. The 1911 is a great pistol and fun to build, since there are so many ways to set the gun up.

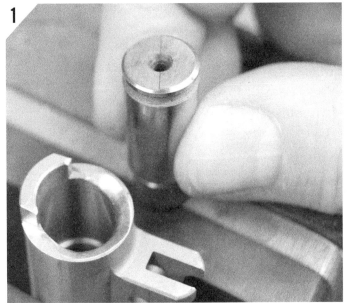

[1] A special headspace gauge made by the author. It's a NO-GO gauge with a step ground in down to GO. One side is GO and the other, higher side is NO-GO. Drop the gauge in the chamber and you can quickly check to see if the chamber is too short or too long. The hood should be flush with the GO side. [2] The Novak Lo-Mount sights have fiber optic inserts for greater visibility. They are installed from right to left, like all dovetailed parts. [3] The Novak fiber optic front sight is also fitted the same way into the dovetail — right to left.

pending on your needs. For a strictly concealed carry, or defensive pistol, there are two options. The little Officer's Model is a short barreled version of the venerable 1911, and Caspian and other makers offer slides and frames in these versions. Also popular are Officer's frames and Commander-length slides. In this version, the longer slide is better concealed down into the wearer's pants, and the smaller exposed portion of the frame is easier concealed under clothing.

Assuming you are building the Officer's Model for concealed carry use, most of the steps to build a Government Model apply to the Officer's version. Although checkering the frontstrap is changed to 30 LPI, the sights are the excellent Novak Lo-profile, and for the pistol I built, the sights have fiber optic inserts

for greater visibility under all lighting conditions. The thumb safety is limited to a strong side only, not an ambi style. All sharp edges on the gun are dehorned to a greater extent, since the gun will be carried in deep concealment and you don't want anything catching on clothing when the pistol is drawn and presented. I usually don't test the Officer's Model in the Ransom Rest, and I'll function test the pistol with 200-300 rounds to make sure it's ready to go before refinishing, since it's a defensive pistol. Also, I regulate the sights to shoot Point of Aim/Point of Impact to 15 yards, not the 25 yards of the full-sized Government version.

For a purely offensive/defensive version of the 1911, Caspian makes a frame with an integral Picatinny rail system to install a tactical light or other accessory. The

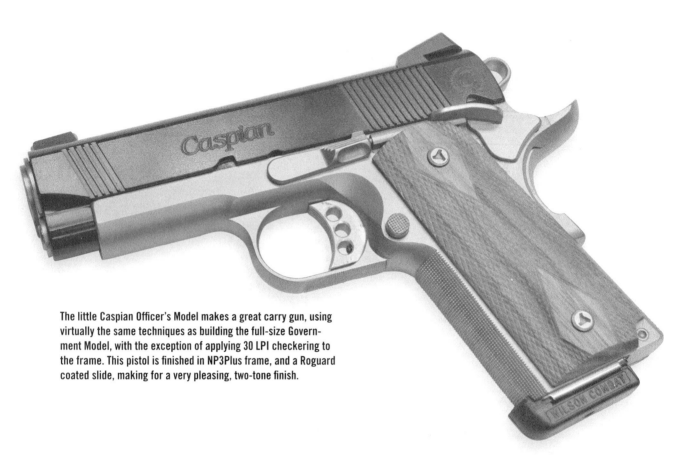

The little Caspian Officer's Model makes a great carry gun, using virtually the same techniques as building the full-size Government Model, with the exception of applying 30 LPI checkering to the frame. This pistol is finished in NP3Plus frame, and a Roguard coated slide, making for a very pleasing, two-tone finish.

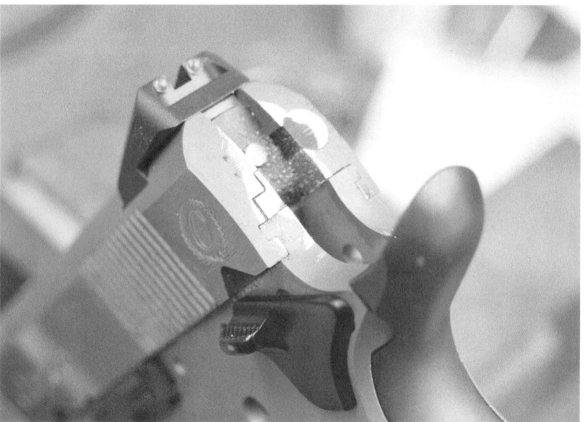

The back of the slide is blended after fitting the beavertail safety.

The beavertail is fitted and then blended with files and #120-grit sanding drums.

frame's dust cover is widened and machined to accommodate the Pic rail. Additionally, the slides offer the Bo-Mar adjustable sight mounted about .150-inch forward to provide additional protection to the rear sight blade when subjected to heavy use and adverse conditions. This pistol would actually be a good choice for IDPA competition, but is really meant for serious use, especially with the tactical light mounted. I built a custom Caspian tactical 1911 for this book, and mounted the excellent Surefire Ultra X300a to its Picatinny rail. Also, for this pistol, I used the superb Kensight with Tritium inserts, and a fiber optic front sight dovetailed into the top of the slide. Img. GUNSMITHING_64.jpg

The author's version of the 1911 Government Model, utilizing a Caspian slide and frame set up as a tactical model, with a Tritium adjustable rear sight, 20 and 30 LPI checkering, Smith and Alexander magazine well, fiber optic front sight, Surefire Ultra X300, and finished in Sniper Gray Cerakote by Accurate Plating.

TIGHTENING SLIDE TO FRAME FIT

If you want to tighten up a loose-fitting slide-to-frame on a used pistol, or a factory pistol that has more generous tolerances, the process is simple. You will need a rail micrometer and a set of 1911 slide-fitting bars. Measure the slide rail for thickness, and select a slide-fitting rail either at the size of, or .001 larger than, the slide rail measurement. Secure the frame in the padded vise jaws, set the appropriate slide rail into the slot of the frame, and using a small ball peen hammer lightly tap the corner of the frame above the fitting rail. Tap

The "squeeze and peen" method of fitting the slide to frame. This technique will eliminate the up and down, or vertical movement of the two parts.

Using the slide-fitting blocks in the vise to squeeze the slide to eliminate side-to-side or horizontal movement.

the two corners on one side of the frame, then switch and do the two on the other side. Favor tapping toward the outside of the frame rails. In other words, try to push the metal outward and downward. File the sides of the frame rails, since this peening will cause them to expand outward. Install the slide on the frame. It should be considerably tighter than when you started. Use the Magic Marker to look for high spots. Take another slide measurement and select the slide bar that exactly fits the thickness of the slide rail, and repeat the process. You should have eliminated almost all of the vertical movement of the slide-to-frame fit at this point.

Now turn your attention to removing the horizontal, or side-to-side play of the slide. This procedure uses the slide-squeezing blocks. Place the slide in the blocks in the vise and tighten the vise for about ten seconds. Try the slide and check for play. You may need a breaker bar on the vise handle for this procedure as it can take some force to squeeze the slide. If you go too far, you can get slide expander bars from Brownells. I have markings scribed on my vise that will tell me incrementally how far I'm squeezing the slide. Once the slide is a slightly force fit, you can lap the slide in with lapping compound. Remember to allow for a little play in the slide when it's moving rearward going out of battery by relieving the front and inside slide rails forward of the

slide stop disassembly notch. This will allow the slide to cycle freely with a little dirt and grit, but still be tight at lockup.

When using lapping compounds, be sure to use plenty of lubricating oil to keep the parts from seizing and/or galling. If the parts start to gall, you will need to thoroughly clean the parts and file away the areas where the galling is occurring and start over. In my opinion, tightening the slide to frame fit on an iron-sighted 1911, or a 1911 with the optical sight mounted on the slide, does not contribute much to the inherent accuracy of the gun, but it does contribute to the reliability by making the slide reciprocate in a more straight line, front to rear motion, enhancing the feeding, extraction and ejection cycles of the gun. In an iron- or slide-mounted, dot-sighted 1911, the slide, sights and barrel are all locked together when the gun is fired, so they are always on the same plane, regardless of how the slide and frame are oriented. This is why slide fitting doesn't contribute that much to accuracy, but no custom gun is complete unless the vertical and horizontal slide to frame movement is eliminated. Once you've lowered the frame rails the appropriate amount, and have tightened the slide, draw file the top of the frame to remove the hammer marks you created when lowering the frame rails.

Chapter 5

BUILDING THE STI 2011 PISTOL

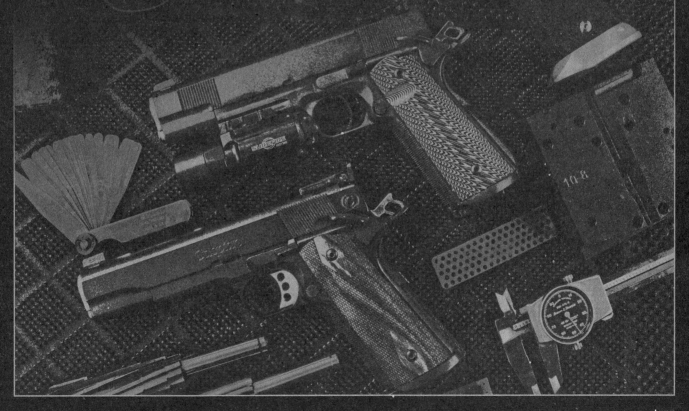

The texture applied by Extreme Shooters for STI on their lower frames is both functional and eye-catching.

That the 1911 design has been used for so long, in so many different roles, from law enforcement to military, competition and more, is a testament to John Browning's genius. Also, the gun's design has remained unchanged from the year 1911. Almost all of the refinements of the gun over the decades have come from either tightening of the tolerances of the original parts, or making parts oversized so the professional pistolsmith can hand fit for improved performance. For example, a popular modification is the beavertail grip safety, which provides a higher grip on the gun for improved recoil control, and extends the number of rounds the shooter can comfortably fire in a given range session by spreading the recoil over a wider area of the web of the hand. But the manner in which the grip safety functions, by blocking the rearward motion of the trigger and preventing the pistol from firing if not gripped properly, has not changed with the new style part from the way John Moses originally designed it.

That all changed in 1993 when a CAD engineer named Sandy Strayer revolutionized the shooting world by designing a new platform using the 1911 as a starting point. The result is the STI 2011, a gun that has a two-piece frame, with the lower half being an injection-molded polymer mated to a steel upper that included the dust cover and frame rails. The result is a high-capacity pistol with frame weight less than half of that of comparable steel guns.

The main difference between the 2011 and the 1911 is the unique two-piece frame. This configuration allows for a very lightweight gun, which handles slightly differently than a traditional model. The two-piece frame is attached to the upper steel section via three screws, two at the upper grip area and one at the front of the trigger guard. The gun also incorporates a high capacity double stack magazine. My gun, in .40 S&W, holds 14 rounds. The polymer frame has the checkering and grips molded in, doing away with expensive metal checkering and screw-on grip panels of the 1911.

TOP: Fitting the ramped STI barrel is no different from a standard barrel. Measure the side of the hood, and fit, then the length of the hood. Lastly, cut and fit the lower lugs. BOTTOM: The barrel fitting rod is inserted, as is the barrel alignment tool and barrel block to verify the barrel is square prior to cutting the lower lugs.

This is good, since I have had to fix many a stripped grip screw bushings and frames in which the bushing threads were stripped. The 2011's polymer construction allows for customization of the lower frame by texturing for improved grip. STI offers this as an option to their custom guns. My gun has this custom texture applied by Extreme Shooters, and it really makes for a solid gripping surface.

Another difference of the 2011 design that I really like is the integrated plunger tube. On a 1911, the plunger tube is a separate piece, attached to the gun by staking the two posts to the inside of the frame. I usually add a dab of red Loctite to ensure it doesn't loosen up. The plunger tube holds a spring and two plungers, one for the thumb safety, while at the other end the plunger acts on the slide stop, keeping it in place until the magazine follower lifts it up. If the plunger tube loosens, it can lift away from the frame. If this happens, it can tie up the thumb safety, preventing the shooter from being able to take the gun off safe, not a good situation if the pistol is used for defensive applications. With an integrated plunger tube like the STI, it's a small but im-

portant difference. Another feature that STI offers is an elongated, full-width dust cover. This adds some weight to the front end of the gun and alters the balance, but in a good way. The frame I have is configured this way, and makes for an excellent Limited Class IPSC pistol. The STI 2011 incorporates most of the internal features that make the 1911 pistol so great, but adds a unique twist to a legendary gun.

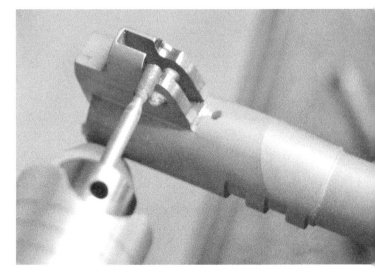

RIGHT: The barrel's lower lugs being initially cut. BELOW: Fitting the bottom lugs with the cobalt grinding tool and a Magic Marker.

TOP: The beavertail has been roughed in, and can now be filed against the slide and frame. BOTTOM: Checkering the back of the slide at 50 LPI using the bench vise as a guide to lay out the horizontal lines.

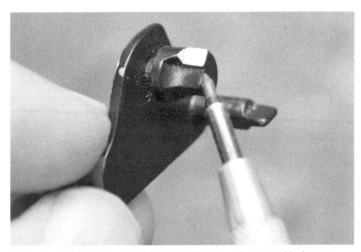

Fitting the stud of the thumb safety where it bears on the sear to block movement when the thumb safety is engaged.

The STI frames are wildly popular for USPSA competition, and the model I received for this book was STI's full frame version. Frames and slides are made from CNC billet steel and are available in a wide range of configurations. Building the gun is similar to a steel frame 1911, but the upper and lower frame pieces are separated. Fit the slide to frame by filing on the bottom of the slide rails, and use the Magic Marker and the frame rail micrometer to measure as you go.

One aspect of 1911 and STI 2011 pistols is that they are configurable for ramped barrels; that is, a barrel that has the feed ramp machined integral to it, not as part of the frame. This makes for a very reliable configuration.

Once the slide to frame fit is achieved, building the 2011 is a straightforward process, and the same techniques used with the 1911 as outlined in the previous chapter are applicable to it, with the exception of the two-piece polymer frame.

Testing the 2011 in the Ransom Rest is a little trickier, since the polymer frame will flex slightly. This is similar to testing the Glock in the Ransom Rest, in that the gun will need to be settled into the rest, usually taking about 25-30 rounds or more.

The finished product. The STI makes a beautiful, functional Limited Class IPSC pistol. The finish is brushed hard chrome applied by Accurate Plating and Weaponry.

Chapter 6

CUSTOM GUNSMITHING THE SERVICE PISTOL

The term 'service pistol,' as generally recognized, is any handgun, either semi-auto or revolver, which is typically issued to a military unit or law enforcement organization's front line personnel as a standard issue sidearm. The firearm typically is issued unmodified, or if modified, is only allowed to be changed by a trained and certified armorer who does not deviate from the factory specifications. In this chapter we'll be working with three common service pistols — the Glock 17, Sig P226, and Smith & Wesson M&P.

UPGRADING A GLOCK G17

The Glock pistol made its debut in 1982. Since that time, it has become one of the most popular handguns in the world. Some people love 'em, and some people hate 'em, but either way, the pistol has some very good features that make it an effective handgun for self-defense, offensive tactical operations, and competition.

I purchased my Glock in the late 1980s, and I've had quite a bit of fun with it in USPSA, IDPA, and many informal practical matches. Since that time, I've added a few items to it to enhance the pistol and make it more personal and "shootable," a word which means different things to different people. In my case, one of the first items I added was the superb Bar-Sto stainless match-grade barrel. Being an old Bullseye competitor with the Army Marksmanship Unit, I view accuracy as the Holy Grail, and the match barrel from Bar-Sto is the best there is. I opted for the oversized barrel, although the drop-in version will give excellent accuracy as well. Being a gunsmith has a few benefits, not the least of which is that I know my way around a #2 Swiss pattern file and an India stone, but even someone

with basic gunsmithing skills can easily install a match barrel in the Glock, since there are only three fitting points, and the amount of material that needs to be removed is not much. As long as you go slow and check your work, fitting the barrel is very straightforward and the benefits are huge. I also installed a set of Trijicon white outline night sights, and a Brooks Tactical Grip System. The Trijicon sights are excellent and glow very bright, but typical night sights only last about ten years and these were much older than that, so the nighttime effectiveness was severely diminished. Lastly, the Brooks Tactical grips give excellent results and actually work better when wet, but they had worn smooth and didn't provide the same gripping surface as they did when initially installed. So, this section will go through the refurbishment of a Glock, with the addition of a 3.5-lb. trigger connector. Note that the addition of a light trigger and a match barrel may change which IDPA classifications you'll be allowed to compete, so check the rules. Also, if the gun is to be used for self-defense, be careful about installing aftermarket parts that affect the feeding, firing, extraction and ejection of the gun. Any time such parts are added, always test the gun with a large quantity of ammunition before entrusting it with your life.

GLOCK UPGRADES

Not that we have that out of the way, let's get started. Installing the Bar-Sto barrel, as I mentioned, is really straightforward. There are two main fitting points — the front of the barrel hood, and the bottom flat of the barrel that sits on the Glock barrel block. First, start by making sure the gun is unloaded (you knew that) and remove the slide from the frame. Remove the recoil spring and

The finished Glock with barrel, sight, trigger and grips installed, ready to go to the range for testing.

guide, and finally, take out the old barrel. The pistol is now field stripped, and you can begin fitting the barrel.

Measure the width and length of the hood of the Bar-Sto replacement, and measure the ejection port opening of the Glock. Subtract the length of the Glock port, from the length of the barrel hood: this is the difference you need to remove from the front edge of the Bar-Sto barrel. Use a #4 Swiss pillar file to take down the edge. Do this by taking a stroke or two on the sides of the barrel hood, then try fitting the barrel into the slide. Press hard to make the barrel go into lockup, and use a soft nylon hammer to tap it into place. Use a blue Magic Marker to check, making sure you are filing the surface square, taking off only the high spots. If you are a little unsure of yourself with a file, use a soft India stone to accomplish the same thing, it will just take longer. With the stone, you don't have a safe (non-cutting) edge as on the pillar file, so be careful not to take off material from two surfaces of the barrel at the same time. Once the sides of the barrel are fitted, fit the front of the barrel. Only the material from the front edge of the barrel hood should be removed. Fit the barrel to the point to where you can push it up into battery and it stays locked, but will also drop out of battery with slight downward pressure of a fingertip on the hood. This is the ideal fit. Once the barrel is fitted to the slide, remove material on the bottom flat of the barrel where the flat sits on the barrel block. Again, use Magic Marker to show the high spots where you need to remove material.

You are finished with the barrel/slide assembly when the assembly will install on the frame. If it won't go onto the frame there is still material to be removed from the barrel flat. Once these two fitting points are taken down so the barrel locks up fully into the slide, and the slide assembly will install onto the frame, you are done. Install the slide onto the frame and cycle the gun a few times.

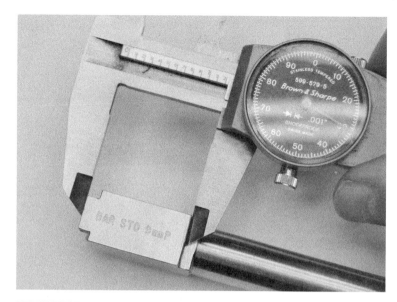

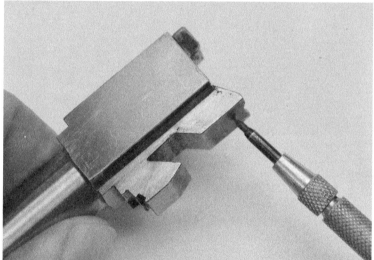

TOP: After fitting the sides of the hood, fit the front edge of the barrel locking surface until the barrel locks up into battery. BOTTOM: The bottom flat needs to be fit to the locking block in the frame. Go slow and check often for fit.

Next are the sights. Again, Trijicon are excellent when they are new, but after 20-some odd years, the Tritium can dim. In my case, it was time to go with something brighter that would give me day/night capability, ergo, the newer fiber optic sights. These sights absolutely are like a huge neon beacon. Since I still want the nighttime visibility afforded by Tritium sights, but also the bright glow of the fiber optic for daytime use, I went with Tru-Glo sights. This sight combines the best of both worlds — Tritium and fiber-optic inserts — providing 24-hour visibility.

Removing the old front sight is straightforward. Just remove the 3/16th -inch nut that holds the front sight in place. It takes a special nut driver to get in there, but

The Glock rear sight pusher works on factory and aftermarket sights equally well.

once it's out, you can install the new sight. Degrease the threads of the new sight screw and, with a toothpick, place a tiny drop of blue Loctite onto the screw threads. Place the sight into the slide, and secure it with the screw. Do not overtighten it or you will strip the threads. Just run it up snug; with the thread locker in place that sight isn't going anywhere. This is how I installed my original Trijicon sight and it's been securely fastened, and has had over 40,000 rounds through it without any issues.

The rear sight is different. It is mounted in a dovetail, and as such, there are certain "best practices" to use when installing into a cross dovetail. The main point is that the part, any part, is ALWAYS installed from right to left into the dovetail, as looking from the rear of the gun. If you install a part from left to right, then the next time you go left to right or vice versa the dovetail slot will be opened up and the part will never be able to be installed tightly. Dovetails are always very slightly

tapered from larger to smaller, from the right side to the left of the dovetail. So, the part gets installed from right to left, and removed from left to right, always! Use the Glock sight tool, because Glock rear sights require downward as well as sideways pressure for removal.

The Tru-Glo rear sight was a perfect fit going into

The Ghost Systems Glock aftermarket trigger is one of many available for the polymer pistol. It gives a great 3.5-lb. trigger pull and is adjustable for overtravel.

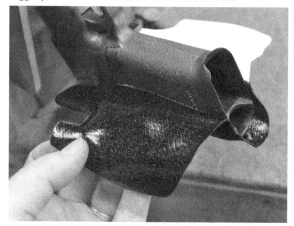

TOP: The Brooks Tactical is a textured wrap-around grip that is easy to apply, works well even with wet or sweaty hands, and is inexpensive. BOTTOM: The Glock is tested after all work is complete with the NRA trigger-weight system. This is the best way to test for precise trigger pull as the weights never go out of calibration. They are what the NRA uses to check for correct trigger pull at all NRA sanctioned matches. Get some!

the Glock M17 dovetail, and all it took was a few good raps with a nylon drift punch and a brass hammer in order to set it in the center with a light-driven, almost press fit. I ran the sight set screw up snug, but didn't use any threadlocker since I'll do that once the gun has been zeroed.

Now that you have the barrel and sight installed, the next step is to install the 3.5-lb. trigger connector. This will provide you a nice, light trigger, but again, if you are using the gun for purely defensive work, I would leave the original factory trigger connector and springs installed.

The Glock is a great service pistol, but it has a service pistol-grade trigger, which is fine for most uses: For example, law enforcement, personal defense and military applications, and even competition and informal plinking if you don't mind the heavy trigger. But if you want to use the gun strictly to compete in the various types of practical pistol competitions, then the service grade trigger is not ideal, and that's where the 3.5-lb. trigger connector comes in.

There are a number of lightweight Glock trigger connectors available, and I chose the Ghost trigger from Ghost Industries. It comes with a 3.5-lb. trigger connector, and a variety of springs to set its weight. I installed the 3.5 connector, but opted for the heavier 6-lb. trigger and firing pin springs that will yield a little heavier trigger pull in case I do want to carry the gun out and about. The result is a trigger that breaks a little over 4.5 lbs. The trigger connector is a direct replacement, and removing the old connector allows for replacement of the new, Ghost Industries part. The Ghost trigger connector comes with a small tab on the connector, which requires minor fitting. This tab acts as a trigger stop — a nice feature to have on a competition gun. The kit also comes with a clear slide backplate in order to view the sear and firing pin engagement when fitting the trigger connector.

The last step is to remove the old Brooks Tactical Grip, and install the new one from the same company. This is the exact same grip that I originally installed over twenty years ago, but the old one had worn with age. Installation is simple. Once the old one is peeled off, degrease the grip area with brake cleaner, and wipe it down with the alcohol pad supplied with the new grip. Since the grip covers the magazine button on both sides, the instructions demonstrate that the area around the mag button on both sides needs to have a tiny amount of oil applied so the grip doesn't adhere to the mag release. Again, I've had the old Brooks Tactical grip installed on my Glock forever and have never had an issue with the magazine release not functioning properly. Wrap the new grip onto the pistol's frame per the instructions. If it isn't applied exactly correct, you can lift it and move it, but try not to do that too many times. (The grip overwraps itself, so if you wrap it together, it's difficult to remove it.)

Once the grip is installed, the entire pistol gets reassembled, and function checks are done, along with functioning using dummy rounds. Checking the trigger pull with the NRA weights, mine came in at just over 4 ¾ lbs. That's not too light or too heavy, and has minimal overtravel.

So there you have it — a pistol that is extremely accurate with the Bar-Sto barrel, has excellent sights with 24/7 visibility, a light, crisp trigger, and excellent textured grips that work in all environments — even better with wet or sweaty hands. Now I just need to take it out to the next IDPA match and run it through its paces.

GUNSMITHING THE SIG P226

One of the outgrowths of the XM9 Joint Service Small Arms Program was that there was a flurry of innovation and interest in a new service pistol for the U.S. Military. One of the new designs resulting from that effort was the Sig P226. It is arguably one of the most successful double-action/single-action (DA/SA) handguns ever developed. As a testament to its design, the P226 and the Beretta were the only pistols to successfully pass all of the tests, and were accepted into service. The Beretta became the M9 service pistol and the P226 was adopted by the U.S. Navy SEAL Teams, with the P228, the smaller version of the P226, being pressed into service as the compact service pistol, used by units

such as the Criminal Investigation Division (CID) and others needing to carry a smaller, more compact duty pistol. The P226 is also carried by Israeli Special Forces, the German SEK, or Spezialeinsatzkommandos (Special Deployment Commandos) and the elite French GIGN, the French version of the U.S. Delta operators, as well as the British Army and Canadian Special Forces.

As good as the P226 is, and make no mistake, the pistol is very well engineered and manufactured, like any other firearm it can always be improved upon. I attended the SIG Armorers Course at the Sig facility headquarters in Exeter, NH. Throughout the course I could see where the gun could be improved upon by tapping into aftermarket parts manufacturers.

As with most handguns, there are three areas in which the P226 can improve most: sights, trigger quality, and accuracy. Actually, Sig sights were addressed by the factory later on, when the pistol was offered with Tritium night sights, a major improvement though they are still a little small for my liking, although for the purposes of this article, they were left alone.

The second area, trigger quality/weight, is something

The Sig ready to be accurized with the addition of the barrel, hammer spring kit and an SRT trigger. The author added the Surefire X300a tactical light.

with which most service pistols are hampered. This is because the pistol has to be reliable in all types of harsh field and weather conditions, when shot with military grade ball ammunition. Basically, the gun has to go bang every time with little regard for the quality of the trigger pull. By having a heavy trigger there is a fairly large margin of reliability built in — the gun will fire the round if it has been properly chambered, regardless of the condition of that round or of the gun, within reason. The P226 and other service-type pistols don't necessarily have poor trigger quality, it's just that the trigger reset distance may be too long, a little gritty or uneven.

The third area, accuracy, can be improved very easily with the addition of a quality match barrel. The barrel I chose was the Match Target from Bar-Sto Precision. The factory barrel will give good, serviceable accuracy, generally around 2-3 inches for five shots at 25 yards. But with the addition of a match barrel, this group size can be cut in half or more.

You can improve the trigger quality and still maintain that level of reliability by spending a little bit of money on aftermarket parts and some time at the workbench. Since my P226 came with excellent Tritium sights from the factory, I decided to leave those on for now, and turn to trigger quality and accuracy. I will probably install the newer fiber optic sights on the gun in the future, but for now, they seem to be pretty visible in day/night conditions, and work fairly well.

One complaint leveled at the P226 is the distance the

trigger needs in order to reset itself after firing. The factory has addressed this by offering a Short Reset Trigger, also known as the SRT, which consists of the SRT sear and SRT safety lever. Both of these parts should be installed by either a factory-trained Sig Armorer, or a qualified gunsmith. The process is, first the old sear and safety lever are removed, the SRT sear installed, and the sear spring tensioned. The SRT safety lever is installed by reassembling the pistol with the exception of the grips, the sear spring de-tensioned and the sear pin pushed to the left until there is room to install the safety lever. Once the safety lever is in place, the sear pin can be pushed back in until flush.

This handy upgrade enables the trigger to reset sooner, which gives the competitive action shooter quicker split times, and also helps the CCW holder when the pistol is used in defensive situations.

The heavy trigger pull, while necessary for a military or LE pistol, can be lightened for the civilian shooter. You can maintain the same level of reliability by simply replacing the factory hammer spring with an aftermarket part, in this case, the excellent Wolff hammer spring. The hammer spring is replaced very easily by lifting up and out on the hammer spring retainer, replacing the factory spring with the Wolff spring and easing the hammer spring retainer back into place. Doing this will reduce the double-action trigger pull by about 3 pounds, and the single-action pull by about 1 to 1 ½ pounds. One caveat when replacing parts like

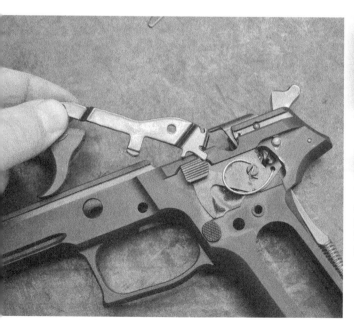

The Sig is disassembled for installation of the SRT trigger.

The Wolff hammer spring is an excellent replacement part to improve the Sig P226's trigger pull.

the hammer spring to reduce the trigger pull weight or any aftermarket part that involves the functioning of the gun: If the handgun is going to be used for defensive purposes, it must be tested for reliability by firing a minimum of 500 rounds through it with zero malfunctions before entrusting your life to it.

Finally, the third way we talked about improving the gun, by enhancing its accuracy, is very easily accomplished by installing the outstanding match barrel from Bar-Sto Precision. Founded in 1967, and currently run by Irv Stone III, Bar-Sto barrels have been used by the Marine Corps MTU since 1977, and have won every major pistol tournament, including Camp Perry, USPSA Nationals, Steel Challenge, and hundreds of regional and state championships across the country and around the world. Manufactured from stainless steel, and machined and rifled in-house, the barrels, when properly fitted, are capable of incredible accuracy. I've toured the Bar-Sto facility while working as a Senior Gunsmith for a classified DoD facility building 1911s for the Special Operations community. We were using a competing product for our customer's guns, and although the accuracy was good, we thought it could be better. We purchased a small batch of Bar-Sto barrels for testing and found that on average we were getting about a 3/8th-inch improvement in overall group size which, when taken in context with the amount of guns we were building at the time, was a significant improvement. We made the switch to Bar-Sto barrels then, and I continue to rely on them for my own gunsmithing projects today.

I've installed literally hundreds of the Bar-Sto match barrels in 1911, Glock, Sig, and S&W M&P handguns, and have always found them to be consistently accurate, very well machined and finished, and capable of delivering outstanding accuracy. They make two stainless versions: Drop-in, which require very little if any fitting, and the Match Target, which is a gunsmith-fit part. Bar-Sto will also install these barrels for you for a small fee.

To fit the Match Target barrel to the Sig, you need to understand how the barrel locks up into the slide. Unlike locking systems like the 1911, which have the locking lugs machined into the barrel, and corresponding grooves machined into the slide for the barrel to lock into, the Sig barrel (as well as Glock, and S&W M&P) locks up by extending the barrel hood to fit into the ejection port. This area is left slightly long in the Bar-Sto Match Target barrel, so you can fit it to each individual slide for best accuracy. First remove material from the sides of the hood so it fits up into the slide. Then remove a small amount of material from the front of the barrel's locking surface. Use a #2 flat Swiss file, but if it's your first barrel, you may want to try an India stone. Just remember, the stone doesn't have a safe edge like a file does, so be careful you don't remove material where you don't want to. Once the barrel fits up into the full lock position, make sure the sides of the barrel

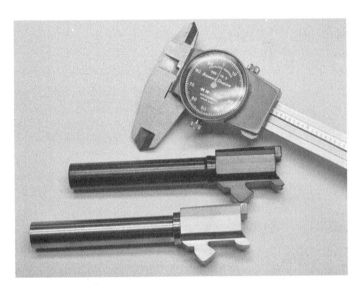

TOP: The Bar-Sto match barrel is an excellent replacement for the factory tube, and is a great project part for the custom gunsmith. BOTTOM: The factory barrel crown is on the left and the Bar-Sto 11-degree target crown on the right. The 11-degree crown is used by rifle barrel makers and custom riflesmiths for its inherent accuracy.

The Sig field stripped and the Bar-Sto barrel ready for fitting.

hood are clear of their corresponding recess in the slide. When properly fitted, the barrel should stay up into the locked position, and drop out of battery with just a slight amount of finger pressure.

The next area to fit is the bottom locking surface, which makes contact on the barrel locking block. Use a blue Magic Marker to show the high spots when fitting any parts, but especially barrels, because a good fit greatly contributes to the accuracy of the finished product. Only a small amount of material needs to be removed in order for the slide to go back on the frame. You should see a contact area on the bottom locking surface of the barrel where it makes contact with the locking block. Strive for obtaining as much contact as possible as this is where the lower barrel locks up when the upper receiver assembly goes into battery and will greatly contribute to the overall accuracy of the gun. Once the upper and lower locking surfaces have been fitted, cycle the slide several times to make sure the barrel locks and unlocks properly.

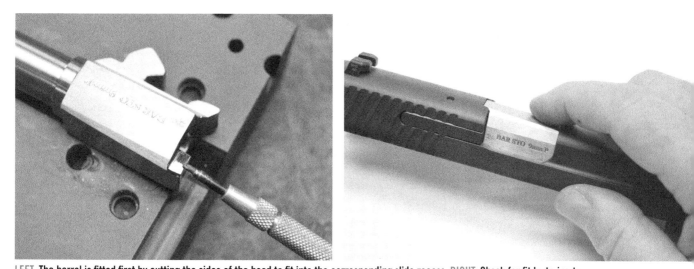

LEFT: The barrel is fitted first by cutting the sides of the hood to fit into the corresponding slide recess. RIGHT: Check for fit by trying to push the barrel down out of battery after you've fitted the sides and front of the barrel's locking surface. A very small amount of drag is ideal. The barrel should stay up on its own, and drop out with light finger pressure. This may be too tight for some pistols.

Check to see if the slide is a little sticky either going into or out of battery and especially make sure it goes fully into battery. If the gun is too sticky when cycling, carefully remove material from either the upper or lower contact locking surfaces. Then use dummy rounds to check for proper cycling and, finally, take the gun to the range for live fire.

For this pistol, I obtained a set of Ransom Rest inserts for the P226. I normally use the Ransom Rest for the 1911 pistols I build, but I wanted to see what the P226 would do out of the rest, with the match target

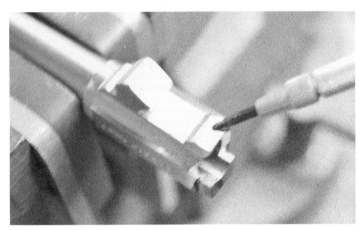

barrel and good ammunition. I used the Ransom Rest with the factory barrel installed, and obtained groups of about 2.5 inches at 25 yards with the excellent Hornady 115-grain Critical Defense FTX ammunition. Swapping out the factory barrel for the fitted, Bar-Sto MT barrel immediately shrank those five-shot groups down to a little over an inch.

The following is a test I ran with the Sig, in which I compared the factory barrel's accuracy with the Match Target from Bar-Sto. In the handgun world, whether it's competitive shooting, informal plinking or defensive pistolcraft, accuracy is one of the three critical aspects, along with power and speed. I'm of the opinion that you can never have too much accuracy in a handgun. The accuracy of today's handguns is excellent for the most part. They are designed to feed and function through the widest variety of ammunition types and configurations as possible. Defensive pistols and ammunition absolutely need to be as close to 100 percent reliable as humans can make them, and today's manu-

ABOVE: The lower locking surface is filed or stoned to provide clearance in order to properly sit on the barrel locking block.
BELOW: The Sig P226, with the Bar-Sto barrel in place, and ready for testing.

Accuracy testing the Sig in the Ransom Rest.

facturers do an outstanding job in achieving that goal.

But we are always looking for ways to improve things, and pistols are no exception. Factory handguns sacrifice a little accuracy to achieve reliability by loosening manufacturing tolerances. This is not necessarily a bad thing, but a cottage industry has sprung up to make parts — in this case, handgun barrels — that increase accuracy without sacrificing reliability.

I knew what an impact the Bar-Sto Match Target barrel had on the accuracy of the 1911 platform, and I've had them in my Glock 17, delivering extremely tight groups and absolute reliability with every type of ammo I've run through it, included several handloads. But I was interested in doing a side-by-side comparison of the factory and the Bar-Sto barrel, in the Sig P226 to further confirm the theory.

The semi-fit barrels may need to be fitted, or could possibly just drop in due to variations of manufacturing tolerances. If you elect to buy a Bar-Sto barrel, make sure you understand the difference between the two variations. Bear in mind that the accuracy of a semi-fit or drop-in is usually very close to the accuracy level you will achieve with the fitted barrel. Most of the accuracy of a match target barrel comes from the more uniform bore and groove dimensions of the bore itself.

Now you have a pistol with a new match barrel, but how does it shoot? This is where the Ransom Rest comes into play. It's the only way to test a handgun, and handgun ammunition, properly. It removes all human error and influence on accuracy. It does take some technique to set up and get the most out of it, but it's

very simple to use. The key is consistency.

Once I had the Ransom Rest set up on the bench, and the Sig clamped into it, it was time to start shooting. Since the Bar-Sto barrel was already installed in the gun, I went with that as the initial test. I used a good selection of defensive ammunition for the evaluation, including Nosler's 124-grain JHP match-grade round, Federal's 124-grain HST tactical round, Hornady's 115-grain FTX Critical Defense load, Black

TOP: The Bar-Sto barrel is removed and the factory barrel installed as the test continues. MIDDLE: The Ransom Rest is the best way to test handguns and ammunition for accuracy and consistency, especially if you have performed custom gunsmithing. BOTTOM: The Ransom Rest recoils consistently from shot to shot.

Good technique when manipulating the trigger actuator gives consistent results.

The Hornady Critical Defense load shot almost a five-shot, one-inch group at 25 yards.

Hill's 115-grain TAC-XP +P round, and Remington's 124-grain JHP Ultimate Defense load. The target was set at 25 yards, and I shot a single five-shot group with all brands of ammo in order to produce a sample group size from both the factory and match barrel. Time precluded from shooting more groups from each to produce an average, but since I was just conducting a test to see if the barrel made an improvement and not conducting an ammunition test, per se, a single group from each load would still give me a large enough sample size to draw some conclusions.

Once all ammunition was tested with the Bar-Sto barrel, I removed the slide from the frame, and with the pistol still in the Ransom Rest, installed the factory barrel and repeated the test using the same ammunition and firing five-shot groups. The results were a little surprising, but as expected, the group sizes with the match barrel were practically cut in half, although the Sig factory barrel did produce a good group with one of the factory loads. This is why you should test your guns with a variety of ammunition types, and use group averages, rather than a single good group to get a truer picture of the gun's accuracy. Time also precluded me from testing handloads, which may have also produced

some better groups than the factory loads. That's why it's always a good idea to test a gun with a variety of ammunition; you never know which gun/load combination will work best in your particular firearm. The results of the test were remarkable: with the addition of a Bar-Sto match barrel accuracy was improved by over an inch in the average group size compared to the factory barrel, cutting the group size average almost in half. A service-type pistol that can produce 2 ½-inch groups with factory ammunition and a factory barrel is not bad, but more accuracy is always a good thing, especially as the range increases. The Ransom Rest really showed the true accuracy of all of the ammunition, as well as the accuracy potential of the excellent Sig P226 pistol. The addition of a quality match barrel like the Bar-Sto improved the accuracy of the Sig, and will definitely give the accuracy edge to any gun.

The entire job only took me about two hours to complete, including installing the SRT trigger, hammer spring and Bar-Sto Match Target barrel, with a minimum of tools, not including range time. Now I have a pistol that's accurate, reliable, and a great tool for concealed carry, IDPA or IPSC competition.

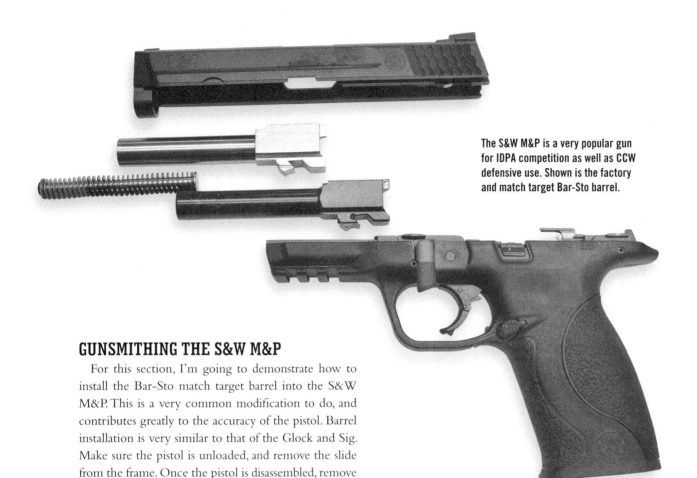

The S&W M&P is a very popular gun for IDPA competition as well as CCW defensive use. Shown is the factory and match target Bar-Sto barrel.

GUNSMITHING THE S&W M&P

For this section, I'm going to demonstrate how to install the Bar-Sto match target barrel into the S&W M&P. This is a very common modification to do, and contributes greatly to the accuracy of the pistol. Barrel installation is very similar to that of the Glock and Sig. Make sure the pistol is unloaded, and remove the slide from the frame. Once the pistol is disassembled, remove material from the sides of the barrel until it goes up into battery. The front of the barrel's hood is left long to provide solid lockup, so remove material from this area very carefully until the barrel goes fully into battery, just like you did with the Glock and the Sig.

Once the barrel goes up into battery, turn your attention to the lockup surface on the barrel's flat where it bears on the locking block. Again, use the Magic Marker to check for high spots as you remove material to fit the lower barrel lug to the locking block. Keep trying to install the barrel and slide assembly to the

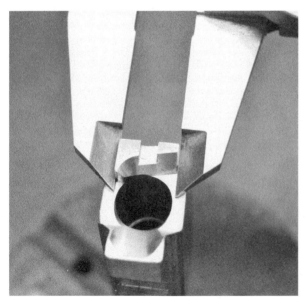

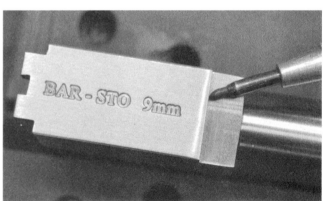

LEFT: The sides of the hood of the match target barrel are fitted first. RIGHT: Fit the front of the hood until the barrel goes into lockup with the slide.

Fitting the front of the locking surface of the match target barrel for proper fit.

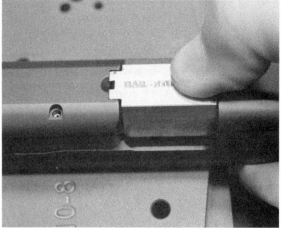

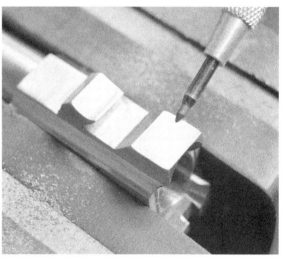

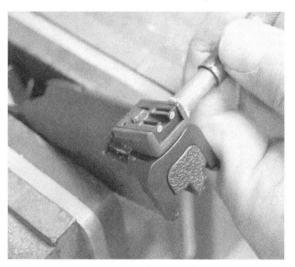

TOP: The barrel might be a little sticky at this point. Try to push it down and out of battery. Then do a final fitting. MIDDLE: The barrel flat is fitted so it bears on the barrel locking block, similar to the Glock and Sig. Use the Magic Marker to show the high spots and file or stone for the best fit. BOTTOM: The rear sight is drifted into place with light taps using a brass punch. A nylon punch would also be appropriate.

frame until enough material has been removed. Cycle the slide assembly and it should be a little sticky in the locking and unlocking cycle. Look again for tiny high spots on the hood length and/or the bottom of the barrel locking surface. Leave it a little sticky, and shoot about 100 rounds through the pistol to seat everything in. Usually this is enough to get the barrel seated and functioning correctly. If it's still a little sticky after firing 100 rounds, remove a little more material.

Once the barrel is installed, the sights are replaced with hi-visibility fiber-optic versions. These are great sights to use for any service-type or competition pistol as they gather in all of the available light and work very well even in dim lighting conditions. To remove the existing sights, drive out the old ones from left to right using a soft brass punch. If you want to reuse the sights and keep them for another time, use the handy sight pusher available from Brownells to drive out the old, and install the new sights. Remember, drive out any part that is installed into a dovetail from left to right, and install the new part from right to left. Once the new sights are installed into the slide, take the pistol to the range and test it for functioning with the new barrel in place, and to ensure the sights are regulated to point of aim/point of impact at 25 yards.

Chapter 7

GUNSMITHING SMITH & WESSON REVOLVERS

The S&W customized with an action job, Leupold Delta Point sight, and a signature Jerry Miculek grip is a great revolver for an Action Steel-type event.

The Smith & Wesson 686 revolver was designed as Smith's answer to the success of the Colt Python. The 686 has ruled various action shooting events going back to the original PPC matches of the mid- to late-1950s as characterized by the S&W M10, which later had a heavy barrel and a sight rib attached. The gun also had extensive trigger work done to it, as well as other match-grade enhancements. Later, IPCS and NRA Action pistol came about, and these games have either a revolver division, or are shot revolver neutral, meaning you shoot the stage with no more than six rounds, therefore no one gains an advantage by going to the semi-auto.

Today, revolvers are a niche within competitive pistol shooting, but the competitors who use them are very die-hard fans of the gun. The revolver can still be a very competitive choice, as anyone who has seen Jerry Miculek shoot can testify.

So, the S&W revolver is a great project gun not only because of its competitive lineage, but because if you can work on a S&W 686, you can work on all S&W revolvers. And if you can work on them, you can work on most other double-action revolvers, with the exception of the Colt Python, which has an action unique unto itself.

The gun that S&W sent me for this project will be used as a competition revolver for steel matches. Why

Steel? Because they are revolver neutral matches with five targets shot from start to finish, so they are a lot of fun with pretty much any gun, but especially the revolver, which provides a unique challenge and requires additional shooting skills.

Let's assume you have a new, serviceable handgun. To make a service grade wheelgun competitive, there are basically three areas to address: sights, trigger, and accuracy. Since shooting steel is done at fairly close range, a match barrel is not needed as the gun has enough accuracy to be competitive. And while more accuracy is always a good thing, leave the accuracy as is and concentrate on sights and trigger work for this project.

SIGHT UPGRADE

The S&W front and rear sights are pretty good as they are for normal, everyday shooting at the range, or for defensive or CCW carrying duties, but for competition work, especially shooting steel where speed is important, need to be larger and of better visibility. I'm also going to put a Leupold Delta Point optical sight on this project gun.

The S&W front sight is a ramped style, with a red insert. The red ramp is OK, but for competition work something larger and brighter is needed. Enter the fiber-optic sight. First used on competition shotguns, the fiber-optic sight found its way over to handguns and has really taken off, with sight sets available for virtually all of the major handguns, like the Glock, S&W M&P, and the Springfield XD lineup.

To replace the front sight, it's really a pretty straightforward operation, but there are a couple of points to remember. The front sight is held in place with a roll pin, but on some older guns it was secured with a solid pin. If your gun has a solid pin, use the proper cup-tipped punch. The cup tip will sit on the rounded end of the solid pin and not slip off when trying to drive out the pin, as sometimes can happen with a standard flat punch pin. If you gun has a roll pin, use the regular 1/16th-inch pin punch to drive it out from either direction. (Note it's not a good idea to reuse roll pins. Once installed they are compressed in the hole to provide holding power. After being driven out, they won't have the same holding power, so discard and use a fresh pin, they're cheap.)

Once you have the old front sight removed, install the new one and drill the sight hole using a drill press with a fresh #53 drill bit. Only use drill bits a half dozen times before discarding. The TiN-coated drills have quite a bit of life, I've drilled ten or more holes with them, which is something I would never do with a standard drill. The TiN, or Titanium Nitride coating, greatly extends their life. Once the sight hole is drilled, degrease everything and use a very small amount of blue Loctite to hold everything in place. Don't rely on the roll pin to hold the sight. Remember, this is a competition gun, and will be shot much more than a weekend plinker, so you need to make sure the sight stays on. Once the sight is in place, install the fiber insert that comes in red or green. I tend to opt for red, since that's the most visible under various lighting conditions. When installing the fiber insert, use a small drop of super glue in the center bar to secure it in place.

The next step is to install a larger blade on the rear sight. Some may ask why not a fiber optic rear sight, too — a combination some people like. However, for speed shooting in steel class the focus is on the front sight, and the rear is just there as a reference. There's no time to line up front and rear. So use a big, highly visible front sight, and a big blade in the back to provide reference. This is a fast combination. Before you rebuild the rear sight, or install an aftermarket part, some explanation of the sight itself is needed. The Weigand rear sight blade comes from the shop of Jack Weigand, former President of the American Pistolsmith's Guild, the professional organization dedicated to elevating the professionalism of the pistolsmithing profession. He was the 1999 Pistolsmith of the Year, and has been featured on numerous magazine covers. Weigand Combat makes great parts for the competitive shooter. The rear sight is installed just like a regular S&W rear sight, but the blade is substantially larger. To rebuild the rear sight, or install a new blade on the rear sight assembly, you need to break the original sight. That's right, to fix it, you need to break it. That's because the screw is secured in place with the nut on the end of the screw, and is staked in place. The screw is an inexpensive part, and the easiest way to remove it is to turn the screw in clockwise until it stops, then keep turning it until it breaks. Remove the parts by pushing out the screw and nut, being careful to secure the spring and plunger in the screw head. Install the new blade, with the spring and plunger, keeping the screw nut on the end. Center the new blade. Secure the nut in place with the windage nut staking tool. This is a special tool made just for this purpose. You should purchase a 10 pack of windage springs and plungers. They are cheap and you will lose a few trying to get the windage screw in. When I attended the S&W Armorer's Course for revolvers most of us were launching springs and plungers all day long. Most in the class were police officers who were not used to handling such small springs. If you are in a hurry or don't want to mess with the small springs and plungers, you can send the sight assembly to Weigand and for $15 they will install the blade for you.

Once the rear sight assembly is installed, remove it in order to install the scope mount base for the Leupold Delta Point. Leupold provides a very good mount and base for mounting the optics, but the aftermarket parts are also good. This gives you another option to mount the sight, and the brushed aluminum base looks really nice with the stainless steel frame. Simply remove the rear sight assembly and install the base to the topstrap of the revolver with the screws provided. Mount the Delta Point onto this base. Always use a small amount of blue Loctite between the base and the topstrap of the frame to secure the screws. Do not use Loctite on the screws that mount the optic to the mount.

S&W TRIGGER JOBS

One of the first aspects of doing a trigger job on any revolver is to decide if you really need it in the first place. If it's used for everyday carry or home defense, I would recommend leaving the gun alone. Many people will want to lighten the trigger, thinking it will be more accurate or whatever, and that's true, but in a home in-

The strain screw can be used to lower the weight of the trigger pull, but it is never a recommended method since the gun can misfire or even hangfire.

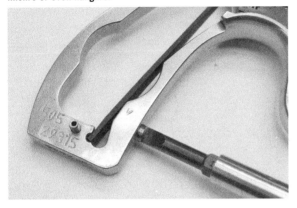

vasion your adrenaline will be sky high, and you probably won't even remember if the trigger was heavy or light or anything else for that matter.

Having said that, if you are set on doing any kind of action work on a defensive revolver, I would limit the work to just lightly polishing some of the more non-critical contact internal surfaces. It's very easy to polish too much. In doing this kind of work, you are trying to smooth the trigger pull, not lighten it. Keep the mainspring and rebound slide spring untouched. There are many tricks to improve the trigger pull on the revolver, but again, if the gun is used for defensive purposes, keeping it as close as possible to factory trim will always be the best choice.

I see and hear many comments from shooters from a wide variety of backgrounds and levels of experience. One time at the range not too long ago, I heard a shooter make this statement. "Why should I pay a gunsmith to do a trigger job when I can just unscrew the mainspring screw and accomplish the same thing?" That is a factual statement. If you back out the strain screw on the mainspring, it will definitely make the trigger pull lighter, but here's the problem: by backing out the screw, it will do nothing about the quality of the trigger pull of the gun. In other words, the gritty, rough trigger pull will not be affected at all by easing out the tension on the mainspring strain screw. The second, and most important point is by unscrewing the strain screw the weight of the trigger pull is lessened, but it will also lighten the inertia of the hammer, making the possibility of a light hammer strike and a potential misfire or hangfire likely. If this is a competition gun that's OK, you get a refire. If it's a defensive pistol, you won't get a second chance. Some people will try all sorts of tricks to make the trigger pull lighter, includ-

ing clipping coils on the rebound slide (don't do this), thinning the mainspring, shortening the mainspring strain screw and a host of other methods. The bottom line is, if it's a defensive pistol, lightly polish the contact areas to smoothen the trigger pull but leave the factory springs as they are.

Since the project gun is strictly a competition pistol, it's primarily being used for steel-type matches, but also would be a great option for NRA Action Pistol with either the iron sights reinstalled for Metallic Sight Division, or with an electronic optic and a couple of other parts like a set of wings. This would make the gun excellent for an NRA Action Pistol in Open Division, perhaps with the addition of a match barrel and crane lock. You can do all sorts of modifications to the gun to make it more competitive.

The first thing to do is to detail strip the gun and conduct an inspection. Since this revolver was sent to me directly from S&W, and is not a used gun, I don't need to check the headspace, cylinder end shake and barrel/cylinder gap, or cylinder timing, so I won't cover that here, but if yours is a used gun, for example, make sure you or a competent gunsmith familiar with S&W revolvers do a thorough function check on the gun. Make sure the cylinder timing is correct and there is no excessive end shake. If the gun needs work, all of these areas are correctable. Remove the Leupold sight for now, and set it aside. Remove the screw for the Hogue wood grip, and the grip. Now you can remove the sideplate. This is really easy, but if you don't know how to do it, it can be a bit puzzling. I used to work as a gunsmith for a fairly large gunshop in Southern California, and one day a customer came in with a box of parts. He said he had sent the gun off to be reblued and had taken it apart, but couldn't get it back together again. Not an uncommon occurrence in the shop at which I worked, we had people come in from time to time with their guns completely apart in a box. I looked in the box and noticed it was a nicely polished and blued, S&W M19 4-inch Smith, all in parts. I told the customer that I could have it back together for him in about 30 minutes, until I noticed the sideplate. It was bent at about a 30-degree angle. I asked the customer what had happened, and he said he had taken it apart in order to send it off to a shop for bluing. Obviously, the customer was unfamiliar with how to get a sideplate off of a S&W revolver. He had pried the sideplate off the gun. The only fix was to send the entire thing back to Smith & Wesson to fit a new sideplate.

First things first. Make sure you have the proper

The sideplate is removed by unscrewing the sideplate screws and tapping the frame with a soft hammer.

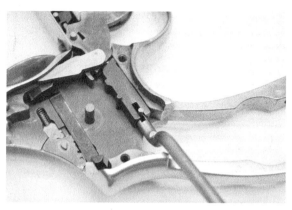

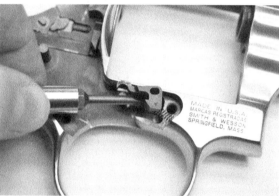

TOP: The rebound slide tool makes quick work of removing the rebound slide. MIDDLE: The cylinder bolt lifts straight up and out, be careful to capture the spring. BOTTOM: The ejector rod can be held in a padded vise and unscrewed by turning the cylinder clockwise to remove.

screwdriver bits. Brownells sells a kit with the correct screwdriver blades specifically for the S&W revolver. Make sure you have them. Then, remove the front sideplate screw first. This screw holds the cylinder crane in place. Open the cylinder and swing it out, remove the cylinder and crane, and set them aside. Remove the two remaining screws. Now, with a soft-faced nylon hammer, tap on the frame, either at the front around the trigger guard, or at the grip strap. Anywhere you tap will cause the sideplate to "pop up" so it can be removed. If the hammer block pops out, don't worry, it just kind of floats in there anyway. It will go back in easily. Now unscrew the mainspring and remove it. Pull the cylinder bolt and the hammer back at the same time and remove the hammer. Use the special tool to remove the rebound slide and spring.

The rebound slide spring is under quite a bit of tension so be careful. Pull the cylinder hand back slightly and lift the trigger out, working a screwdriver bit under the cylinder stop and pop it out. Remember, there are many springs under tension, so have spares on hand and wear eye protection. Remove the cylinder bolt by lifting it up and out, being careful to capture the bolt spring. Polish the sides of the cylinder bolt. Remove the crane from the cylinder assembly. Place the ejector rod in a padded vise and turn the cylinder clockwise. The ejector rod is threaded onto the extractor with left-hand threads. To unscrew, turn it in reverse. Once that is disassembled, remove the extractor and set everything aside. Chamfer the charge holes, but do not touch the extractor. With the tool of your choice, (I use a deburring tool because it leaves an even, smooth finish) lightly chamfer the cylinder holes, clean out any chips and set it aside. Do not overdo this step, as it's easy to take off too much.

You are not going to use the original trigger so set it aside. For this project we are using the Ron Power drop-in trigger kit. This kit comes with a match trigger, lightweight rebound spring and a couple of trigger stops. The trigger stops will need to be fitted. Using an India stone, lightly polish the rebound slide's bottom and side, and the surfaces in the frame where it moves. Lightly polish the cylinder stop where the trigger nose rolls over. Just break the edge with a hard Arkansas stone. Strive to keep all surfaces true, lightly polishing these parts. Thoroughly clean all of the parts you've pol-

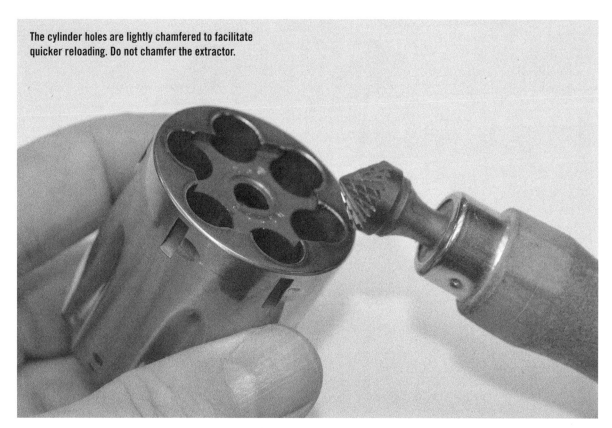

The cylinder holes are lightly chamfered to facilitate quicker reloading. Do not chamfer the extractor.

ished and clean the frame. I always use the Ron Power hammer and trigger shims in all S&W revolver trigger jobs. They keep the hammer and trigger off of the frame and reduce the friction.

Now you can reassemble the gun. Reinstall the cylinder stop, being careful not to launch the actuator spring. Install the trigger shim and reinstall the trigger. Pull the trigger a few times to make sure it actuates the cylinder stop. Install the rebound slide with the 12-pound reduced power rebound slide spring. Actuate the trigger again to make sure everything is functioning correctly. Do not polish the hammer at all. The hammer and trigger are both case hardened, and if you polish these parts you will cut through the case hardening and into the soft metal. Case hardening is only a thousandth or two inches in thickness, so pretty much any polishing will destroy the parts. Also, the hammer engagement notch is too small to do anything with, anyway. Leave this part alone. You can, however, remove the hammer nose or hammer fly.

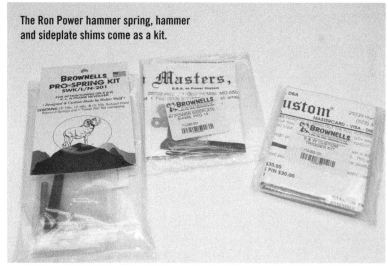

The Ron Power hammer spring, hammer and sideplate shims come as a kit.

Polish the tip where it rides on top of the trigger when the gun is fired in double action. Optionally, polish the corresponding area on the trigger, though the finish of the part is pretty good as it comes from Power Mfg. Install the hammer fly on the hammer and reinstall the hammer, putting the hammer shim on the frame first.

Install the mainspring, and secure with its setscrew. Tighten the set screw completely. Now you have the gun almost reassembled, but you want to do a function check to make sure everything is put back together

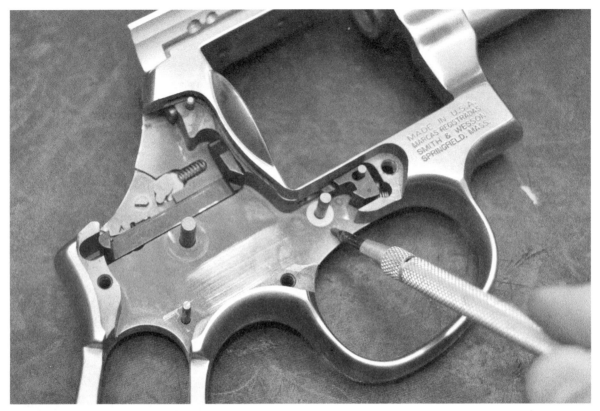

ABOVE: The shim applied to the S&W frame. LEFT: The Ransom Rest can also be used for revolvers, and is a great way to test ammunition.

assembly back into the gun and lock the cylinder into place. Slide the hammer block onto the gun with the notch of the hammer block riding on the stud of the rebound slide.

Put the sideplate back onto the frame by sliding the tab at its top into the notch in the frame. Gently tap it into place and reinstall the screws. Reinstall the grip and the Leupold Delta Point and you're done! Cycle the action a few times, and pull the trigger both in single and double action. It's perfectly fine to dry fire the gun. The trigger is now much smoother and lighter. Single-action pull is 3.1 lbs. and double action is 7.7 lbs.

This is a fun project, and the gun is now ready to be competitive at the range. Are these the only modifications you could have done to this gun? Absolutely not. Were these all of the areas that could have been polished? No, there was actually quite a bit more polishing and fitting that could have been done to this gun, but this is a pretty good start. You now have a reliable and highly competitive revolver, perfect for Steel-type shooting or even NRA Action Pistol. If you have a S&W revolver, or are thinking about getting one, get yourself some tools and get started.

properly. Apply a small amount of oil on the gun at the hammer and trigger posts, the rebound slide, and the cylinder stop.

Reassemble the extractor and ejector rod back onto the cylinder. Install the crane, and reinstall the cylinder

Chapter 8

SETTING UP & USING THE RANSOM REST

Acquiring a new, custom pistol is a wonderful thing. When you save your hard-earned money and put it down on a new pistol or revolver, it's a great day to take it to the range for the first time and blaze away. Also, if you reload for this new, custom pistol, it's even more satisfying to take a couple hundred or so carefully assembled pet handloads and shoot some really nice groups with them. But what happens if that new custom handgun — or even a new factory gun — doesn't perform the way you expected?

Going beyond that, how do you know what kind of accuracy to expect from a particular gun or load? Many custom 1911 builders provide an accuracy guarantee with their pistols, and that's a good thing, but many do not. Plus, there are many variables to take into account when discussing accuracy potential of any gun/load combination. Guns can be really finicky. I've shot many for which the groups opened or tightened up just by slightly changing one component of a handload, or by switching lot numbers on a batch of ammunition. Not only that, the human variable probably is the largest factor affecting the measurement of accurate results of the gun/load combination. How many of us are National Champion Bullseye shooters, or Olympic competitors? Even those shooters have good and bad days.

Taking away the human variable is why the Ransom Rest was invented. I was first introduced to it when I was hired by a DoD contractor to build 1911 pistols for the government. I personally have built over 500 1911s and have used the Ransom Rest for each one of them. It has been around since 1969 and really is the gold standard for gun and ammo testing.

Getting the most from a Ransom Rest means building a mounting a board for it so it can be secured to the shooting bench at your local range. Most ranges have shooting pedestals made from cinder block with a concrete top. This is a very sturdy basis for attaching the mounting board with the Ransom Rest attached. Remember, you are trying to remove as much movement as possible, in order to make sure the pistol returns to the exact same spot after each shot. If the bench to which you are attaching the mounting board is wobbly, you are just wasting your time.

Building a mounting board is pretty straightforward and anyone who is even mildly handy with power tools can construct one in a couple of hours. The Ransom Rest company sends pretty good instructions, but if you are like me, if the instructions say ½-inch thick plywood, I go with ¾ or 1 inch. Ransom recommends three C-clamps so, of course, I use four — one on each corner.

Go to your local range and measure the dimensions of the shooting tables and make a paper template. With those dimensions it's a simple matter to lay everything out using a single sheet of ¾- or 1-inch plywood. Then screw and glue 1/2x3-inch strips to the bottom of the plywood. This is to make sure that the plywood is suspended off of the concrete table top. The mounting board should only contact the table on the front and rear. Put additional 1/2x3-inch strips on the side to add a little more stiffness to the board. The board should not make any contact with the table top.

Once the board is roughed out and the supporting strips are installed, add 4-inch square metal plates to the

Lay out the board and trim to length. Use the strips to raise the board off of the table top.

TOP: This mounting method did not use the Windage base, an option that's handy for quickly setting the pistol up on the target. BOTTOM: The Ransom Rest mounted to the board and the metal plates glued to the four corners is ready to take to the range.

The Ransom Rest is bolted to the bench, and ready for testing.

four corners. These keep the C-clamps, which will be used to secure the board to the table top, from cracking and splitting the wood by spreading the clamping force over a wider area. They are available in your local, friendly big home improvement store where you will also get the plywood mounting board and wood strips.

Once the board is made, and the wood strips and metal corner plates added, affix the Ransom Rest. The instructions included with it spell out very specifically how and where to place the rest onto the board for best results, and it's a good idea to follow those instructions (certainly the company has the most experience with their tool). The left side, or gun side should be on the centerline of the board, and the Rest should be placed two-thirds of the way to the rear of the board. Lay the Rest on the board, mark the mounting holes so you can go back and drill pilot holes for the mounting screws. Once the pilot holes are drilled, screw the Ransom Rest onto the board with the #10 wood screws provided.

Ransom makes a windage base into which the Ransom Rest mounts. The windage base gets installed onto the mounting board first, and then the rest gets installed onto the base. It makes it easier to center the pistol on the target. Once the rest is mounted and the glue has set on the metal corner pieces, make sure the handgun is unloaded. Mount it into the Ransom Rest and adjust the trigger actuating lever. With any pistol prior to testing, you need to take a box cutter or Exacto knife and cut away areas that will interfere with the proper functioning of the pistol. Things like extended thumb safeties and Ed Brown-type magazine wells need to be relieved for proper clamping into the rest and for functioning. It's best to do this in the workshop or garage, rather than getting to the range and realizing the gun won't clamp correctly into the rest because it doesn't exactly fit into the inserts. When you add an aftermarket part, make sure the gun can still be clamped into the rest prior to going to the range.

Remember that the trigger actuator will have to be adjusted specifically for autopistols and revolvers. Polymer-framed guns are a little different and can be a challenge to use with the Ransom Rest. Because of the flexibility of their frame, such guns cannot be clamped down as hard as a steel-framed gun. More rounds must be fired from polymer-framed guns before they will "settle" into the inserts. With a 1911-type autopistol, typically 5-10 rounds are enough to get the gun to settle into the inserts to create tight, uniform groups. With the Glock or other polymer-framed pistols, don't tighten down as much, and fire around 30 "settling" shots before you start testing.

One nice feature about using a Ransom Rest is that

ABOVE: The author's old Bullseye 1911 gets a workout at the range from the Ransom Rest. Note the Oehler 35P chronograph to the side.

LEFT: A bullseye pistol shown from the shooter's point of view. Testing some excellent Black Hills ammo.

later at home when you have more time to assess the results. This lets you find the best gun/load combination and "tweak" the handloads to see exactly what the results are. You can also take small batches of slightly different handloads to the range and run them through testing to see how slight variations affect group sizes.

RANSOM REST TIPS AND TRICKS

There is a definite process to mounting the gun into the Ransom Rest and getting it ready to fire. Starting with the 1911, remove the stocks and place the pistol into the right insert, then install the left insert. Before you clamp everything down, make sure the grip safety and thumb safeties are both fully depressed. Install the left plate, washers and the star knobs. The three knobs are labeled A, B and C. The best routine is to tighten A and B, then snug up C. Make sure the gun cycles, the magazine can be inserted and falls free, and the trigger resets. Do this adjustment by hand, do not use tools to tighten the star knobs on the rest. Once that

you can combine accuracy testing with velocity testing by running it in conjunction with a good chronograph. I paired up mine with an Oehler 35P and was able see, in real time, which loads produced the smallest, most uniform groups, with the smallest standard deviation and most uniform velocity. What makes this pairing even better is that you have hard copies of the targets, and the printout from the chronograph for comparison

LEFT: The Ransom Rest is needed for optimum consistency in measurement when testing handloads. RIGHT: The revolver has its own special techniques when using the Ransom Rest in order to get the best results.

is set, make sure the gap between the two inserts is equal. An uneven gap means that the inserts were not tightened correctly.

Large-caliber revolvers and the TC Contender in large calibers are special situations. The TC has a long barrel which, when combined with heavy calibers, generates vicious recoil. The only TC I ever tested in a Ransom Rest was in .223 with a muzzle brake, so recoil was not an issue, but I can see where firing a .30/30, 7/30 Waters or .45/70 Govt. would generate some stout recoil. The castle nut on the back acts as a recoil stop for semi-automatic pistols in case they go full-auto, and needs to be removed for large calibers. I've tested several 1911s that would double in a Ransom Rest but shot fine when handheld. Always keep the castle nut stop in place for semi-autos. Be sure to stand to the side when testing autopistols just for that reason. It's a little eye-opening when you expect to fire a single shot and three or more go downrange causing the pistol to climb! That third shot is almost straight up in the air.

Installing revolvers is a similar process to the autopistol, but adjusting the trigger actuator is a little trickier since the trigger travel of the revolver tends to be much longer. Again, make sure the gap between the inserts is uniform, and fire 10 to 15 settling shots prior to testing. Remember that it's normal for the initial "settling" groups to string vertically while the handgun settles in, regardless of whether it's an autopistol or revolver.

Never return the handgun to the lowered position by grabbing the pistol itself. Always use the shelf on the rest to lower it. Anytime you touch the pistol other than for loading and unloading, you run the risk of shifting it, destroying that group until the pistol "settles." Repeatability is the key to shooting, and the Ransom Rest does this automatically, but you as the fixture operator have to use the same technique when mounting the gun into the inserts, loading, and actuating the trigger. Varying the pressure on the trigger actuator can influence shot groups. Consistency and repeatability are keys to good results.

Another best practice is to always make sure that the part of the trigger actuator that actually touches the trigger is placed in the center of the trigger each time so it's pulling straight back. The actuator has two adjustments for this and they are easy to use. Take a small set of tools to the range to make sure you're able to make any adjustments that are needed. Another adjustment is the elevation stop, which has a stop nut that needs to be tight while testing. Always remember that the Ransom Rest has two friction plates and a spring, so the entire mechanism acts like a disc brake when firing. Never make any adjustments to the spring.

The Ransom Rest can give you confidence that your gun/load combo is performing at a peak level. It is a niche product not intended for the casual shooter, but for the serious hobbyist or professional, whether a gunsmith or avid reloader, using a Ransom Rest for testing gun/ammo combinations will pay off big time in not only time savings, but also general knowledge for what works best in your specific guns.

Chapter 9

GUNSMITHING THE REMINGTON 700

This book presents two Remington Model 700 project rifles. One will be turned into a tactical rifle with a match-grade barrel and a McMillan stock. The other will get the full treatment, including stock fitting, glass bedding and finishing a new semi-inletted walnut stock, plus installing the recoil pad, and sling swivel studs. We'll install and fit a new match-grade trigger, stainless match-grade barrel (to include accurizing the action and setting the minimal headspace), new firing pin, and finally learn how to glass bed an H-S Precision fiberglass stock with their bedding block system in order to get maximum accuracy from the system. I'll talk about and demonstrate tools, tips and techniques to get the most accuracy out of just about any bolt-action rifle.

Accurizing the rifle using the stock you already have starts with glass bedding. If unfamiliar with the term, glass bedding the rifle means that you are going to remove the spaces between the rifle's action and the stock itself using some sort of epoxy. You won't permanently glue the action and barrel together, al-

though if done wrong, bedding the action and stock can become glued together, so you have to use a release agent and techniques to prevent this. As a side note, semi-permanently glued-in actions have actually been used in benchrest competitions for decades with great success but you don't want to do that here.

Before you get to work, I want to go over some rifle bedding terms and why the technique contributes to a rifle's accuracy. First off, the terms: Glass bedding, pillar bedding, skim bedding and spot bedding.

GLASS BEDDING

"Glass bedding" is really somewhat of a misnomer these days, since you don't actually use fiberglass as a bedding material any longer. Glass bedding refers to the process of applying some type of two-part fiberglass epoxy to the stock of a rifle, in order to remove the gaps between the stock and the barreled action. This stabilizes the stock and keeps the barreled action from shifting during firing. Brownells was a pioneer in this area and created the product Acraglass, which was used by the shooting community for many years, and is still carried in their catalog today.

There are many forces at work when the cartridge is fired. Depending on caliber, the pressure inside the chamber can be over 50,000 CUP's, or Copper Units of Pressure, which is similar to, but not equal to PSI. Small shifts in the barreled action will have a huge impact on the size of the group at the

Bolt-action rifles can be made to fire much smaller groups when properly bedded and accurized.

target downrange. Tightening the action screws won't help, because this will only compress the wood fibers between the barreled action on top, and the floorplate metal on the bottom and, after a few shots, the barreled action will start to shift again, especially in the larger calibers. Back in the 1960s and early 70s, benchrest competitors found that applying a thin film of fiberglass epoxy stabilized the barreled action in the wood stock. Remember, accuracy is all about consistency from shot to shot. Not only in the consistent application of the marksmanship fundamentals from the shooter, but also consistency from the bullet/powder/primer/case combination, and also in the interaction between the stock, action, and barrel when the cartridge is fired. Applying glass epoxy between the wood stock and barreled action contributes greatly to consistency by preventing any minute shifting.

PILLAR BEDDING

This led to the development of pillar bedding. Pillar bedding came about when those same benchrest shooters found that when they tightened the action screws, accuracy would change. The amount of force needed to properly tighten the screws varied because the wood between the barreled action and the floorplate metal was being compressed at different rates. Some of this variance was due to the wood stock itself. Since wood is made of a non-inert material, the stock has a moisture content that will vary from stock to stock, and from wood type to wood type. American walnut used in the firearms industry has moisture content be-

Aluminum pillars used between the rifle receiver and the floorplate that keep the stock from compressing when tightening the front and rear guard screws.

tween 6 and 8 percent, and this ratio can vary depending on many factors. Rifle stocks in Arizona will have different moisture content than ones in Mississippi. Wood stocks will shrink, swell and warp depending on the outside humidity levels and the conditions in which the rifle is stored. Shooters would detect this when they would tighten the action screws, and the tension on the screws would vary based on outside humidity levels.

Pillar bedding eliminated the compression effects from wood stocks that shrunk and swelled. Pillar bedding is performed by inserting aluminum pillars, or sleeves, into the stock between the barreled action and the bottom metal, so when you apply 65 in.-lbs. of torque to the action screws, it will tighten up against the pillars with the same tension every time. Indeed, it was the inherent instability of wood that led to the development of the fiberglass rifle stock.

SKIM BEDDING

Skim bedding is used under one of two circumstances: when you have already glass bedded the rifle, and there are voids, pinholes or other imperfections in the bedding job that are not severe enough to rip out the entire epoxy. Here you just want to apply a thin film of epoxy that will patch up the job. If you find yourself in this situation, you cannot apply bedding compound to a specific spot, you have to apply it over the entire existing bedding surface, or you may create a high spot in the bedding where the action is only sitting on this high spot. Not a good situation. I won't go over this technique in this book, since hopefully you won't need it.

SPOT BEDDING

The other method is spot bedding, where you apply a small amount of bedding material behind the recoil lug, and at the rear of the receiver tang. This technique is great for the hobbyist gunsmith that doesn't want to plunge into a full pillar bedding job, but still wants some of the accuracy enhancement that glass bedding provides. This is the technique I'll demonstrate using the factory Remington laminated wood stock.

TOOLS FOR GLASS BEDDING

Ok, I've given some history, terminology and context to the principals and techniques of glass bedding a modern bolt-action rifle. I'll also cover some of the tools needed to perform this work. In order to spot bed the first project rifle, you'll need scrapers to remove the polyurethane finish from the stock where the epoxy will go; you want the epoxy to stick to the wood. You'll also need inletting pins and stockmakers' screws. A couple of other items to get are bedding tape and modeling clay. In a pinch you can use electrical or duct tape. You'll also want some sort of release agent, which is applied to the metal parts of the rifle to ensure you don't glue the whole thing together. Brownells sells a great spray release that I've used for years. In a pinch you can use Pam, the cooking spray. It actually works pretty well and doesn't add calories! I also use a good grade of paste floor wax along with the spray; using both ensures that when you screw the rifle together with the epoxy, it will come apart easily. The spray works well for covering large areas, and the paste works on internal and external screw threads and other small areas.

BEDDING COMPOUNDS

Over the years, many types of bedding compounds have been tried and used and all are of the two-part epoxy variety. In the early years, fiberglass liquids and gels were used, and Brownells' Acraglas was the primary material. Acraglas is a two-part epoxy, requiring mixing the resin with the hardener together in a specific ratio. It comes in either a liquid version or the gel, and was the compound I learned to use when going through gunsmithing school. I also used it at the National Match Gunsmithing Course at Rock Island Arsenal, where I was taught how to accurize the M1A rifle for National Match competition. Acraglas is still a good choice to use on wood stocks where you want to hide the fact that you have used a bedding material. If I'm fitting a really high-end grade of wood stock to the rifle I'm building, I don't want to use an epoxy like Devcon that will be visible afterward. Using Acraglas, when mixed with a wood coloring, can hide the tiny gaps and spaces between the wood and metal and be almost invisible. The Marine Corps used to use Marine-Tex, which many people, myself included, found very difficult to work with. Benchrest shooters once again came up with a very good epoxy, the aforementioned Devcon — a two-part epoxy made of a semi-viscous steel-based resin. When mixed with the hardener, it becomes a putty with the consistency of peanut butter, which is very easy to work with. It hardens into a very strong steel block that can actually be drilled and tapped, or otherwise machined. It's used to rebuild steel machinery and gears in many industries. Brownells sells a similar product called Steel-Bed that also works well. The downside to this steel epoxy is that it's not

cheap. One pound runs about $40, and you will get only two or three rifles from it if you are doing a full pillar bedding job. If you are doing a spot bed, you will get several jobs out of a 1-pound tub. Devcon is also made in aluminum and titanium, and I've used all of them at various times with great success, although I will say the titanium Devcon, when used as a bedding material, while quite strong, has a very short working time. In other words, when you mix the two parts together, you only have a few short minutes before it starts to harden. Devcon steel, and Brownell's Steel-Bed have very generous working times, giving you plenty of time to get the rifle screwed together and the excess epoxy cleaned up before it starts to set up.

BEFORE YOU GET STARTED...

Before you get to work, shoot the rifle with a variety of factory loads and old-standby handloads to establish a baseline accuracy standard for the gun. Remember, the better the gun shoots initially, the smaller the results you'll get. In other words, if you are starting out with a rifle that shoots 5-shot groups of 2 inches at 100 yards, it will be fairly easy to cut the group sizes in half at least, depending on caliber and other factors, all things being equal. Conversely, if you take for example a heavy-barreled rifle in .22-250 and it already shoots under 1 inch at 100 yards, it may take a large amount of work and money to get that group size to shrink in half with consistency. There is a rule of diminishing returns between money spent and reduction in group size. Once you get groups substantially under an inch, you'll spend more money and effort to get small increments in reductions in group size. Sometimes it takes

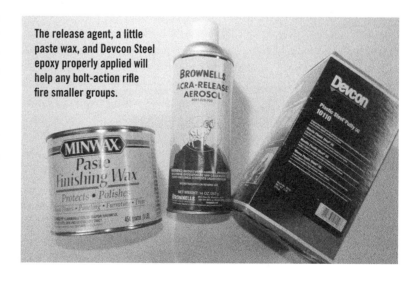

The release agent, a little paste wax, and Devcon Steel epoxy properly applied will help any bolt-action rifle fire smaller groups.

Firing the Remington rifle after bedding with a Nightforce varmint scope.

working on the rifle, and sometimes it takes carefully developing quality handloads, but that's half the fun of rifles, gunsmithing and reloading. Testing and trying to achieve tiny groups is what it's all about!

RANGE TESTING THE PROJECT GUN

For this initial range session, I took several factory loads, and two handloads. The factory loads were Federal's 50-gr load utilizing Barnes' Triple-Shok bullet, and their 60-grain offering using the Nosler Partition. This load would be a good one requiring deeper penetration, such as a coyote load. The 60-grain bullet is on the ragged edge of stability with the 1-in-14 twist of the factory Remington varmint barrel. We'll correct this when we rebarrel the rifle later with a Shilen stainless match barrel, which sports a faster 1-in-7 twist. That twist will stabilize even 70-grain .22-caliber bullets for long-range shooting. I also chose Federal's 55-grain softpoint as a kind of standard general purpose varmint load and Federal's 55-grain loads utilizing the Nosler Ballistic Tip.

Two more factory loads I used in the testing phase were the Hornady 40- and 55-grain V-Max rounds. For handloads, I chose the Hornady 50-grain Z-Max bullet, over 36.0 grains of Reloader 15, with a Federal case and Winchester Large Rifle primer, and the Berger

52-grain Varmint bullet. The Berger is basically a very accurate match-grade bullet with a large hollow point for great expansion. I used 36.0 grains of Reloader 15 with a Federal case and a Winchester primer for it. All handloads were assembled with the outstanding Redding Big Boss press and a Redding Competition micrometer seating die. This seating die lets you set the seating depth of the bullet to .001-inch increments. This way, you can seat the bullet a few thousandths of an inch off from the lands of the barrel for best accuracy. The scope used was the Leupold 6.5x20 VX-3L Varmint scope, and the spotting scope was the Nightforce 20x70 tactical spotting scope, which made finding those little .22 caliber holes much easier.

The rifle shot really well. I shot one Hornady load, two Federal loads and two handloads. The Federal load with the Nosler Ballistic Tip shot the best, turning in a 5-shot group of 1.049. My handload with the Berger 52-grain FB Varmint load, ahead of 36.0 grains of Reloader 15, Federal cases, and Winchester primers shot the second best, with a 5-shot group size of 1.103. The group was actually better than that, with four shots going into one tiny hole. This shows the difference between inherent accuracy and potential accuracy. In the next chapter, we will see how a basic bedding job improves this rifle's accuracy.

BEDDING THE WOOD STOCK

In the previous chapter I covered the different methods, tools, terminology and techniques in glass bedding a Remington M700 rifle. This chapter, we are going to dive in and really get our hands dirty. If you remember, I discussed a technique called "spot bedding," in which a small amount of bedding material is applied in the recoil lug area, at the rear of the receiver tang, and around the front and rear receiver screws at the trigger guard area.

This bedding material will stabilize the barreled action in the wood stock, and help prevent it from minute shifts when firing, making the rifle more accurate.

What this technique won't do is prevent the stock from compressing and swelling from shifts in humidity and temperature — pillar bedding is a better technique to prevent this. We'll use the other techniques in subsequent chapters, bedding the Wenig Riflestocks walnut wood stock, McMillan stock on our tactical rifle, and for the current .22-250 varmint rifle utilizing the aluminum bedding block of the H-S stock.

But for now, we are going to use the spot bedding technique, which is an excellent way to get started in learning rifle bedding techniques without getting in way over our heads.

Getting the rifle ready to glass bed.

Using woodworking tools like scrapers to remove the urethane finish in order to get down to the bare wood, so the epoxy that you are going to apply will stick.

SPOT BEDDING PROJECT

So, to get started, you need to prep the stock. Factory wood stocks have a polyurethane finish applied over the wood in order to make the wood more impervious to moisture. The stock on our project gun is a laminated wood stock, which has thin layers of wood glued together to form a stock blank, which is then shaped. The stock is finished with the polyurethane; between the glue used in the manufacture and the polyurethane applied as a stock finish, the laminated stocks are very stable and make a great option for varmint stocks, or when you are concerned about accuracy. You can make them better by bedding, but first need to remove the urethane finish. The steel epoxy we'll use for the bedding material won't stick to the urethane, so we need to remove that finish and get down to the raw wood. There are several tools you'll need for this, the go-to being the Fischer scraper. As you can see by the photos, Fischers come in different sizes and types; small round and large round, and a flat blade for getting into corners. These scrapers really remove material in the large curved areas, as well as down into small spots like the corners of the

recoil lug. Make sure that you get all of the urethane finish off, and are truly down to the raw wood. You will know when you are into the wood by sight, sound and feel. The urethane finish will be white, whereas when you are into the wood you'll see the brown wood material. The sound is different, too. The urethane makes a squeaking sound when scraped, whereas the wood will be a crunch. By feel you will skate over the urethane whereas the Fischer tool will really dig into the wood. The other required tool is the curling scraper.

Just get through the urethane and into the wood, don't take off too much material. You are just trying to put a small skim layer of steel epoxy bedding material around the recoil lug and at the rear of the receiver at the receiver tang. Taking off too much material between the stock and the receiver will show a large gap between the wood and metal. You are looking for a very thin gap between the two. Scrape out the urethane down in the recoil lug area, and behind the recoil lug, the rear of the receiver tang and around the bottom of the stock around the screw holes at the front and rear of the floorplate.

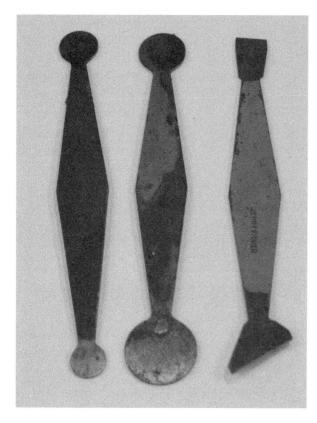

ABOVE: A small strip of electrical tape is applied to the bottom of the recoil lug. This will provide a bit of spacing between the steel and the epoxy. The stock will compress slightly when you screw it together, you do not want the action to teeter on the recoil lug. The only contact should be at the rear of the recoil lug, not the bottom.

LEFT: The Fischer scrapers are the author's go-to tool for removing small amounts of wood or existing finishes to prep the stock.

The next step is to tape off and dam these areas so you can control the flow of the steel epoxy, keeping it out of areas you don't want it. The first step is to place a layer of electrical tape on the bottom of the recoil lug. The reason for this is that there will always be a slight bit of compression when the front and rear guard screws are torqued, and the idea is that when the screws are tightened, if the recoil lug bottoms out, the receiver will teeter slightly on the bottom of the lug. A single layer of electrical tape on the bottom of the lug will provide clearance. Use an Exacto knife, or a box cutter to perfectly shape the tape, fitting it just on the bottom of the lug without overlapping onto the front, back or sides of the lug. There should be just a small strip on the bottom of the recoil lug.

Remember, the whole idea of bedding the rifle is to mate the stock and receiver as a single unit. You want contact primarily at the rear of the recoil lug so that when the rifle recoils, the recoil lug is doing its job.

Next place a layer of bedding tape from the front of the recoil lug forward. This will allow you to lift the excess epoxy off the front area. There are different theories on bedding a rifle. Some people like to have the barrel completely free-floated, and others want a pad of an inch to an inch and a half of support from the

bedding material in front of the lug. I normally like a 1-inch pad of bedding material extending out from the front of the lug to help support the heaviest barrels. For this rifle, with its thinner factory barrel and the fact that I'm demonstrating a beginning technique, I'm going to go with a completely free-floated barrel. Some people may not agree and that's OK. Every gunsmith has to develop a technique that they feel will deliver the best performance. I will show how to pillar bed the next three rifles and for those, I'll put the pad of epoxy in front of the lug. I built tactical rifles for many years and have developed techniques that work well.

Now, you've scraped the areas you want the epoxy to stick, and have placed tape where you want to be able to lift off the excess epoxy. The next step is to use modeling clay to plug the holes you don't want the epoxy to flow into. Modeling clay is great to use because it does a great job, and the clay will never dry out. You need to plug the gas port hole, and the trigger slot and both of the trigger retaining pin holes. Once everything is taped off and the clay has plugged up holes and recesses, degrease the receiver using brake cleaner, and screw everything together to make sure the barreled action will go together, and the receiver is level and square to the stock. You don't want to find out that the stockmakers'

ABOVE: Taping off areas to keep epoxy from flowing where it shouldn't go. This is spot bedding — applying a small spot of bedding around the recoil lug and the rear of the tang. You will also place some bedding material around the floorplate.

RIGHT: Once mixed, the epoxy gets placed into the recoil lug area, around the barreled action, and around the floorplate.

screws won't go through or the receiver is not level, although since this is just a spot bedding job, all should be good to go.

The next step is to apply your release agent. Remove the barreled action and dip the stockmakers' screws into the paste wax, and screw them into the receiver to lube the threads. You want to be able to unscrew the rifle easily, and this step makes sure you can do that. Brownells makes a spray release agent that works really well. Apply two thin coats of release agent on the outside of all receiver surfaces, making sure you coat all surfaces. You don't want to apply too much since you are striving for a tight fit between the epoxy and the metal surfaces. You definitely don't want the release agent to drip, that's too much and will affect the fit you are going after. If you apply too much, wipe it off and start over. Don't forget to apply the release agent to the stockmakers' screws, and the area inside the receiver in the bolt lug section. Don't worry about getting oil inside the chamber; it will all get cleaned up later.

Now that you have taped off the rifle parts, plugged the holes with modeling clay, and applied release agent to the entire barreled action and floorplate, it's time to mix up the epoxy and apply it to our stock.

Mixing and Applying Bedding Compound

The Devcon steel putty mixture is 2.5:1 by volume, meaning mix 2.5 times the amount of resin to hardener.

Use a mixing pad, basically a notepad and Popsicle stick or tongue depressor to stir up a batch. Once you've started mixing, the working time is about 16 hours, so you have plenty of time to get it mixed up and into the stock. One of the most common mistakes is to rush once the epoxy is mixed up. Remember, you have 16 hours of set time and 24 hours of cure time. Having said that, don't mix your epoxy and go eat a sandwich.

Place the stock into some type of cradle for support. Use a small Popsicle stick and spread the epoxy down into and behind the recoil lug, back of the receiver tang and around the front and rear guard screws on the floorplate. Lower the barreled action into the stock, and hold it in place. Take the floorplate and raise it up into the stock and hold it in place. With the other hand, screw the stockmakers' screws into place — snug, not too tight. You will see the epoxy ooze out from under the receiver. Look for the epoxy to come out uniformly. If there is a gap in the ooze that means that there is probably an air pocket. Depending on how big

 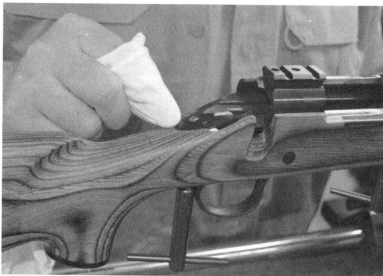

LEFT: The epoxy will flow out a little around the sides of the stock. This is desirable. You'll remove the overspill later. RIGHT: The excess epoxy is cleaned up after screwing the rifle together with a little bit of Shooters Choice cleaning solvent on a rag.

the pocket is will determine whether or not you have to rip out the epoxy once it's cured, and do the bedding job all over again.

Wipe off the excess from the stock using a clean rag. I like to put a little Shooter's Choice solvent on the rag to help clean things up. Once the excess has been removed, leave the stock to set in a rifle cradle and don't touch it for 24 hours.

I showed how to prep the rifle stock to control epoxy overflow. I also showed how to use modeling clay and bedding/electrical tape to prep the stock, then how to scrape out the urethane finish and prep the wood in order to lay down your steel bedding compound. I stressed that paste floor wax and Brownells release agents are your friends, and that less is more. Don't

overdo the release agent or it'll compromises the close fit between the barreled action and the stock. Use just enough to ensure that the rifle will part from the stock.

After curing for at least 24 hours, break out the action from the stock and see what you have. Once the rifle is separated from the stock, the first things to check for are voids, gaps, air pockets or any place where there is insufficient bedding material. The first question novice gunsmiths ask at this phase of the build is how big of a void/air pocket is too big. At what point do you have to rip the bedding material out and redo it because of a void or air pocket. When I was building precision rifles, if one of the gunsmiths that worked for me had a void that was larger than a matchhead, we would redo it. Not because the void would affect the accuracy of the

The stock, once screwed together with the stockmakers' screws, gets put aside overnight to allow the epoxy to cure.

The bedding job gets inspected for voids and pinholes. Poke at the bedding with a dental pick to look for them.

gun, but because we wanted it to look professional, and we only put out quality work. Voids and pinholes look sloppy. There may be larger voids and pockets hidden underneath the surface that you can't see. Fortunately, we only had a couple that had to be re-bedded. Stuff happens sometimes.

If there is a small pinhole or air pocket you can poke it with a dental pick. Sometimes, the tiny pin hole is really a larger air pocket, but you won't know until you poke at it.

One thing you don't want to do is to fill the void or pinhole with bedding material and try to fill it in. Doing a patch job like this will not work. That's because applying bedding material to a void and screwing the rifle back together will create a raised spot where you applied the compound, so you will only have contact at that tiny spot, which is not a good situation. It's best to leave the small pinholes alone.

To get the rifle apart, unscrew the stockmakers' screws. You've applied enough release agent on them that they should twist right out. Once out, put the rifle barrel into your padded vise with the bottom of the rifle facing you, and try to pull the stock off the barreled action. If it doesn't come off easily, you can use

The Foredom Tool is a great choice when used with various bits for the cleanup job on the stock.

more forceful means. To do that, hold the rifle at the low ready, and bring the muzzle end of the barrel down on the padded benchtop with a fair amount of force. That should pop it out. If it doesn't, then Houston, we have a problem! Let's assume at this point that you were able to get the barreled action out of the stock. If not, you'll have to use some significant heat or cold to break the bond of the epoxy. Putting the rifle in a freezer usually works.

Now you can inspect the job you did at spot bedding the rifle. When you look down at the recoil lug

LEFT: These bits, when used in the Foredom Tool, work great on all types of materials. They are structured-tooth carbide and are available from Brownells and other machine shop supply houses like MSC and McMaster and Carr.

BELOW: The guard screws are torqued with a torque wrench to 65 in.-lbs. for best results.

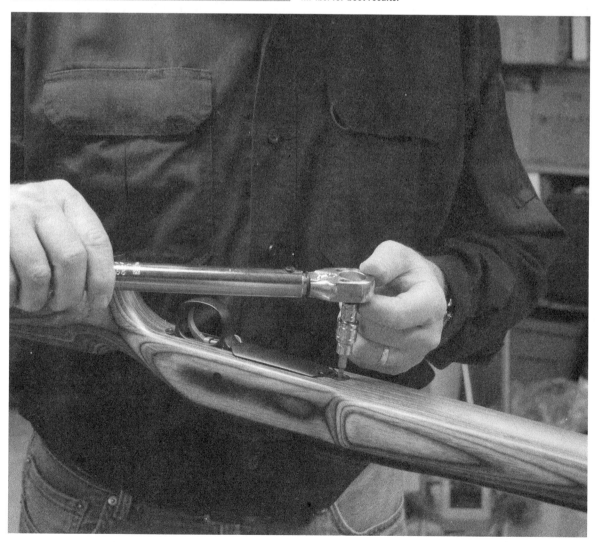

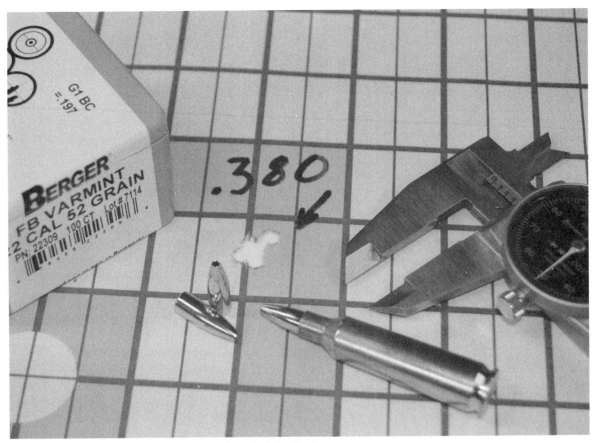

The rifle shot pretty well after the bedding job with the author's handloads.

area where you applied the steel epoxy, you should see a perfect reverse image of the bottom of the barreled action, free of voids, gaps and pinholes. You also need to remove the floorplate assembly from the stock. The best way to do this is to set the stock in a cradle, and use a wood dowel or something soft to tap the floorplate down and away from the stock.

Remove the bedding tape, and clean up the excess bedding material from the receiver and floorplate area of the stock. A Foredom tool works really well for this cleanup job. I have found that the structured tooth carbide bits from Kutzall do a very quick job of cutting through the steel or aluminum epoxy during the cleanup process. They are available from Brownells and come in cylindrical, straight and ball end. They're a little expensive, but indispensable.

Drill out the guard screw holes and the rifle can be reassembled and the guard screws torqued. Once you have the rifle back together, you can take it to the range.

I tested the project rifle bedded in this chapter with handloads using Berger's excellent 52-grain flat-based varmint bullet. The best group of the day was shot by my son, measuring at a tidy .380 inches, for five shots at 100 yards. Not bad with a factory barrel — and a huge improvement over the baseline groups measured in the last chapter before bedding.

INSTALLING THE TITANIUM FIRING PIN

One of the great features of the Remington Model 700 is the wealth of aftermarket parts available for the gun. Some parts are just cosmetic, while others perform a certain function to enhance the accuracy, reliability or functioning of the rifle. So it is with the installation of the titanium firing pin — an important upgrade.

One of the factors affecting accuracy in rifles, and to a lesser extent pistols, is the length of time between the release of the trigger/sear mechanism, and the moment of impact of the firing pin to the primer. During the time when the hammer or striker falls, the shooter is constantly influencing the aim and movement of the rifle to the target. Movement is imparted in the system by the shooter's heart beating, and simply by holding the rifle, ultimately affecting aim. This length of time between sear disengagement and primer strike is known as locktime. The greater the locktime, the more time the shooter has to adversely affect aim, and subsequently, the quality of the shot. Conversely, it follows that the shorter this length of time is, the less opportunity the shooter has to screw up the shot. Many decades ago, some enterprising shooters tried to come up with electronic triggers and ignition systems for firearms in order to get locktime down as close to zero as possible. These systems never worked, so we are left with mechanical means to fire the rifle and send the bullet on its way.

Locktime is actually measured on sophisticated equipment. The locktime of most rifles is somewhere between 2.6 and 9.0 milliseconds. How long is a millisecond? One thousandth of a second. The Remington M700 is at the low end of this scale, with locktimes in the 2.6-2.9 millisecond range, which is one reason the rifle is inherently accurate and why it has an advantage over other factory rifles. But you can get this lower, and there are a couple of ways to do it. One way is to make the factory firing pin lighter by reducing mass. Remington picked up on this by manufacturing lightening cuts into the body of the firing pin. This lightens it, speeding it up. We would often use titanium firing pins on the custom tactical rifles we were building on Remington M700 actions. The factory firing pins were solid body back then, it seems as though Remington has picked up on the advantages of the lighter firing pin, and now lightens them up some.

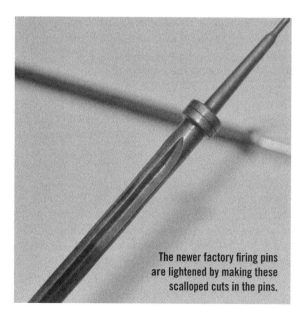

The newer factory firing pins are lightened by making these scalloped cuts in the pins.

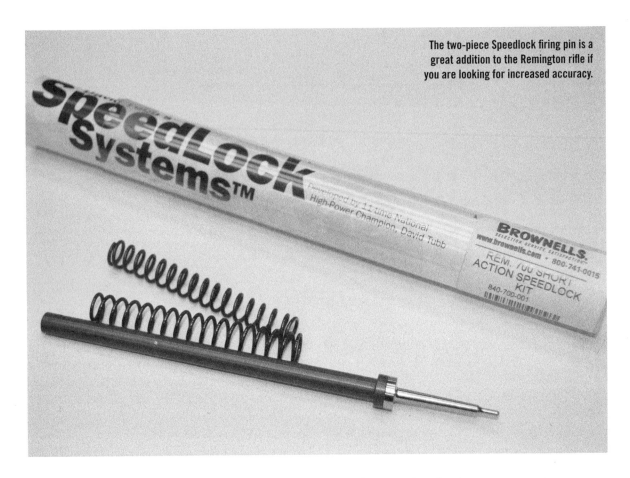

The two-piece Speedlock firing pin is a great addition to the Remington rifle if you are looking for increased accuracy.

There is also a downside to most good things, and the titanium firing pins were no exception. We found that the stock factory firing pin, being steel, not only had weight, but mass, and with that, had momentum. So if the operators were using any ammunition other than factory match grade, misfires would sometimes result. We tested our rifles for function and accuracy with factory Federal 168-grain match ammunition before shipping. We did not know that some units would use military Lake City ammunition, with thicker military primer cups. This resulted in misfires.

SPEEDLOCK SYSTEMS TITANIUM FIRING PIN

The new Speedlock Systems titanium firing pin is shipped with a duo-coil spring, which imparts more energy than factory springs previously supplied with the pins. Nevertheless, if you are using a titanium spring on a tactical rifle, make sure you test it thoroughly with the type and brand of ammunition the rifle will be deployed with, as per your agency's testing protocol. The Speedlock firing pins are actually part aluminum and part titanium. The front of the pin is tough titanium,

the red rear portion aluminum.

Now that we know why we are performing this operation, let's get into how. Fortunately, this is a really easy job, and actually takes longer to explain than it does to do. First, anytime you are doing any work on a firearm, make sure the rifle is unloaded, and remove the bolt. There are a couple of tools you need in order to complete this job. The firing pin assembly consists of the firing pin, firing pin spring, cocking piece, cocking piece retaining pin, and the bolt shroud. You need to remove this as a single assembly. One word of caution: Whenever you are working with compressed springs, always wear good quality eye protection. Firing pins are under very strong compression.

FIRING PIN REMOVAL AND TOOLS

You can use tools specifically designed to remove this assembly, or a simple coin to capture the firing pin, and unscrew the assembly from the bolt. To do this, clamp the bottom of the cocking piece into a padded vise, and retract it until the disassembly notch is exposed. Then insert a coin into the notch and release, capturing the firing pin and the firing pin assembly so they can be

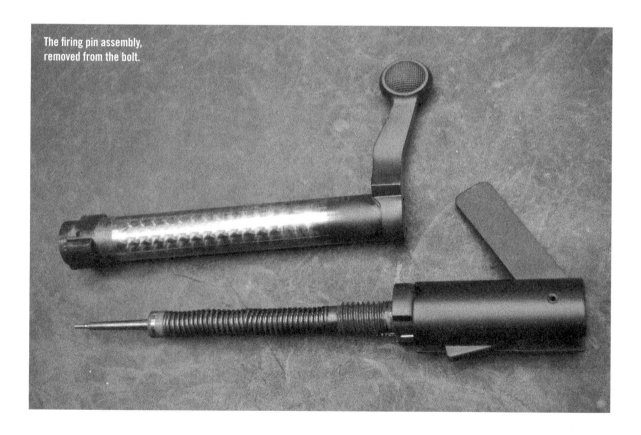

The Kleinendorst bolt disassembly tool is a great solution to keep in the range bag, for a quick way to remove the firing pin for cleaning.

unscrewed from the bolt. A handy tool made by Kleinendorst Mfg. does the same thing, and it's a good idea to keep one in your range bag or accessory container. To use the Kleinendorst tool, simply place it over the bolt shroud, then place the hook over the edge of the cocking piece and swing the lever over. Unscrew the firing pin assembly from the bolt.

Once you have the firing pin assembly removed from the bolt, Kleinendorst also makes another tool to take apart the assembly into its component parts. It's a very simple tool to use. Screw the firing pin assembly into the tool, and run the large screw into the face of the firing pin to compress the firing pin spring. As the spring

is compressed, it will expose the cocking piece from the bolt shroud. Keep screwing the large screw in until the cocking piece retaining pin is exposed. Once the pin is exposed, drive it out with a pin punch. I usually use a short, stubby starter punch to get the pin going, followed by the long 3/32nd-inch punch to drive it out. This is a good practice with any pins you are driving out. I have several starter punches that I have made from broken 1/16th-inch punches. After you work on firearms for a while, you will accumulate broken punches. Use your bench grinder to grind them to the diameter and

The firing pin assembly, removed from the bolt.

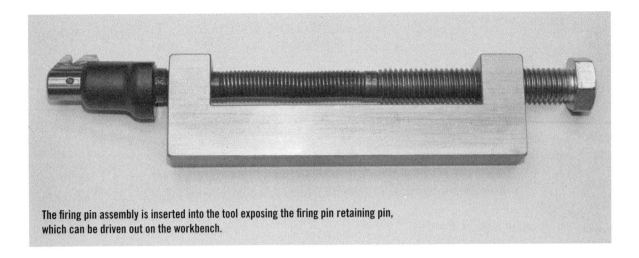

The firing pin assembly is inserted into the tool exposing the firing pin retaining pin, which can be driven out on the workbench.

length you need, and keep them on the bench where they're handy.

Once the cocking piece retaining pin has been driven out, remove the cocking piece from the back of the firing pin. Unscrew the large screw from the firing pin tool in order to relax the firing pin spring, unscrew it almost all the way off, but do not unscrew it all the way. Once the large screw is back out almost all the way, you can unscrew the bolt shroud from the disassembly tool and remove the entire firing pin assembly from the tool. Now that you have everything taken apart, insert the new titanium firing pin into the firing pin tool you just used. Insert the Duo spring onto the firing pin. Then take the bolt shroud and compress the spring until it starts to screw onto the tool, and use the large screw to compress the firing pin spring until the cocking piece hole is exposed outside the bolt shroud. Once the hole is exposed, install the cocking piece back onto the rear of the firing pin and drive the pin back in. I use a brass drift punch for this task. Once you have the pin back in, make sure it's below flush on both sides. You don't want the retaining pin dragging on the inside of the bolt shroud, as this can cause inconsistent firing pin fall, which can translate to inconsistent firing pin strike on the primer, and inconsistent ignition — all of which negatively impacts group size.

Check to make sure the retain-

ing pin is flush by running a soft India stone over both sides of the pin. If it raises a shiny spot, that's a high spot and needs to be taken down below flush of the cocking piece. Once the retaining pin is in place, unscrew the large screw on the bolt disassembly tool to relax the firing pin spring, and install the firing pin removal tool back on and unscrew the entire reassembled firing assembly from the bolt tool. Screw the firing pin assembly back onto the bolt, and reinstall the bolt back into the rifle. Dry fire the rifle several times and you will notice the difference, especially if you have the Jewell trigger installed. When you take the rifle to the range, dry fire the rifle again, and notice how little the

The retaining pin is removed in order to completely disassemble the firing pin assembly.

The Remington M700 rifle shot really well after installing the Speedlock system. In .22-250 it would make a great medium-range varmint rifle.

crosshairs will jump when the rifle is dry fired. This is because there is so little mass of the firing pin coming to an abrupt halt when the rifle is dry fired.

RANGE TESTING

This project gun produced excellent results at the range. I took two handloads and several factory loads. The handloads were 52-grain Sierra Matchking, and 52-grain Speer Varmint bullets in front of 37 grains of Reloader 15. Factory loads included two from Federal, the 55-grain Fusion hunting round, and the 55-grain

offering loaded with the Barnes all-copper bullet. I also shot two from Hornady, the 40- and 55-grain V-Max.

The scope used was the excellent Nightforce, and spotting duties were performed with the Nightforce spotting scope. This combination has been invaluable in my rifle testing, the spotting scope makes viewing the small .22-caliber holes a breeze, no matter at which yardage we shoot.

We had many targets with factory loads in the ½ to ¾-inch range, and handloads going into the ½ and below range. The firing pin allowed for more consistency, and the targets proved it.

BLOCK BEDDING
A SYNTHETIC-STOCK

In this chapter we are going to do another type of bedding technique to the Remington 700, but this gun will utilize a synthetic factory stock. The technique is called block bedding, and is very effective when using some of the newer factory synthetic stocks that have internally structured compartments in the forend and around the action area. As a review, the three types of rifle bedding techniques for the bolt-action rifle are spot bedding, block bedding, and pillar bedding. I'll cover pillar bedding in subsequent chapters when we convert this .22-250 varmint rifle into a tack-driving .308 tactical sniper system.

So, what is block bedding? Basically, block bedding involves surrounding the recoil lug of the rifle with a giant block of solid steel. It's accomplished by filling in the structural chambers in front of and behind the recoil lug. There are two chambers directly in front of the lug that measure about .750 of an inch, and two chambers behind the lug that measure about 1.25 inches, which becomes our 2-inch block of steel.

To get started, ensure the rifle is unloaded, and remove the two stock screws and the bolt. Take the floorplate off, along with the magazine box. Separate the stock from the rifle. Notice on the forend's tip that there are two pads of material. Fire up your Dremel or Foredom

tool, and remove these two pads. They are there to provide upward pressure on the barrel when the stock is screwed on, and keep reverberation to a minimum upon firing. Old-time benchrest shooters tried this technique with varying levels of success in the 1960s with wood stocks, and it's an inexpensive way for a mass produced firearm to achieve a decent level of accuracy out of the box, but you can do better. You are going to bed this rifle at four points, in similar fashion to the spot bedding technique used on the other M700 — bedding the recoil lug, back of the tang, and around the two guard screws underneath the rifle at the trigger guard.

First scrape out the stock material where the bedding

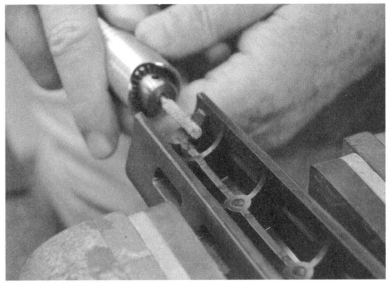

The contact pads of the forend are removed, since you are bedding the rifle in order to provide the stabilization needed for best accuracy.

Modeling clay is used to block off the area where you do not want epoxy to flow.

material will go. This ensures a large enough gap for the bedding material, as you don't want stock-to-metal contact. Always maintain a gap between the stock and the firearm, this will make room for the epoxy. Also, by scraping, it will rough up the stock so the epoxy will stick to it. You will need to use sandpaper to really rough it up. I use #120 grit, and if I had access to a bead blasting cabinet, I would tape off the stock and bead blast the epoxy areas to further rough it up. After scraping and sanding, spray it out with brake cleaner and blow it dry.

Next step is to tape the barrel. You want to free float the barrel, but you need to extend the bedding material out in front of the recoil lug about ¾ of an inch, rather than have the barrel completely free floating like

you would when using the spot bedding technique. Tape off the front of the barrel at the forend tip, and wrap tape around the barrel ¾-inches in front of the recoil lug. Look down the muzzle of the rifle to make sure the barreled action is exactly on center and you haven't used too much tape, causing it to sit too high. Everything should be leveled and centered at this point. Next get out the modeling clay, and fill the barrel channel chambers in front of the two chambers you are using that are located in front of the recoil lug. That is, from front to back, epoxy goes in the two chambers in front of the lug, then the lug chamber, and two chambers behind the lug. See the photo if this is not perfectly clear. You want to fill the two chambers in front of and behind the recoil lug, but don't waste expensive epoxy by allowing it to flow into chambers where it's not needed. Next, spray release agent onto the areas of the barreled action, the stockmakers' screws and the floorplate. Remove the magazine follower and spring from the floorplate, as these just get in the way.

Once you have everything taped off, greased up with release agent, and modeling clay applied in places you don't want the epoxy to flow, mix Devcon in a 2.5 to 1 ratio. Apply it to the four points within the stock, starting with the chambers in and around the recoil lug. There is a special technique to use when filling in deep areas like that with an epoxy that has a thick consistency such as Devcon. Use a Popsicle stick to apply a thick glob of epoxy down into the cham-

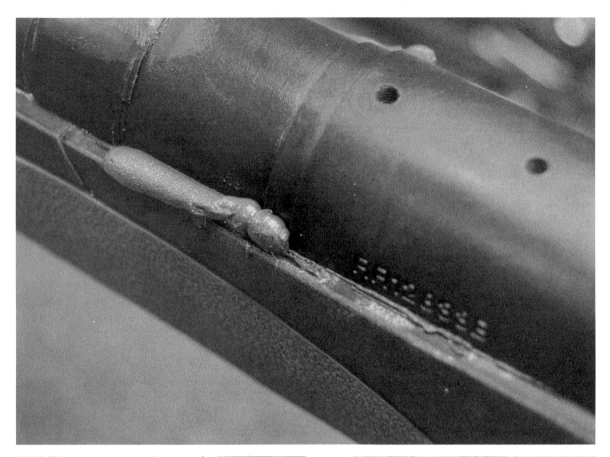

ABOVE: Make sure you get a good squeeze of epoxy. This will give a visual assurance that the bedding material has flowed into all of the areas where support is needed.

RIGHT: Screw the rifle together with the stockmakers' screws to allow everything to set up overnight.

ber, stir with a butter-churn action to get the bubbles out; otherwise, large voids and bubbles will form, negating the beneficial effects of a big block of steel around the recoil lug, which is the whole reason for doing this job. You'll know you are getting the air bubbles out by the popping noises. Once you have all of the epoxy in place, screw the rifle together, being careful to not screw it together too tightly, just enough to snug it up. Set the rifle in a cradle to let the epoxy set up, do not put the stock or the barrel in a vise during the curing process. You want the stock to sit as stress-free as possible. Wipe off the excess epoxy, and let the rifle sit overnight.

The next day, break it apart and take a look. It should look like the photos. Use the Dremel or Foredom tools with the structured tooth carbide bit to grind off the excess steel epoxy where it overflowed, and degrease the entire rifle. Put everything back together, and give it a good function test, making sure all of the safeties work and that the rifle will feed dummy ammunition.

ABOVE: Once the epoxy has cured, the barreled action and stock are broken apart and the bedding surface is inspected for voids and pinholes.

RIGHT: The front and rear guard screws are torqued to 65 in.-lbs. for best results.

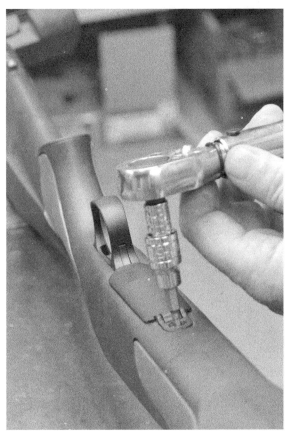

Set the torque on the front and rear guard screws to 65 in.-lbs. and mount the scope.

That completes block bedding a bolt-action rifle in a nutshell. It's a basic yet very good technique to improve accuracy, especially with heavy-barreled rifles, or rifles that generate quite a bit of recoil that use a synthetic stock with compartments in the forend. Notice that, in this project, you applied a bedding block in front of the recoil lug, and also bedded the barrel for about ¾ of an inch in front of the lug. Free floating the entire barrel is another option, but which technique is correct, or most effective? It depends on who you ask. I've used both methods and have had good results with both.

In most cases, placing a small amount of bedding on the barrel in front of the recoil lug produces more consistent results, especially with very heavy varmint barrels. I believe that is due to the fact that supporting that section of the barrel tends to dampen the harmonics in

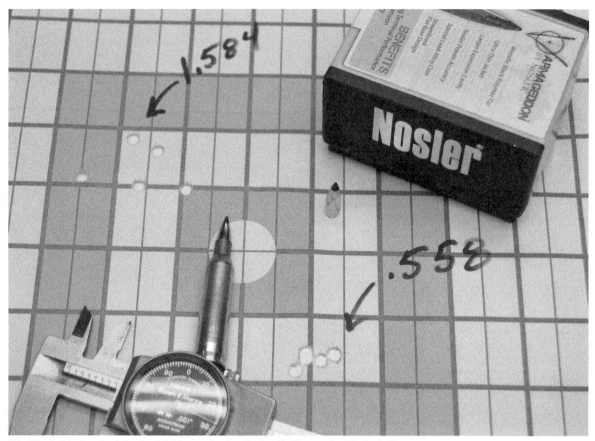

This rifle shot factory loads to about 1.5 inches, but handloads with the excellent Nosler bullet went into about ½ inches at 100 yards, or .5 MOA.

a positive way. Remember, when the rifle is fired and the bullet is traveling down the barrel, the barrel is acting like a whip, but is also rotating around in a circle as it's snapping whip-like. I think this block reduces this whip-like effect, makes it more consistent, and better controls the barrel's harmonics. So why did you remove the pads at the front of the forend on this stock? Wouldn't that have the same positive effect? The short answer is no. Applying upward pressure at the forend exerts pressure unevenly, and causes a very inconsistent bounce or slapping effect from the stock and the forend out toward the end of the barrel. It's an OK way to get a decent amount of accuracy from a mass produced rifle, but you are trying for more than just decent accuracy, especially from a potentially tack-driving caliber like

the .22-250 — one intended for small targets at long range. This is why I'll free float the barrel, except for the first ¾ of an inch or sometimes a full inch and a half past the front of the recoil lug with a really heavy barrel.

Some barrels may not respond to this technique. If the rifle won't shoot and you've exhausted all other possibilities, you can always easily remove the block in front of the lug and free float the entire barrel to see if that improves accuracy. Remember that none of these techniques involve pillar bedding. These are techniques that you as a beginning home gunsmith can use to get your "feet wet" in the technique of custom riflesmithing. In later chapters of the book I'll show how to pillar bed and finish a semi-inletted wood stock, and a McMillan fiberglass stock.

REBARRELING THE REMINGTON MODEL 700

The Remington action is constructed and engineered in such a way that taking off the old barrel and installing a new, match-grade one, and setting the headspace to the minimum SAAMI chamber dimensions greatly improves the accuracy of the rifle. That's because the bore and groove dimension, chamber dimensions, bore and groove uniformity from land to land and groove to groove, as well as uniformity over the length of the barrel are all held to very, very tight tolerances. For example, bore and groove dimensions of a typical match-grade barrel such as a Shilen are on the order of .0005 for the overall dimension and less than .0003 for uniformity from end to end. Considering that the average width of the human hair is on the order of .004, you can see that the modern match-grade rifle barrel is very straight, tight and uniform throughout its length. This is one of the reasons match-grade tubes shoot better than factory barrels. The factory barrel, being a mass produced part, is still an excellent, quality part, it's just that the mass production process negates the ability to hold those precise tolerances.

One of the critical areas of the modern match barrel is the rifling process, with each manufacturer producing theirs in one of four unique ways. Additionally, most shops that make match barrels have proprietary methods or techniques that make theirs shoot well. The four ways to make a rifle or pistol barrel are: Button, Broach, Single Point Cut, or Hammer forging. Button-rifled barrels are cut with a carbide slug, or button, which is pulled through the barrel and effectively "irons" the rifling into the barrel. These barrels are then hand-lapped

and air-gauged for uniformity and quality control. Broach cutting employs a cutter that has all of the teeth machined on it, and is pulled through the barrel. Factories use this method for handgun barrels. Single point is used by small custom barrelmakers and employs a single cutter to meticulously remove barrel material. Hammer forging is exactly that — a series of hammers to form the barrel around a mandrel. Shotgun barrels and some European gunmakers employ this method. This book does not have enough space for me to explain about hand lapping or air gauging, but in a nutshell, air gauging is a device to measure uniformity by using air pressure flowing around a barrel mandrel of precise size to measure barrel uniformity. I used to have one in my shop when I was working for the DoD and used it to verify and Q/C the match pistol barrels we received from various vendors.

This chapter we continue with the riflesmithing project, and move over to the Model 700 that we are setting up as a tactical rifle for military and law enforcement. This is the beauty of the M700 bolt action platform: it can be set up for virtually any type of functionality, depending on the caliber. Whether it's for long-range varmint hunting, big game like moose or bear, or law enforcement, the M700 is really that versatile.

Caliber of the rifle will dictate its use, and to that end, the M700 is offered in three sizes of bolt face — small for .223-sized calibers; medium-sized, which accommodates .308 classes of calibers; and finally, the belted magnums. So, for example, our Precision Tactical Rifle Project gun is starting out as a .22-250 Rem., but because of the size of the bolt face open-

The Remington barreled action, after installing the new Shilen match barrel.

ing, it can accommodate a wide variety of cartridges, including the .308 Win. So this rifle will be rebarreled and converted from the .22-250 to the .308 by doing nothing more than swapping out barrels. Even the magazine box and follower will work with both cartridges. If you were converting from .22-250 to a longer cartridge, one with the same sized bolt face such as the .30-06, it would not be possible since the cartridge requires a long action. You must stick with calibers that will fit into the short action. Calibers like the .22-250, .243, .308, 7mm-08, etc. are excellent choices. In the late 1980s and into the 90s, you could not simply buy an action from Remington, you had to purchase the barreled action from them, or a complete rifle from a gun show. Nowadays, you can just buy the action, sans barrel from Brownells, saving about $60.

Since we're starting from a complete rifle, we have to remove the original barrel before we can convert it to another caliber. Removing the barrel also allows us to do something else — accurize the action. To borrow a term from the automotive racing industry, this

is "blueprinting" the action, with the goal of truing it and the bolt, prior to installing the barrel. So, what does it mean to "blueprint" or true the action? You are going to make the receiver, bolt and barrel perpendicular, parallel and on center. This will give you the accuracy you are looking for.

STURDY WORKBENCH MANDATORY

First you have to remove the barrel, but in order to do that, you need to set up your barrel vise and get your inserts molded so you can properly clamp the barrel into the vise. If you don't get a good grip on the barrel with the vise, it will just spin when you try to remove the barrel, thus properly fitted inserts are essential. There are several ways to accomplish this, but the way I do it is to install the straight steel inserts into the barrel vise and make a mold of the individual barrel. This way, you can use the vise and the insert for any size barrel taper, from a featherweight tapered barrel, all the way up to a straight, no taper barrel. The mold material

The Remington barreled action, with the barrel removed, ready for the action to be accurized.

is the same material that you use to pillar bed the rifle — Devcon or alternatively, Steel Bed from Brownells.

The first step in the process is to mount the barrel vise on the workbench as solidly as possible. As an alternative, if you have a concrete wall or cinderblock wall in your basement, the barrel vise can be mounted to it. There are several barrel vises available and a couple of ways to remove the barrel. Remember, removing the Remington barrel is one thing, but down the road you may want to get into rebarreling Mausers, Lee Enfields, Arisakas, or others. Some of these barrels can be extremely difficult to remove, so in order to ensure the bench can take the torquing action of unscrewing the barrel, it must be solidly mounted. My bench is 1-inch thick plywood, which is stout enough, but if I were anticipating removing other types of barrels, I would probably add another 1-inch reinforcing piece of plywood, or possibly a piece of 2x8 under the top bench, with longer anchor bolts securing everything in place.

MAKING INSERT MOLDS

Having secured the vise to the bench, you need to mold your inserts. The barrel vise and inserts are split, so you'll make a shim between the upper and lower halves and split them apart later. Make the shims out of anything, even cardboard works. Once used, you can throw them away. For a more permanent solution, make them out of plastic. The shim needs to be as close to the barrel contour as possible so you don't get steel putty flowing between the two halves. If it does, you'll have to use a cutoff wheel on the Dremel tool to split the two halves apart. Block off both ends of the vise to keep the putty from flowing out the ends as well. Install the vise, and clamp the barrel as close to the front of the receiver as possible in order to keep the torque of the unit to a minimum. The farther out on the barrel you get, the more torque is placed on the barrel, and the more it is going to want to spin; consequently, the more clamping power is needed. Once you have your shims made, put everything together to check alignment before mixing up putty and making the mold. Personally, I have the barrel supported on the front and back so the barreled action is centered in the inserts. I also use a cardboard piece as a dam at the front of the vise to keep the epoxy from oozing out.

Now that everything is ready, put release agent on all exposed metal parts, a quick spray is all that's needed in order to make sure everything separates. Mix up the Steel Bed according to instructions. You'll need quite a lot since the shim is a couple of inches long. Lay the epoxy into the bottom and top of each of the inserts, then lay the lower insert into the barrel vise, place the barrel in position, put the shims in place, lay the upper half of the insert onto the top of the barrel and finally, put the top half of the barrel vise in place. Use the vise screws to line everything up by screwing them down slightly, but don't tighten anything, since that will squeeze out all of the epoxy. Let everything set up overnight, allowing at least 24 hours to cure.

Now that you have a mold of the exact barrel taper, take the upper half apart and separate the two halves of the mold. Use a good, quality brake cleaner to thoroughly degrease everything and then put some rosin into the upper and lower halves of the inserts you just created between the barrel and the epoxy inserts, and put it all back together. Clamp everything down tightly using the top bolts of the barrel vise, and remember, you can't get it too tight, you are not going to damage the old barrel. You can use the same breaker bar you're going to use on the action wrench to tighten the top bolts on the barrel vise. You need to get the barreled action in the vise oriented so the wrench is positioned properly. Since some of these barrels can be installed pretty tight from the factory, you'll need to

The old Remington barrel being removed.

You may need to use a breaker bar to remove older barrels, although the new ones tend to come off easily.

have the wrench handle pointed in the upright position at around 10 o'clock so you can put a breaker bar on it if additional leverage is needed.

Today's Remington barrels come off the action quite a bit easier than they did 20 years ago. Back then, heavy clamping power and leverage on the action wrench was needed. By comparison, our project gun's barrel came off the receiver with just a slight pull of the breaker bar, and I probably didn't need the breaker bar at all, except to tighten the top screws on the vise. Once the receiver is loosened, you can remove the action wrench and unscrew the action by hand.

TRUING THE ACTION

With the old barrel off, and the receiver stripped, you're ready to install the new match barrel. First, you'll need to true the action to make sure it is fully prepped and ready to go. There are three terms to understand when accurizing a rifle action, especially as it relates to the receiver. If any of them are off accuracy will suffer. The three areas are: parallel, perpendicular, and on center. In other words, the axis of all four

parts — receiver, bolt, barrel, and recoil lug — have to be as perpendicular, parallel, and on center with each other as possible. These dimensions are all taken from the axis of the bolt. The truing of the action and machining of the parts are known by the aforementioned "blueprinting" the action. You want to make sure the receiver ring face is square to the axis of the action, bolt and barrel, and that the front and rear face of the recoil lug is parallel and square with the front of the receiver and the shoulder of the barrel. The closer to exact that you can make the action, bolt, recoil lug and barrel, the more "potential" accuracy the rifle will have. Conversely, the more you deviate from this ideal, the more of a chance the rifle will not shoot up to par. In the end, you should be able to draw an imaginary line exactly through the center of the action, bolt, barrel, and cartridge from front to back. Anything that deviates from these parts being perpendicular, parallel and on center will result in diminished accuracy.

Barrel manufacturers have gone to great lengths to make their parts as true and square as possible, but you need to do the same to the bolt and action. You would normally do all of this machining with a lathe, but since we're assuming you don't have one in the garage, you need to turn to the good folks at Brownells to provide the tooling to allow you to true the action and bolt without a lathe. These handtools will allow you to true, or square the bolt face; true or square the face of the receiver; and lap the locking lugs of the bolt for maximum contact between the bolt locking lugs and the corresponding lug seats in the receiver.

The first step in the process, once you have the barrel removed, is to run a tap through the receiver threads. This will take care of any tightness or uniformity issues. I usually do this step in a lathe to make sure the tap is square and perpendicular to the receiver, but if you put the receiver upright in the vise, and run the tap down into it, it will keep the tap from leaning and will remain fairly square. Always use cutting oil when using these cutting tools, and flush out any chips after each procedure with your solvent and a blast of compressed air (wear safety glasses!). Once you have the receiver threads tapped, the next step is to lap the locking lugs. Do this with a bolt lug lapping tool, and a small amount of 800-grit lapping compound and a little dab of cutting oil. The lapping tool puts pressure

TOP: The front face is squared with a squaring tool from Brownells. The pointer shows where the low spots are that will be evened out with the tool. BOTTOM: The bolt squaring tool trues the bolt face by careful hand-turning.

on the bolt face. Actuating the bolt by opening and closing it will soon show where the bluing is removed and the bolt lugs are making contact. On the bolt of the project gun, only one of the lugs was making contact, a condition that can make the rifle string its shots vertically on the target. Actuate the bolt about ten times, then take a rag and wipe off the lapping compound, apply some fresh compound and a little oil, and go at it again. Once you have full contact on both locking lugs, clean off the lapping compound thoroughly with solvent and compressed air from both the bolt and the action, and move on to the next step. Remember, performing these steps will affect the final headspace dimension, so you are starting with a short-chambered

rifle barrel and, by lapping the locking lugs you have, in effect, decreased the short chamber dimension. In other words, you have increased the overall headspace dimension. If you do not clean off the lapping compound, it will continue to lap the lugs, potentially increasing the headspace over time. Also, do not lap locking lugs on a rifle you are not rebarreling, as the lapping process will increase the headspace dimension.

The next step is to true the front face of the receiver ring with a squaring tool. This tool is used with a light touch, as you only want to take off enough material to get to fresh metal. Always use a little cutting oil with the tool. You may get chatter, but it will not affect the accuracy as long as it's kept square. Next, the bolt face

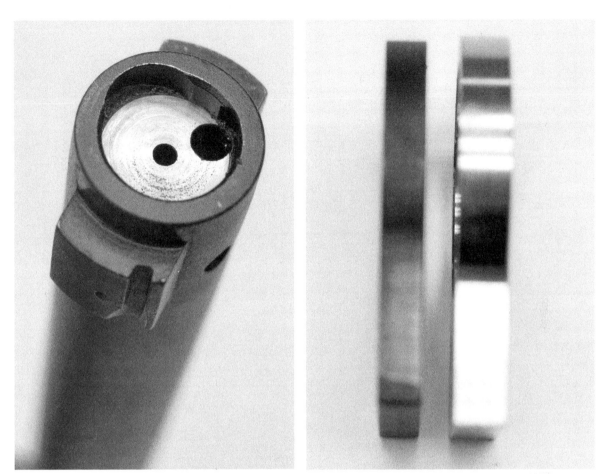

LEFT: The bolt face, after being squared with the squaring tool. RIGHT: The recoil lugs are shown. The factory lug is about .186 and the oversized lug is about .250 inches.

is trued with a … bolt squaring tool. This tool is used with the extractor in place. Put the tool under the extractor lip, and with a cordless drill, slowly turn the burr to lightly take off a slight amount of material until the bolt face is cleaned up. Remember, lapping the lugs increases headspace, taking material off the receiver rings reduces headspace, and squaring the bolt face increases headspace. Since the amount of material you are taking off is so low, the cumulative effect should be a barrel that is short-chambered. Chambering the barrel then becomes the final step.

BARREL CHAMBERING

To begin barrel chambering, clean the chamber, bolt, recoil lug and the action, and the headspace gauges. Make sure the firing pin assembly and the ejector are removed, and keep cutting oil, a chamber brush and compressed air at hand. The ejector and firing pin assembly are removed so you don't get a false reading with the headspace gauge. First you must make sure you still have a short chamber. Insert the GO gauge, screw the action onto the barrel with the bolt in the action and the recoil lug in place. You'll be replacing the factory lug with an oversized one, and the barrel was set to short chambered configuration using the oversized lug. Do not mix and match recoil lugs. Once everything is screwed together, make sure the bolt is fully closed and check the gap between the barrel shoulder and the front of the recoil lug. Since this is a short-chambered barrel, there should be about a .020 gap in between the receiver and the recoil lug. If there is no gap and the bolt is fully closed on a GO gauge, then check with the NO-GO Gauge. Another way to check is to screw the action onto the barrel shank without the bolt, then insert the GO gauge, and try to close the bolt handle. The bolt handle should not drop to the fully closed position. If it does, remove the GO gauge and insert the NO-GO and try the bolt again. If the bolt fully closes on the NO-GO gauge, then the headspace is excessive, and the barrel will need to be sent back to the manufacturer to have the shoulder set back to restore the short chamber.

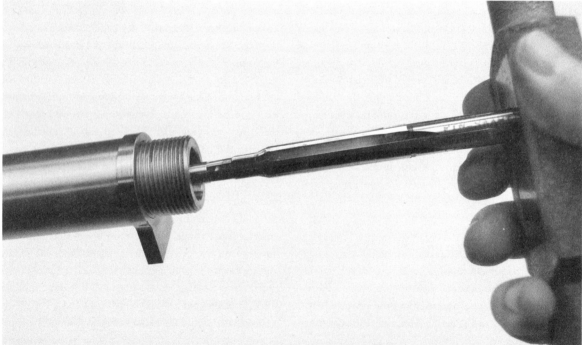

TOP: The recoil lug alignment tool is mounted to the action to orientate the recoil lug properly during installation. BOTTOM: The reamer is used to remove a small amount of material to properly fit and headspace the barrel.

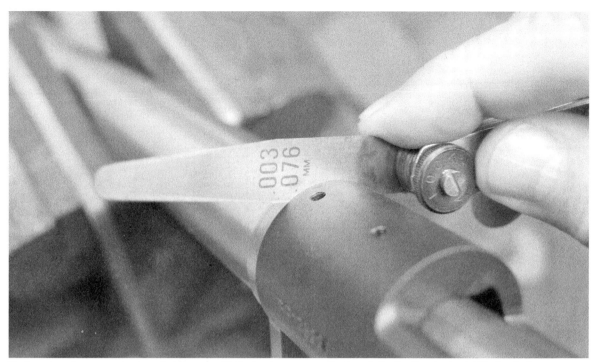

The barrel gap is measured using a feeler gauge with the headspace gauge in place, indicating there's about .003 of an inch of chamber left to cut.

Assuming that the bolt does not close on the GO gauge, slightly deepen the chamber to the minimum SAAMI specifications with a finishing reamer. Mount the finishing reamer into a tap handle, and secure the barrel into the vise. Typically, I like to mount the barrel so the chamber is facing up toward the ceiling, with the muzzle pointing toward the ground. If the barrel is held sideways, gravity can cause the reamer to apply more pressure downward, which could make the chamber slightly out of round. However, since you are not taking much material off the throat and shoulder with the finish reamer, the barrel can be held sideways in the vise. Apply a dab of cutting oil to the reamer at the shoulder, and insert it into the chamber. When the reamer gets to the bottom, start to turn the reamer lightly. This is an operation that takes a little "feel." You want the reamer to actually be cutting, to be making "chips." If you are not making metal chips, then the reamer is not cutting and will quickly dull. But if you use too much pressure, you run the risk of taking too much material off the chamber and going in too deep. This is definitely an operation where you measure twice and cut once. I usually make a couple of light turns with the reamer, then stop and remove the reamer. Always move the reamer straight out of the chamber so you don't scratch the chamber walls. Once the reamer is removed, brush out the chips from the chamber and the reamer with the

brush and solvent, and blow out any remaining debris with the air hose. Reapply the cutting oil to the reamer, reinsert it into the chamber and take a few more turns, repeating until you are a few thousandths of an inch out. Check your progress with the GO gauge. You are only taking off about .020 inches total and each couple of turns with the reamer should only remove about .002-.003 inches. So progress should be slow.

Measure progress with a feeler gauge. With the GO gauge in place in the chamber, and the recoil lug mounted on the barrel shank, screw the action onto the barrel with the bolt in place. When it stops, place a feeler gauge in between the recoil lug and front of the receiver ring. The gap between the two is the distance that needs to be removed in order to set the headspace correctly. Once the bolt will fully close on the GO gauge — with just a slight drag at the end where the bolt is fully closed — stop. That chamber is fully cut to the minimum SAAMI specifications. If the bolt fully closes on the GO without slight resistance, then you need to make sure you have not taken off too much material. Clean the chamber again, and insert the NO-GO gauge into the chamber, install the receiver and try to lightly close the bolt. It should not close on the NO-GO gauge. If it does, remove the barrel and send it back to the manufacturer; you have taken too much material from the chamber and the headspace is excessive.

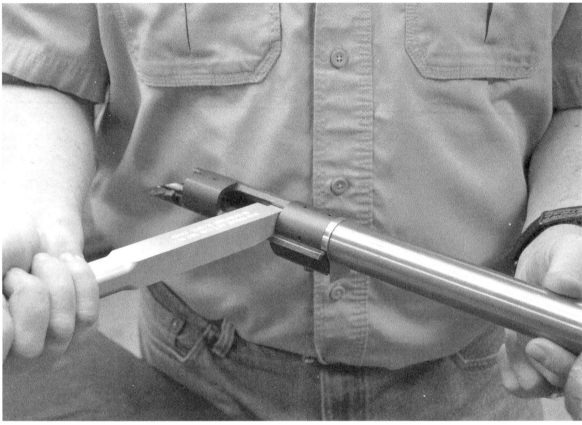

The action wrench is used to install and tighten the new match barrel.

Request they restore the barrel back to short chamber configuration. Let me repeat. If the bolt fully closes on the NO-GO gauge, the rifle is unsafe to fire live ammunition. This rifle has excessive headspace, and if fired serious injury or death could result. The barrel should be returned to the manufacturer to be headspaced.

INSTALLING THE MATCH BARREL

Assuming you have cut the chamber to the proper dimension, and the bolt fully closes on the GO gauge, ideally with a little bit of drag on closing, but does not close on the NO-GO, the final step is to mount the recoil lug alignment tool onto the receiver and, with the action wrench, tighten the receiver onto the barrel. I like to run the receiver up, tightening and loosening it, and then retighten it about 10 times. This will really seat the receiver into place, and was a technique recommended to me by Master Rifle Builder Kenny Jarrett of Jarrett Rifles.

Finally, clean the chamber, bore, bolt and all parts. Now that you have the chamber cut, and the barrel properly installed, the next step is to bed the barreled action into a McMillan Tactical Stock.

The barrel, about to be installed with the oversized recoil lug.

.308 Winchester. Courtesy of SAAMI

SAAMI
SPORTING ARMS AND AMMUNITION MANUFACTURERS' INSTITUTE, INC.
Since 1926

MAXIMUM CARTRIDGE / MINIMUM CHAMBER

308 WINCHESTER

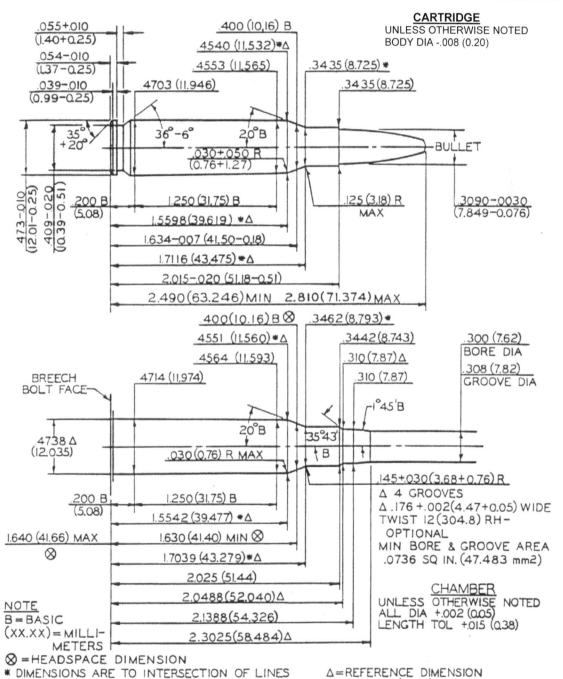

CARTRIDGE
UNLESS OTHERWISE NOTED
BODY DIA -.008 (0.20)

.055+.010 (1.40+0.25)
.054-.010 (1.37-0.25)
.039-.010 (0.99-0.25)
.4703 (11.946)
.400 (10.16) B
.4540 (11.532) *Δ
.4553 (11.565)
.3435 (8.725) *
.3435 (8.725)
35° +20°
36°-6°
20°B
.030+.050 R (0.76+1.27)
BULLET
.473-.010 (12.01-0.25)
.409-.020 (0.39-0.51)
.200 B (5.08)
1.250 (31.75) B
1.5598 (39.619) *Δ
1.634-.007 (41.50-0.18)
1.7116 (43.475) *Δ
2.015-.020 (51.18-0.51)
2.490 (63.246) MIN   2.810 (71.374) MAX
.125 (3.18) R MAX
.3090-.0030 (7.849-0.076)

.400 (10.16) B ⊗
.4551 (11.560) *Δ
.4564 (11.593)
.4714 (11.974)
.3462 (8.793) *
.3442 (8.743)
.310 (7.87) Δ
.310 (7.87)
.300 (7.62) BORE DIA
.308 (7.82) GROOVE DIA
BREECH BOLT FACE
1°45'B
.4738 Δ (12.035)
20°B
35°43'
B
.030 (0.76) R MAX
.145+.030 (3.68+0.76) R
.200 B (5.08)
1.250 (31.75) B
1.5542 (39.477) *Δ
1.630 (41.40) MIN ⊗
1.640 (41.66) MAX ⊗
1.7039 (43.279) *Δ
2.025 (51.44)
2.0488 (52.040) Δ
2.1388 (54.326)
2.3025 (58.484) Δ

Δ 4 GROOVES
Δ .176 +.002 (4.47+0.05) WIDE
TWIST 12 (304.8) RH- OPTIONAL
MIN BORE & GROOVE AREA
.0736 SQ IN. (47.483 mm2)

CHAMBER
UNLESS OTHERWISE NOTED
ALL DIA +.002 (0.05)
LENGTH TOL +.015 (0.38)

NOTE
B = BASIC
(XX.XX) = MILLI-METERS
⊗ = HEADSPACE DIMENSION
* DIMENSIONS ARE TO INTERSECTION OF LINES   Δ = REFERENCE DIMENSION
ALL CALCULATIONS APPLY AT MAXIMUM MATERIAL CONDITION (MMC)

PILLAR BEDDING IN A McMILLAN STOCK

Doing a full pillar bedding job on any rifle, especially the Remington M700, is one of the easiest ways to achieve accuracy and consistency. Our project gun has been re-barreled with a #8 taper Shilen match barrel. Now you need to glass bed it. To begin, drill out the front and rear guard screw holes to accept the aluminum pillars from Brownells. You can order 5/8ths-inch pillars and slim them down to ½-inch, if your drill press only accepts a ½-inch drill bit. With a barrel this heavy, I especially like to put a pad of bedding material about 1 ½ inches in front of the barrel to support and stabilize it. I have no scientific proof this is beneficial, it's a

trick that comes from years of building precision rifles for the DoD, and figuring out what works. Some gunsmiths completely free float the barrel and that's fine, as long as you get the results you are looking for.

Always degrease the barreled action before you do the final fitting as you don't want oil or grease in the fiberglass stock. This will keep the epoxy from sticking to the stock when you bed it. Make sure you can screw everything together before applying the epoxy. With the pillars in place, screw everything together, including the bottom metal, (you can leave out the mag box and mag spring and follower) and use the stockmakers' screws. Make sure the barrel has about .010 clearance the entire length of the forearm.

Wrap the rear of the barrel with bedding tape, either right at the recoil lug, or starting an inch or inch and a half ahead of the lug. Also wrap the barrel at the forend tip to center the barreled action. Make certain the barreled action can be screwed together, and everything is squared and centered in the stock. If it's not, figure out what's causing it to be off center; you may have to scrape out the stock until it's centered and squared.

The next step is to use modeling clay to plug off the areas you don't want epoxy to run into. Use a combination of release agent spray and paste wax on all of the action

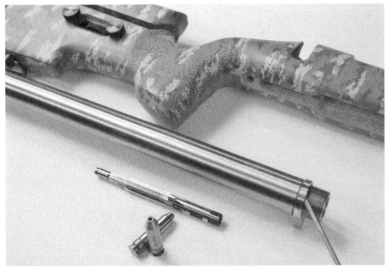

The Shilen barrel, McMillan stock, Clymer reamers, and headspace gauges make for an excellent rifle.

ABOVE: A properly bedded Remington M700 rifle, with a Nightforce scope and spotting scope, ABM tactical ammo and BlackHawk! drag bag is an excellent tactical setup.

RIGHT: The pillars are installed once the stock has been drilled out.

and bottom metal parts. First run a 1/4x28 tap into the front and rear guard screw threads to make them uniform, then apply the release agent. Dip the guard screws into floor wax and run them up into the front and rear guard screw holes. Apply two light, uniform coats of spray release agent. Too much release agent and you will sacrifice the close fit of the bedding material you are trying to achieve; too little and you risk gluing the barreled action together, which is not as bad as you may think. Remember, a little goes a long way. If the rifle comes out of the stock too easily after bedding, you are not getting the full benefits of your work. It should be held tightly when it comes out.

At this point you've taped off the barrel and applied release agent to all of the parts of the gun that could possibly come in contact with the steel epoxy. Once you've applied the release agent, do not place the barreled action back into the stock for any reason — you don't want the release agent to contact the stock as the

The bedding tape is applied around the end of the barrel to provide the proper gap, and to help center the barreled action in the stock.

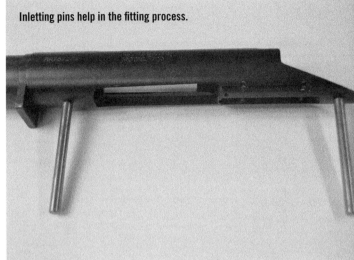

Inletting pins help in the fitting process.

epoxy won't adhere to it. Mix up your bedding compound, I recommend Devcon steel epoxy. (I've used Devcon steel putty, aluminum putty and titanium putty. Titanium is a little expensive, but it sets up way too fast. It does have the advantage of not rusting, and steel is more durable than aluminum. Brownells also sells a steel bedding epoxy that works really well.)

Mix the epoxy per the instructions. I like to use two Popsicle sticks, one wide, and one narrow. Use the narrow stick to start the epoxy into the recoil lug recess. Push down into it a few times to get the air bubbles out of it. Apply the epoxy to the outside of the pillars, and insert those into the stock holes. Use the large stick to spread the epoxy over the large surfaces. Once the epoxy has been spread over the action area, screw the rifle together with the stockmakers' screws. You did apply release agent to these screws, right? Don't tighten them too much, just run those up lightly snug. You should see the epoxy ooze out all around the barrel, action, and bottom metal area. Take a rag soaked with Shooter's Choice and wipe off the excess epoxy, the stuff cleans it up nicely and doesn't hurt the stock. Once everything has been cleaned off, put the rifle in a cradle and let it sit overnight. Allow it to fully cure for 24 hours.

Once it's dried and cured, unscrew the stockmakers' screws. They may be a little tough to turn, and this is normal. If they don't turn at all, you have a problem. Assuming you were able to unscrew them, clamp the barrel into the padded vise with the floorplate pointing toward you, and try to wiggle the stock off from the barreled action. It should be tight, that's what you are striving for. If it won't come off, take the rifle out of the vise and, with two hands, slap the barrel only down onto the bench. This should break the barrel loose from the stock. Once you have the barreled action separated from the stock, take a look at your

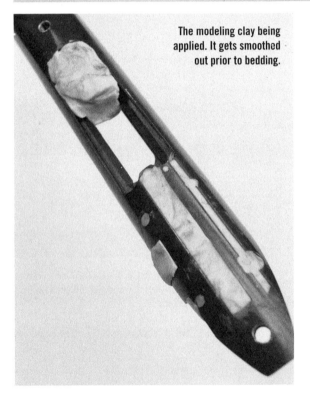

The modeling clay being applied. It gets smoothed out prior to bedding.

The stockmakers' screws keep everything together while the epoxy sets up.

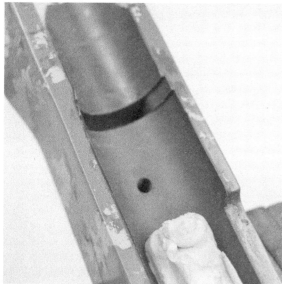

ABOVE: The epoxy gets a good squeeze from the stockmakers' screws when bedding the rifle.

LEFT: The bedding, as it looks after removing the barreled action.

BELOW: The cutoff wheel is used to remove the front pad of material that you don't want. Once it's cut off, lift it out with the tape.

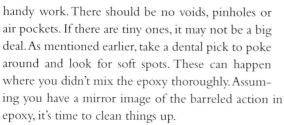

handy work. There should be no voids, pinholes or air pockets. If there are tiny ones, it may not be a big deal. As mentioned earlier, take a dental pick to poke around and look for soft spots. These can happen where you didn't mix the epoxy thoroughly. Assuming you have a mirror image of the barreled action in epoxy, it's time to clean things up.

Take out the modeling clay, remove the bedding tape, and use your Foredom tool with a cutoff wheel to cut

the packing tape in front of the pad of epoxy, and lift the tape off. Use a nylon punch to tap on the floorplate to drop it out the bottom of the stock. A structured tooth carbide bit cleans up the excess around the action area best. Drill out the pillar holes with a J drill, or some

ABOVE: The stock holes get drilled out for clearance after taking the rifle apart.

RIGHT: The Jewell trigger is installed, and the bolt stop actuated to make sure it functions properly.

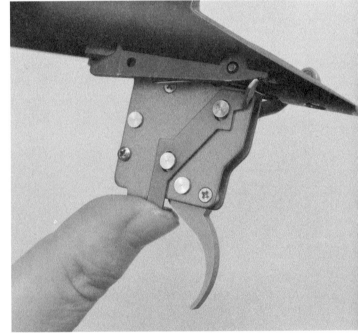

size similar. The stock screws have a shank diameter of ¼ inch, so I like to go larger to get the epoxy out of the pillars. You should drill them out until you get to fresh aluminum. Once the excess epoxy has been removed, and the modeling clay has been cleaned up, the next step is to clean off all traces of release agent. A good solvent and an air hose work well. Once that's done, install the extractor and ejector.

EXTRACTOR AND EJECTOR INSTALLATION

The ejector is pretty straightforward. Put the spring and plunger in and keep it in place with the crosspin. The extractor is slid in place by starting it in the opening slot provided for re-assembly. Replace the trigger, bolt stop and spring — in this case, I used a Jewell trigger factory set to 1 ½ pounds, which is way too light for a tactical rifle, so I changed it to 2 ½ lbs. The overtravel

stop was also set too far out, which is actually not a bad thing for an operational tactical rifle, but since this rifle was built for this book I'll set the stop as close as I can for best accuracy. The way to do this is to screw the stop

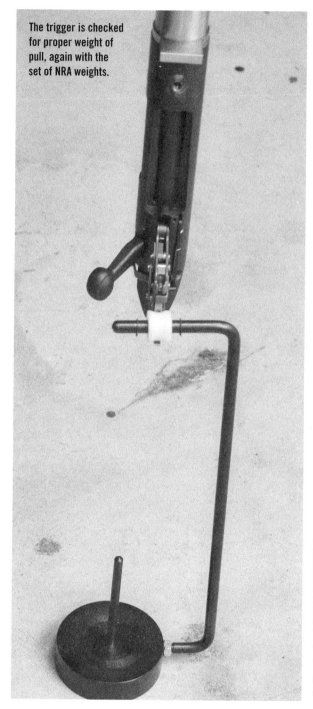

The trigger is checked for proper weight of pull, again with the set of NRA weights.

TOP: The rifle, still unfinished, gets a workout at the range from the author's son. MIDDLE: The rifle shot a .568 group right out of the gate, using the Hornady match round. BOTTOM: The project gun after being refinished in Poly-T2 finish by Robar, with a Leupold Mk 4 scope and Leupold spotting scope, set up at the range.

in until the rifle won't fire, then cock the rifle and pull the trigger while backing out the set screw. When the rifle fires, you can stop there, or give it an extra margin of safety by backing out the stop screw an extra 1/8th turn, and you're done.

Now you can screw the rifle together with the magazine box and magazine spring in place, and do a function check with dummy ammo. Make sure the rifle feeds and ejects, the safety works properly, and the rifle's bolt release functions. The floorplate should drop freely. When you screw the rifle together, torque the front and rear guard screws to 65 in.-lbs. On this rifle, I mounted a Leupold Mk 4 scope and torqued the ring keeper nuts also to 65 in.-lbs. The last task is to run a cleaning rod through the rifle to make sure there isn't any dust, release agent or debris in the barrel before you take it to the range.

THE SEMI-INLETTED WOOD STOCK

Inletting a semi-fitted wood stock can be a great project, if you know what you're getting into ahead of time. Semi-inletted means the stock is shaped fairly close on the outside, with enough room and extra material to allow a little creativity by the riflesmith. The action area, likewise, is fitted fairly close, but is undersized to allow a close fit between metal and wood. The barrel channel is left with a small half round groove to fit the forend to any barrel contour. This will actually be the hardest part of the job. There is a lot of material to fit, and over a long distance.

To fit the barreled action, establish a layout line. The top of the stock has been planed smooth and level, which you'll use as a surface upon which to do the layout. Start with a machinist square and a mechanical pencil. Hold the pencil next to the corner of the square, and run the square and pencil along the barrel contour the full length. This will etch a line to follow while removing wood. Remember, hold the pencil inside the edge at the corner of the square to ensure you are laying out a line inside the outer contour of the barrel. This is to ensure removal of wood up to the line, leaving enough wood to do the final shaping for the actual barrel contour — a safety margin. You will free float the barrel, but don't want a giant gap, either. It's always easier to remove material than to put it back on.

INLETTING TOOLS

Two required tools for stock inletting are the curling scraper and the barrel channel inletting tool. The barrel channel tool takes wood off fast, while the curling scraper is for small amounts. Two key items to have on hand are inletting black and inletting pins. The black is brushed on with an acid brush or other small brush on the bottom of the action, then the action is placed into the stock and removed, the black ink showing the high spots. The machinists' square is also used to show when the barrel channel is being opened up evenly. Turn the square with the point down toward the bottom of the channel. The point and the sides of the square should all be touching the wood at the bottom and the sides at the same time as you are inletting the barrel channel. Any gaps mean you have taken too much material off, and need to switch to another area. In other words, if there is a gap

Stock inletting with a machinist square keeps the barrel channel from getting too large, which will create an unsightly gap.

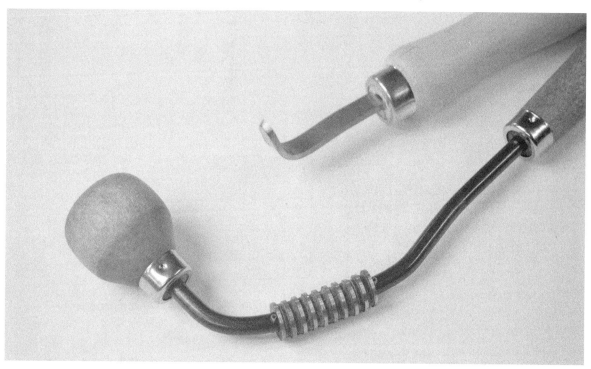

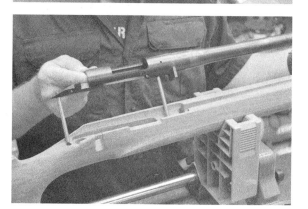

ABOVE: The curling scraper and barrel channel tool. The channel tool comes in different sizes for exact cuts.

TOP LEFT: The barrel channel tool allows you to open up the barrel channel.

BOTTOM LEFT: Inletting pins help guide the action into the stock.

on the bottom, work on the sides, and vice versa. Use it as a guide to gauge where to take off wood.

Once the stock has been fully inletted, install the pillars and bed the stock. The best way to drill straight holes in wood is with the Forstner bit. Once the holes are drilled, you can assemble the rifle to make sure everything fits. Install the pillars, barreled action and the floorplate, and, using the factory screws, secure everything together. Cycle the bolt a few times, and once you're satisfied the rifle is ready, disassemble everything and pillar bed the rifle in the same manner as explained in the previous chapter with the McMillan fiberglass stock. Once the rifle has cured, break apart. Drill out the guard screw holes, and sand off the excess epoxy.

You can now sand the stock down, and prep it to apply the finish. Sand the stock using the orbital sander with progressively finer grits of sandpaper. When you

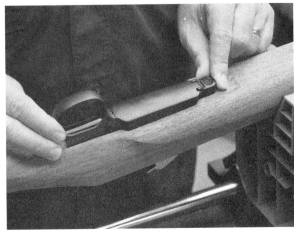

TOP: The Forstner bit is the best tool for cutting straight holes in wood. MIDDLE: Inletting the floorplate is just as important. BOTTOM: Bedding the rifle with an aluminum pillar follows the same process as the McMillan fiberglass stock project.

get down to about #240 grit, you can "whisker" the stock. Do this by wetting its surface with water, allowing it to dry, and sanding off the whiskers that will rise up. Whisker several times until the stock is smooth. You can then start filling in the pores of the stock. This is done by sanding with a little bit of the finishing oil, and creating a type of "slurry" on the stock's surface. Let dry, and repeat several times until the wood pores are filled.

TOP: The stock is bedded and screwed together. MIDDLE: The stock, getting a final fit and check by the author. BOTTOM: "Whiskering" the stock is a very old method of achieving a great wood finish. You only need to wet the wood, not soak it, for best results. Do this a couple of times to remove all of the fine whiskers.

TOP: The stock is hand sanded by creating a slurry of oil finish and wood sanding dust.

BOTTOM: Sanding the stock with the orbital sander and progressively finer grits will yield a smooth finish, then switch to hand sanding for best results.

RECOIL PAD INSTALLATION

You can now install the recoil pad. This is performed with a pad-fitting jig. Screw the pad onto the rifle stock, and scribe a line around the outside of the pad at the edge of the stock. Remove the pad, and install it in reverse on the jig. Use a large machinist square to set the angle of the top of the comb of the stock, and clamp down the jig. Using the belt sander, sand down until you reach the scribe line. Go back to the stock and, using the square, get the angle of the pad at the corporal line, or bottom of the stock. Go back to the belt sander and grind down to the scribe line. Remove the pad from the jig and it should be a very close fit. You can sand it down flush with the orbital sander, but be careful as this will infuse rubber particles into the wood finish. Apply more finish to the wood. You can also install sling swivel studs using the Kleinendorst jig. This tool makes for quick and accurate work when locating the holes for the front and rear studs. That's it for installing and fitting the semi-inletted wood stock.

TOP: The recoil pad is screwed onto the stock and the line around the pad is scribed. MIDDLE: The recoil pad fitting jig in use. BOTTOM: The Kleinendorst sling swivel drilling jig makes it easy to drill straight, accurate holes in both wood and fiberglass.

BUILDING THE H-S PRECISION RIFLE

his rifle will be built similar to the McMillan tactical project. The fiberglass stock I selected for this varmint rifle is the excellent H-S Precision stock. The model is actually one of their tactical models, because I wanted a stock that has a wide forearm to be able to accept the heavy barrel, and one with a fully adjustable cheek piece and buttstock. The reason for that is, since this rifle will be used to hunt coyote and/or other predators in the winter, I knew I'd be wearing heavy winter clothes. The rifle will also be used to hunt woodchuck in the summer when temps reach into the upper 90s. So the temperatures will vary widely and I wanted the stock to be able to accommodate the clothing I'll be wearing. I also wanted an adjustable cheek piece since I test many different brands and types of varmint scopes, with varying sizes of objective bells, so scope height will vary. I chose the woodland camo pattern for the stock.

The H-S precision stock has an aluminum bedding block, which negates the need for a traditional bedding job. I have used many tactical stocks when building precision rifles for the government, but we would always machine out the area around the recoil lug and use Devcon aluminum epoxy to bed the rifles — always with very good results. You are not going to be able to machine out the recoil lug area, but there is enough space around the lug so you can fill it in with the epoxy.

I also obtained a stainless match barrel from Shilen. The Shilen name has been associated with accurate rifles since 1955, and I have used many of their barrels with great success. For this project, I selected the pre-threaded, short-chambered Match-Grade stainless in .22-250, with a #8 taper, an overall length of 24 inches and a 1-in-7 twist. Shilen also makes a Select Match Grade for competition shooters, but for a varmint rifle, Match Grade will deliver all the accuracy you need. There are other variables on the barrel that need to be selected. One of the most important is twist rate. As I stated, I went with the 1-in-7, which means that the rifling in the barrel makes one complete revolution in 7 inches of length. This is a very fast twist for a .22-caliber rifle, but it's needed to stabilize the heavier 70-grain or heavier .22 caliber bullets. I intend to use the rifle as a component test gun at some of the longer ranges, so the 1-in-7 twist will handle the heavier bullets for group shooting, but will also shoot the lighter varmint projectiles in the 50- to 55-grain weights well, too. As mentioned, the Shilen barrel comes pre-threaded, and short-chambered, identical to the one we used for the McMillan rifle. Lathes suitable for rebarreling a rifle can cost 10k or more for a decent one, so to be able to install a match-grade barrel on a rifle without an expensive machine tool is a real advantage.

CRYOGENIC TREATING

Our project rifle will be getting a special cryogenic treatment. The company that does this for the firearms industry is appropriately named 300 Below, because that's exactly what they do. They will submerge the barrel in a cryogenic bath and lower the temperature to 300 below zero. This chapter doesn't allow me to fully explain the procedure or its benefits and advantages to metallurgy, but the process has been performed on rifle

TOP: The H-S Precision stock has an aluminum bedding block, and can deliver good accuracy without bedding, but can also be improved upon with the addition of epoxy bedding. BOTTOM: The Remington action's locking lugs get lapped with a lapping tool and 800-grit lapping compound. The process ensures full contact of the locking lugs to the receiver.

barrels for decades, and in the aerospace and manufacturing industry for even longer. Some shooters do not feel the need for cryo treatment and see no benefit, while many extoll the benefits of easier cleaning and extended barrel life. Does it help accuracy? The jury's still out, sometimes it does and sometimes it doesn't. Is it beneficial? Most shooters say yes. Does it harm the barrel steel somehow? Not in so far as hundreds of shooters have been able to determine. Regardless, this barrel will be off to get treated. Bottom line, there can be big benefits, with nothing detrimental to the barrel or the gun.

OFF WITH THE OLD

You will need some specialized tooling to remove the old factory barrel, plus reamers and headspace gages in the correct caliber to install the new barrel, but once you have those items, the rest is easy. I recommend reamers and headspace gages from Clymer Manufacturing, one of the oldest and best tooling companies in America. The reamer will deepen the chamber about .010 of an inch to minimum SAAMI specifications, and the depth will be verified with headspace gages. Also, by being able to take the barrel off and set the headspace yourself with a new, match-grade barrel, you can do operations to make the rifle more accurate that you would not be able to do with the factory barrel still installed — such as lapping the bolt lugs to the receiver.

Another item I have for this rifle is a Jewell trigger. Arnold Jewell makes the finest trigger on the market today, and I have used his triggers on just about every custom rifle I've ever built. Jewell triggers come in two models, one for hunting, and the other for benchrest. The model I have for the project rifle is the HVR, which stands for Hunting and Varmint. Pull weights on this trigger go down to 1 lb. The benchrest models can come without a safety or bolt release. The various models of Jewell triggers can be had with different configurations, such as having the bolt release on top, and the safety on the left side.

The last item I received for the build isn't a gun part at all. It's a neck sizing die from Redding Reloading. I'm going to use this die on the once-fired brass created when I initially shoot the rifle. Using a neck sizing die with once-fired brass is a great way to tighten up groups

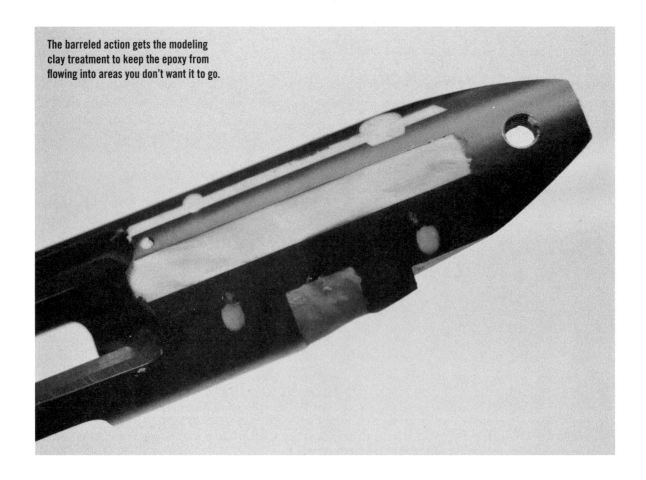

The barreled action gets the modeling clay treatment to keep the epoxy from flowing into areas you don't want it to go.

because the die only reforms the neck of the case, leaving the body of the case the exact size of the chamber. It's a great way to get the most from handloaded ammunition. Once you rebarrel the rifle, use new brass, or full-length size the once-fired brass prior to using, since the chamber dimension will have changed. A very close fit between the chamber and brass is critical to accuracy. Once you've shot the full-length sized brass in the new match chamber, you'll break out the neck sizer and reload those. The difference in accuracy from a rifle with a match-grade barrel, a glass-bedded stock, an excellent trigger and good quality handloaded ammunition to a factory barrel, with factory ammunition is substantial. That's a very quick overview of the parts and tooling that you're going to use to rebuild this rifle into a real tack driver. The rifle is already shooting pretty well, but we can make it much better, learn a few things and have some fun doing it.

BARREL INSTALLATION

Remove the old barrel using the bench vise as you did for the McMillan rifle. Once the barrel is removed, lap the lugs, and perform the other operations to the receiver you did with the tactical rifle, although for this rifle keep the factory recoil lug. Install the new Shilen barrel in the same manner that we installed the .308 barrel on the McMillan rifle, setting the headspace to very lightly drag on your GO headspace gauge.

Remove the trigger, bolt stop and spring. The H-S stock, as mentioned, has the bedding block, so you don't need to use poured or machined pillars, but you can make a few mods to the stock prior to bedding. Back in the day, I would put the stock into the vise in the milling machine and mill a pocket behind the recoil lug, basically enlarging the opening for the recoil lug to hold as much steel epoxy as possible. This essentially put

a big block of steel behind the recoil lug in a very tight fit. Since you can't do this in your garage shop, you'll just have to get by with applying the epoxy to the existing recoil lug slot. Since this is a light-recoiling .22-250, it should be no problem. With harder kicking calibers you would want to open up the slot for more epoxy.

To prep the rifle for bedding, sand down all of the areas of the exposed aluminum block, top and bot-

TOP: The bedding material applied to the stock. BOTTOM: Always look for a good squeeze of bedding material everywhere you've applied it. On this rifle bedding material has been applied all around the action area.

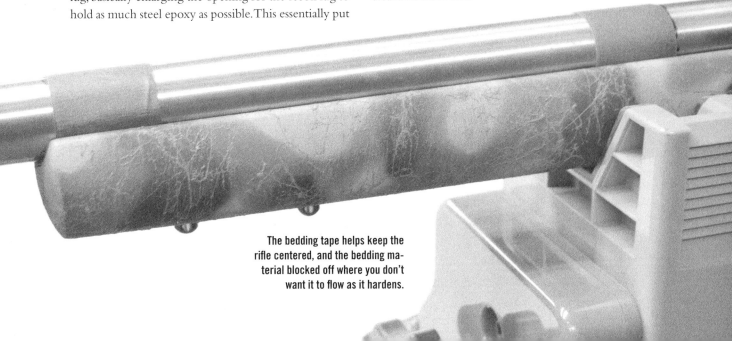

The bedding tape helps keep the rifle centered, and the bedding material blocked off where you don't want it to flow as it hardens.

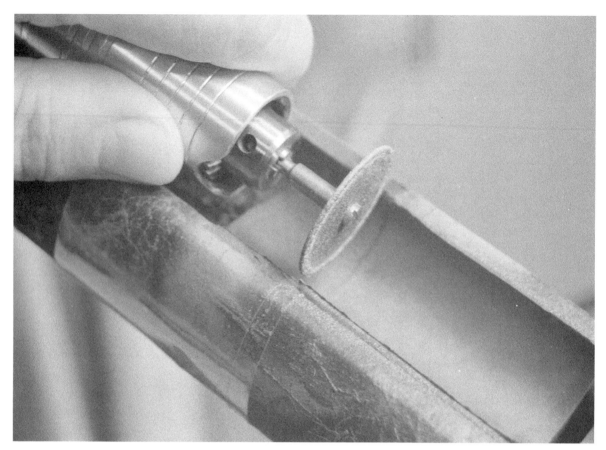

ABOVE: The bedding material is removed from the front bedding area. Note the pad of about 1 ½ inches in front of the recoil lug to support the heavy barrel.

RIGHT: The bedding material is inspected for pinholes and flaws.

tom. Install the newly barreled action into the stock and screw everything together to make sure it all functions correctly without binding.

Remove the barreled action, place your modeling clay in the trigger recesses, and tape off the front of the barrel about 1 ½ inches in from of the recoil lug and at the end of the barrel around at the forend tip to maintain your spacing. Add a strip of tape under the barrel to lift off excess epoxy. Don't forget to place the layer of electrical tape underneath the recoil lug. Thoroughly apply release agent to all of the parts, including the front and rear guard screw threads, and the exterior surfaces of the barreled action where the epoxy will flow.

Mix up Devcon, using the 2.5:1 ratio and,

TOP: The newly bedded rifle gives the Leupold scope a test at the range. BOTTOM: The rifle also gave a Nightforce riflescope and spotting scope a workout.

The H-S stock with adjustable cheek piece works well when using scopes with large objectives.

with Popsicle sticks apply the epoxy, starting with the recoil lug slot to the front and rear guard screw holes, action area, and the bottom metal. For this rifle, I taped off the barrel to give a pad of about 1 ½ inches in front of the recoil lug for the barrel to sit on, rather than completely free floating it. Again, this is just personal opinion, and is the way I like to do it.

Screw the rifle together with the stockmakers' screws, and wipe off the excess epoxy with Shooter's Choice. Let sit in the rifle cradle overnight. The next day, break out the rifle, drill out the guard screw holes, and remove all of the tape and modeling clay. By now,

you should be an expert at this! Once the tape and modeling clay is removed, thoroughly degrease all of the metal parts, install the Jewell trigger, bolt stop, and spring. Test the trigger and make any necessary final adjustments to weight of pull, engagement and overtravel.

Remove all of the excess epoxy from around the action area. Reinstall the barreled action into the stock, along with the magazine box. Install the bottom metal with the magazine spring and follower. Torque the front and rear guard screws down to 65 in.-lbs., and install the scope. Clean the barrel and chamber area and you should be ready to go to the range for testing.

Chapter 10

GUNSMITHING THE
RUGER
MODEL 77

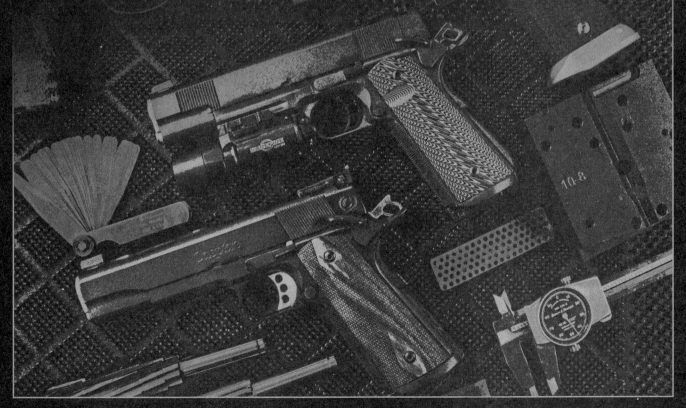

The Ruger Model 77 bolt-action rifle was designed by Jim Sullivan at Ruger, and introduced to the public in 1968. The rifle borrowed heavily from earlier rifle designs and incorporated the Mauser two-lug bolt and a claw extractor. The later version, the M77 MkII, was retooled and reintroduced in 1997. The claw extractor was kept, but the bolt face was opened to incorporate CRF, or controlled round feeding. What is CRF? If you go back and look at some of the dangerous game rifles that were used in Africa in the early 1900s, they were mostly double rifles, but if a professional hunter or their client wanted more than two shots, they had to go with a bolt-action repeater, which gave them four-shot capacity; three in the magazine and one in the chamber, for twice the firepower of a double rifle. The Mauser was a favorite of the day because it could hold more than two rounds and, being a battle rifle, was absolutely reliable for the troops, which is why CRF was first developed. Actually, the Mauser 98 was the first rifle to feature controlled round feeding, a feature that allows the bolt to be in control of the cartridge during the feeding cycle. The bolt pushes the round forward and out of the magazine. When the rear of the cartridge pops up and clears the magazine, the rear of the cartridge rides up the bolt face, and the claw extractor grabs hold of the cartridge while the round is being pushed into the chamber. So, the bolt is in control of the cartridge about halfway through the feeding cycle.

This feature is a good idea to have on a rifle intended for game that could possibly eat you, or stomp you into a bloody puddle on the ground. That's because rifles intended for dangerous game have to be 100 percent reliable. Think about it: If the round is in the process of being chambered, and a feeding malfunction occurs, and your rifle has CRF, you can pull the bolt back before the cartridge is fully chambered, and the offending cartridge will be ejected and a new round fed into the chamber. This can be done in about half a second — a really important feature when a Cape buffalo or rhino is charging you. With a more traditional rifle lacking CRF, you would be pushing the cartridge into the chamber with the nose of the bolt the entire way, with nothing controlling or guiding the cartridge. If the same feeding malfunction were to occur, and the bolt was pulled to the rear to try to clear the malfunction, the offending cartridge would be left in the loading port or jammed halfway into the chamber since the extractor would not be in control of the cartridge. It would then have to be physically removed by hand,

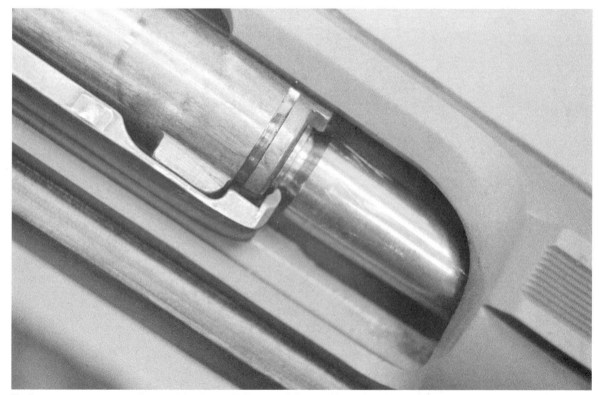

The Ruger system uses controlled round feeding, or CRF to control the cartridge with complete reliability.

which would take precious seconds.

The MkII also got rid of the plunger-type ejector and went back to the original Mauser-style blade ejector. Another feature brought over from some of the military rifles of the early 1900s was the three-position safety. The rifle has one position that's fully safe, where the safety blocks the trigger and prevents the bolt from being opened; a middle position, in which the bolt can be actuated but the trigger cannot; and the fire position, where the bolt and trigger can be actuated. The latest version of the M77, the Hawkeye, was introduced in 2006, with a change to the trigger and stock.

The rifle I received from Ruger for this project gun incorporates CRF, a three-position safety, and other features unique to Ruger rifles, including inte-

gral scope bases that are machined into the top of the receiver rather than separate scope bases. Another feature of all Ruger rifles that separates them from the pack is a one-piece steel bolt. For other makers, the bolt is a two-piece affair with the bolt handle silver-brazed onto the bolt body. Silver brazing is not the same as silver solder; it is many, many times stronger.

The Hawkeye rifle I procured for this project was the Varmint/Target version. This is an all-stainless rifle,

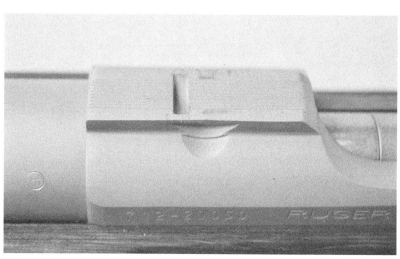

RIGHT: **The integral scope bases are unique to the Ruger rifles.**

BELOW: **The Ruger blade-type ejector is very positive.**

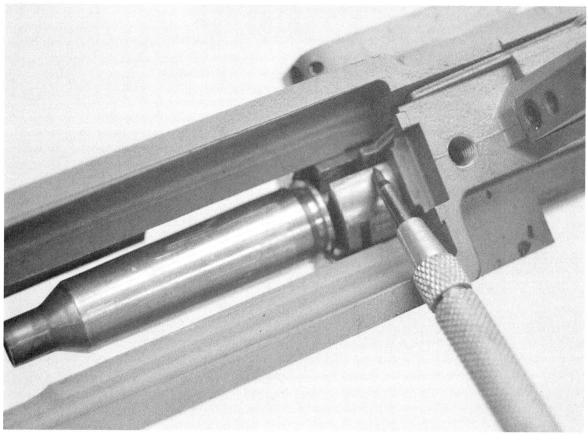

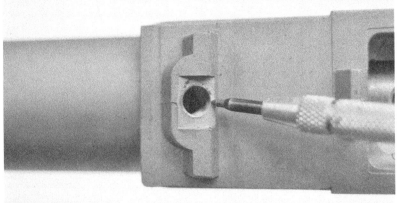

TOP: The Ruger at the range produced good results right from the start, but even good shooting rifles can be made better. BOTTOM: The front guard screw is angled at 45 degrees, which makes it different from other rifles.

that includes the receiver, barrel, bottom metal, swivel studs, and scope rings all made of stainless. Caliber for this rifle is .22-250 Remington. Other vital stats for this rifle include a weight of 9.7 lbs., barrel length of 26 inches, twist rate at 1/14, with a six groove, RH twist, and a 90-degree recessed target crown at the muzzle. The 1/14 twist of the hammer-forged barrel precludes me from testing any bullet heavier than 55 grains. Heavier bullets require a faster twist and I was anxious to try some of the heavier bullets I have from Barnes, Hornady, Speer and Sierra, but for now, I have a good selection of factory loaded ammo as well as bullets in 55-grain persuasion. The stock is a very attractive black laminate, with a wide, beavertail forend, straight comb and a slight swell on both sides of the pistol grip, giving a good hand-filling grip for both righties and lefties. The magazine holds four rounds and features a drop

floorplate upon which the Ruger logo is etched. There's a very positive latch-type bolt release on the left side of the receiver. Two features about the Ruger rifles that depart from tradition are that the front and rear guard screws are not angled the same; that is, the front guard screw is set at a 45-degree angle into the stock, the rear a more traditional 90 degrees to the receiver. The thought is, the 45-degree stock screw pulls the receiver down and back into the stock resulting in increased accuracy because of more positive contract with the recoil lug and the stock. The flip side of this is that some people think that when the front action screw is pulling at an angle, and the rear action screw is pulling straight down, the receiver can be tensioned like a bow, leading to inconsistencies in accuracy. Anytime there's tension in the barrel or action stringing shots creating flyers can occur. That's the theory, but I've never experienced such with any Ruger rifle I've owned, shot or worked on and there have been more than a few. When I get into bedding this rifle, I'll demonstrate some techniques that will secure the stock solidly into the bedding material with the action screws torqued appropriately.

The second feature about Ruger rifles that breaks with tradition is the two-stage trigger. In a two-stage, when the rifle is cocked and ready to fire, the shooter needs to pull the trigger back slightly and, this free travel, or more correctly, pretravel, is a small movement of the trigger to the rear, at which point resistance is felt. This resistance is where the actual trigger is being pressed, the rifle then fires, and the overtravel — or the amount of movement after the sear disengages — is very slight to almost nothing. Some shooters like a two-stage trigger and some don't. The trigger pull on the Ruger rifle was a very light 2.14 lbs. with just a hint of creep, and a fair amount of overtravel.

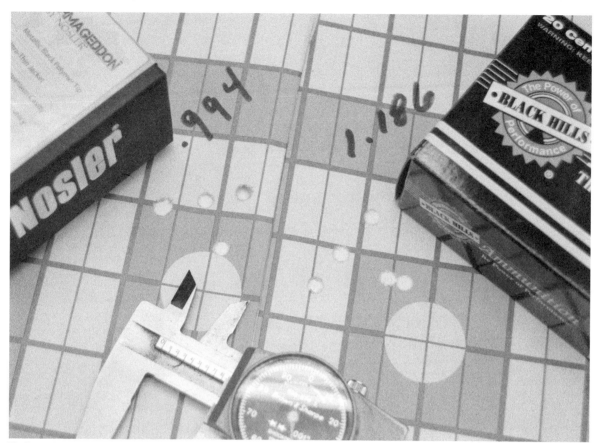

The Ruger Hawkeye Varmint shot really well right out of the box.

OUT OF THE BOX ACCURACY

So, how did the rifle shoot out of the box? I did no initial tuning to the rifle; in fact, I forgot to even run a patch through the bore before taking it to the range. The scope rings provided with the rifle were for a 1-inch diameter scope, and the only one I had in that diameter was a very old fixed 4x Weaver that was mounted on my Ruger 10/22 (and when I say old, this scope is over 30 years old). I did take some really good ammo that shot well through other rifles and some of my handloads, plus some new stuff from Black Hills Ammunition I was anxious to try out. After mounting the scope in the shop, and getting it bore sighted and on paper at the range, I settled in and shot some surprising groups. The best group of the day came from one of my handloads, loaded with the Nosler 55-grain Varmageddon flat-base bullet, which came in under an inch (.994) for 5 shots at 100 yards. Also noteworthy was the new offering from Black Hills, loaded with the excellent Hornady 50-grain V-Max bullet, coming in at a shade over an inch at 1.186. No groups were over two inches.

GLASS BEDDING THE RUGER M77

Glass bedding the Ruger is a little different from typical round-bottom rifles like the Remington and Savage. Brownells makes a set of aluminum pillars that are specifically designed to work with the angled front trigger guard screw. Once the rifle has been disassembled, remove the trigger assembly and set it aside. Drill out the front and rear guard screw holes for the aluminum pillars. This rifle has a laminated wood stock, and as such, the stock finish is a synthetic polyurethane type. This will need to be removed in order to get down into the bare wood areas where you want the steel epoxy to stick. Using scrapers and chisels remove the urethane finish and check the stock for fit. Once you have the stock scraped out, tape off two areas — one at the forend tip to help establish the proper barrel to barrel channel gap, the other around the rear of the barrel about two inches in front of the recoil lug. This will allow the barrel to be free-floated its entire length, with the exception of the pad under the barrel at the chamber area. As explained before in this book, there are two schools of thought: one to completely free float

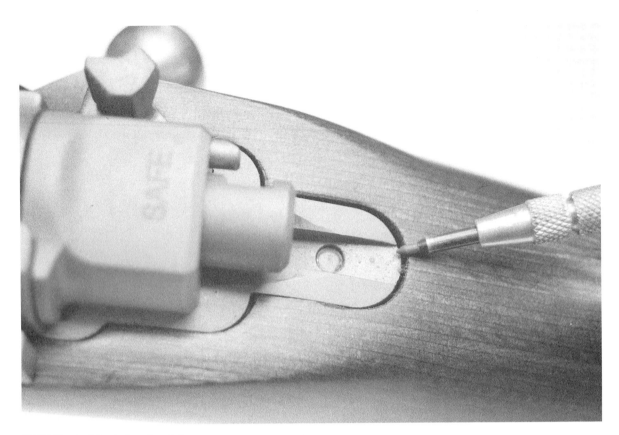

ABOVE: The stock has to be relieved at the rear of the tang for the epoxy to flow around it.

RIGHT: The rifle is ready to get bedded, and everything is screwed together to make sure you have everything correct before the epoxy is mixed.

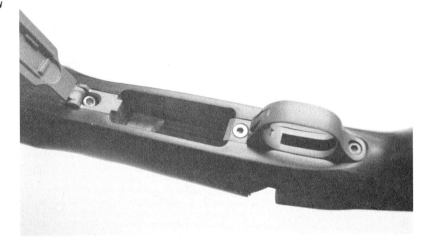

the barrel, the other to float the barrel, with the exception of the pad. I like to install the pad, and shoot the rifle, and if there are issues, the pad can always be removed to see if the rifle responds to that modification.

Once you have the barrel taped off, use the modeling clay to fill in the areas around the action where you don't want the epoxy. The Ruger is a fairly square-bottom action and there are many spots where it's easy to get some epoxy in and lock the barreled action to the stock. Be careful and go slow. Once you have the action's crevices and holes filled in with the modeling clay, reinstall the barreled action with the pillars in place to make sure you can screw everything together. Fit the rifle together one last time.

Once everything is screwed together and the barreled action is checked for squareness and level in the stock, disassemble and apply release agent to all metal parts. I have some paste wax that I use to make sure the threads in the action have been thoroughly coated with release agent. Press the screws into the wax, and turn the screws into the action's guard screw holes. Unscrew and remove any excess wax. You want a good coating of wax and release agent, but too much of the stuff will build up and you'll lose the close fit and all of the ad-

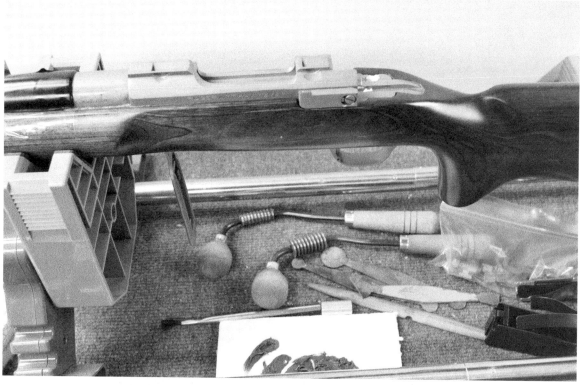

ABOVE: The barrel is bedded and the epoxy curing.

LEFT: The epoxy is applied and ready for the barreled action.

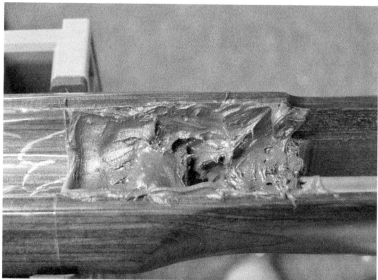

vantages a good bedding job provides. One or two light coats of the spray release agent is usually enough to create a close fit and still provide a good release of the parts when it's time to take the rifle apart after the epoxy is cured. Degrease the aluminum pillars, you don't want them coming out.

Using Devcon Steel putty or Steel-Bed, properly mix with tongue depressors and Popsicle sticks of different widths to get the epoxy down into all of the crevices of the stock. Apply some to the aluminum pil-

lar and install them in the stock. Place the barreled action into the stock and screw everything together. You should notice the epoxy oozing out all around the barreled action top and bottom. If not, you may not have applied enough epoxy. Once you have screwed everything together, remove the excess epoxy with rags and Shooter's Choice bore cleaning solvent. This will quickly remove the excess epoxy, but not harm the stock. Once everything is cleaned up, let the rifle set up overnight. The next day, after the epoxy has cured, you can disassemble the rifle, remove the modeling clay and reinstall the trigger. Drill out the stock's guard screw holes to provide clearance. Remove the tape from the barreled action and screw the rifle together. Torque the guard screws down to 65 in.-lbs. with a torque wrench. At this point, you should be able to take the rifle to the range and see a noticeable improvement in group size.

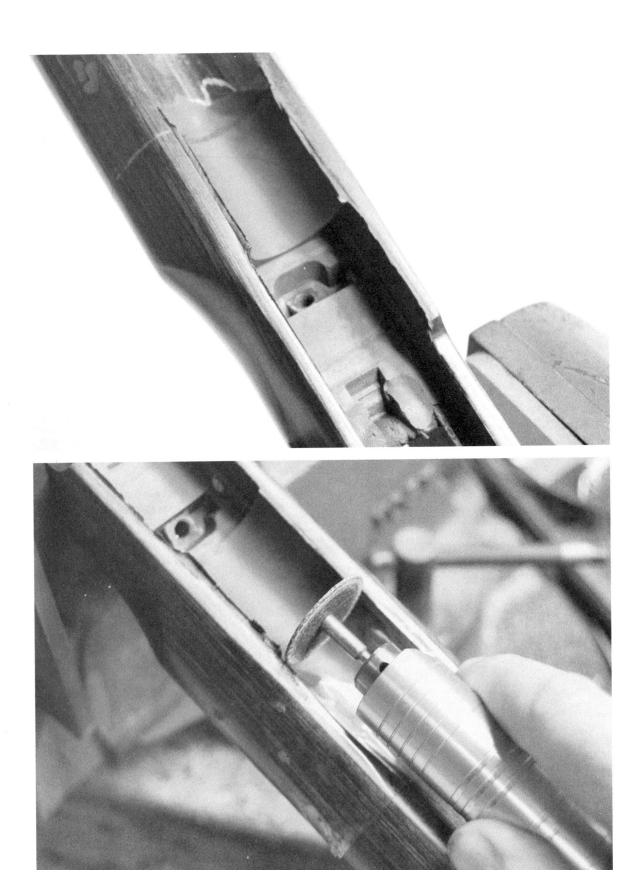

TOP: The bedding as it looks after the barreled action is removed. BOTTOM: The cutoff wheel is used to remove the pad of bedding material in front of the barrel section.

TOP: The bedding complete, and the rifle ready to be reassembled. BOTTOM: The rifle after bedding getting a workout at the range.

Chapter 11

GUNSMITHING THE RUGER 10/22

The Aimpoint made a great accessory for the Ruger 10/22.

The Ruger 10/22 semi-auto rimfire has been manufactured in various forms continuously since it was first introduced in 1964. The rifle is made in a variety of configurations, including a takedown model, sporter model, target and tactical models. Some variants have wood stocks, while others are fitted with synthetic.

The variations and combinations available from Ruger for this popular rifle are too numerous to list here, but suffice it to say, if you include the work that custom shops like Clark Custom Guns and Volquartsen can do, what starts out as a basic .22 semi-auto can turn into a highly specialized, custom rifle. The Ruger 10/22 is very popular with competitive shooters, which drives the aftermarket parts industry.

I purchased my 10/22 in the mid-1980s and have put thousands of rounds through it. It was one of my first gunsmithing projects when I attended the Colorado School of Trades Gunsmithing Course in 1987. Back then, there wasn't much you could really do with the 10/22, other than polish up the internal hammer and sear surfaces, and install a Bullseye spring kit to lighten the trigger pull. I shot it that way for many years and it worked great.

The problem was, even though the trigger pull was lighter, it still wasn't very good, since I didn't do anything to the hammer and sear surfaces themselves. One way to get a really quality trigger pull is to polish those hammer and sear surfaces, but in order to do that, the gunsmith needs to really understand how angles interact, where and where not to polish, and how far to take the work. In order to do the job properly, you need a hammer/sear jig to hold the parts in place while polishing. This also ensures that the angles are kept to original specifications and that the gun remains safe. I cannot stress this enough; anytime you

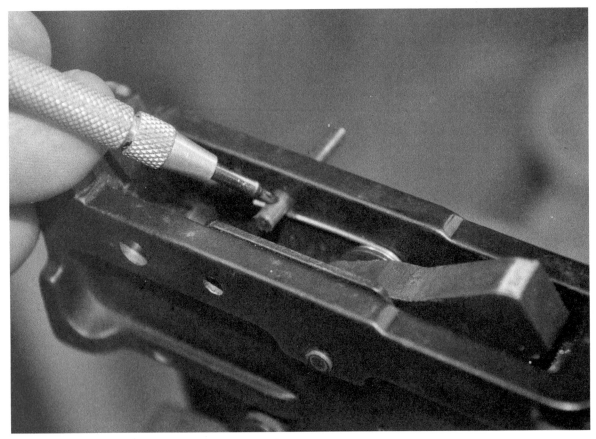

Removing pins is a delicate procedure when they are under spring pressure.

are working on the hammer/sear/disconnector of a firearm, always keep safety in mind — don't stray from factory specifications. Many "gunsmiths" will do things like clip coils off of hammer springs or reduce the engagement of the hammer and sear beyond what is safe. You can get a very good trigger on the 10/22 by a couple of different means, but they always involve keeping safety at the forefront.

RUGER 10/22 TRIGGER KITS

I had obtained a decent trigger pull with the Bullseye spring kit, where I made the trigger pull lighter, but not necessarily better. I wanted both. For this project, I wanted something that would yield a quality trigger with minimum of work, and was something that the average shooter who was fairly skilled with shop tools could do in an afternoon and come up with excellent results. I wanted something that could drop in with little to no fitting and that didn't need expensive fixtures or tooling, and was fairly inexpensive.

Ron Power has been known in shooting circles as the consummate revolversmith. He is a charter member of the American Pistolsmith's Guild and was the 1986 Pistolsmith of the Year. He also makes excellent jigs for the professional pistolsmith and manufactures a line of custom parts for the little 10/22. A quick call to the good folks at Brownells and I had secured a Power Custom drop-in trigger kit for the 10/22.

A quick note about any part by manufacturers claiming to be drop-in. Due to manufacturing tolerances, sometimes this is true and sometimes not. It's not that the parts maker made a mistake, it's just that tolerances being what they are, sometimes parts will fit properly, and sometimes they need to be fitted. Normally, the parts maker will state this on their installation guide, and the gunsmith should just assume that the part may need fitting for proper and safe functioning.

TRIGGER KIT INSTALLATION

Starting with the unloaded rifle, disassembly of the gun is fairly straightforward, and there are many resources to help you if you get stuck. The rifle can be

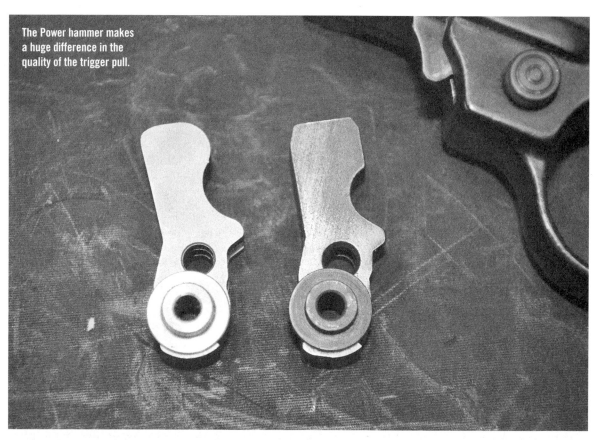

The Power hammer makes a huge difference in the quality of the trigger pull.

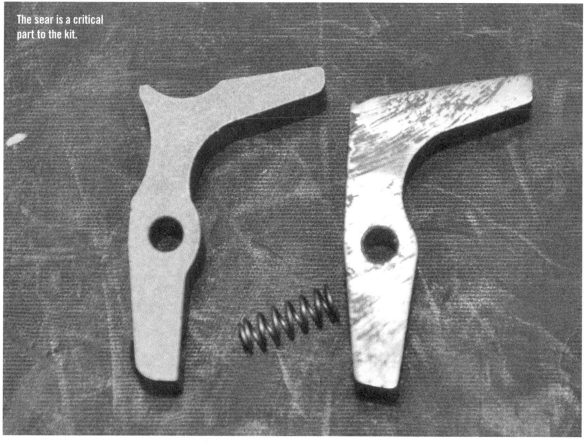

The sear is a critical part to the kit.

disassembled and reassembled with nothing more than a screwdriver and a couple of pin punches. Remove the barrel band and the stock screw. This will allow you to separate the stock from the barrel and action. Push out the two pins holding the trigger group in with an appropriately sized pin punch and remove the trigger group. Push down on the upper arm of the torsion spring to relieve the tension on the upper pin holding in the ejector, which serves as the retainer for the bolt release. Remove the ejector. Push out the magazine catch retaining pin. Remove the bolt release. Push in the magazine catch plunger at the front of the trigger group and drop the magazine release button out the bottom.

Next, make sure the hammer is in the lowered position and push out the hammer pin. Then remove the hammer spring. Remove the sear/trigger pin. There is no need to remove the safety button.

Included with the kit is: Hammer and sear with shims, a cheater pin to help with reassembly, a trigger pivot pin, an extra power hammer spring, hammer bosses, sear spring, and a trigger return spring. The kit has some replacement parts that need to be installed prior to reassembly. One of those parts is the extra pow-

er hammer spring. This is needed because the sear engagement surfaces are so precise, extra power is needed to make sure they stay engaged and that the hammer doesn't follow down when the rifle cycles during firing. Clamp the head of the hammer spring assembly into the vise and compress the spring, then remove the retaining clip, replace the spring and reinstall the clip.

To reassemble, install the trigger, sear and shims and use the cheater pin to hold everything together. Replace the trigger return spring and the disconnector spring. Install the hammer shims between the hammer and the hammer bosses. Make certain you install the torsion spring on the right side hammer boss before you install the hammer and hammer pin.

Once you have the hammer/sear/trigger assembly installed and can cock and release the hammer by pulling the trigger, test it a few times but don't let the hammer fall all the way. Make sure you hold your thumb or finger in front of the hammer to act as a hammer stop to avoid damage to the internal parts. If the hammer does not fall, the pretravel screw needs to be adjusted either in or out until the hammer falls reliably. This will involve a lot of back and forth of assembly, checking, re-

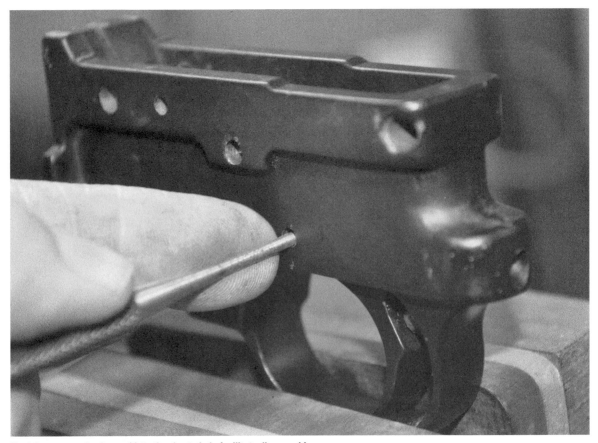

The trigger group is clamped into the vise to help facilitate disassembly.

assembly and checking again. Once the pretravel screw is properly set, apply a small drop of blue Loctite to set the screw. The nose of the sear/disconnector needs to be fitted in order to make sure the safety button can slide under the nose. This is the only real fitting that needs to be accomplished with this kit. Once you have the safety fitted, test it by applying the safety and pull the trigger hard. The hammer should not fall or move forward at all. Slide the safety off and the hammer still should not fall. If the hammer falls during any of these tests, you may have taken off too much material from the nose of the sear or disconnector and the part will need to be replaced. Never dry fire a .22 rimfire rifle or pistol excessively or you can damage the hammer nose, firing pin and chamber.

Replace the remaining ejector, bolt latch, bolt latch spring and plunger and place the upper arm of the torsion spring under the retaining pin. Once the trigger assembly is reassembled, place it back into the rifle using the retaining pins. Cycle the bolt a few times to make sure the hammer stays cocked, and try the safety button again. Assemble the barreled action back into the rifle and install the barrel band and the receiver screw and tighten. Check everything again. Cycle the bolt a few more times. Try the safety again. Cycle some dummy cartridges through the rifle, checking the safeties, pulling the trigger while making sure the hammer doesn't follow the bolt down. After this upgrade, the trigger pull was amazingly crisp and sharp, weighing a shade over 2 pounds.

RANGE TESTING THE 10/22

Once everything was back together, it was time to take the project gun to the range. I mounted the Aimpoint Micro sight onto the rifle and headed out with three different brands of ammunition. I wanted to try the rifle out on static targets and falling plates.

I first loaded the rifle with two rounds, so if it had problems with the sear/hammer engagement, it would only fire twice, not a full magazine. If the rifle doubles even once, then you need to take it back to the bench for diagnosis. I loaded the 25-round Ruger magazine with two rounds, five separate times, then went to five rounds five times, then loaded and shot the full magazine. The rifle functioned flawlessly with the CCI standard velocity and Blazer I fired through it. The Federal HV Gold Medal Match had a couple of hiccups. The combination of a 2-pound trigger and the Aimpoint Micro sight allowed me to knock down the bank of six falling plates at 10 yards, in 2.3 seconds, which for me is not too bad. Once I got the Aimpoint zeroed, I also shot a five-shot group at 15 yards from a supported position that measured about .294.

This rifle project was a fun one. It was a project that was fairly simple for the aspiring gunsmith to take on since the parts were truly drop-in, and only took about 2.5 hours. The results were outstanding, and the cost was very reasonable. It would make a great project for a Saturday. I literally performed the work in the morning, and was on the range shooting after lunch. If you are looking for a great project to start out gunsmithing, you would have a hard time finding a better one than this.

Chapter 12

GUNSMITHING THE SAVAGE MODEL 12 RIFLE

The Timney trigger is fully adjustable for weight of pull and engagement.

The story of Savage Arms is one of entrepreneurial spirit in American ingenuity and the ability to overcome adversity. In the 1800s, the company was able to take on the giants in the industry — Colt, Winchester, and Remington — and not only survive, but innovate and succeed. Today, Savage Arms continues that tradition of innovation with models and features such as the Axis Rifle series and the Accu-Trigger, with specific models for varmint, hunting and target shooting. I have tested two other Savage tactical rifles in .223 and .308 with excellent results using factory barrels, so I was interested to see what I could do with their tactical rifle and a custom barrel in .308 Winchester.

For the project gun, I received the outstanding Savage M12BVSS. This is an all-stainless varmint model in .22-250 with a fluted barrel, laminated stock, and the Accu-Trigger. It has an internal box magazine, which is fine for most types of varmint hunting, but if the rifle is exposed to the elements, or if you want to change ammunition types quickly, it's a bit of a pain. So I wanted to convert this rifle to a detachable magazine, and add a stainless match-grade barrel. Changing the barrel facilitates a change in calibers, from a box-stock .22-250 varminter to a .308 tactical rifle using the same action and trigger. We'll convert the rifle using the factory

bolt and receiver because the .308 and .22-250 cartridge use the same sized bolt face. There are basically three sizes of bolt faces for a centerfire rifle: Small, in cartridges like the .222 and .223; mid-sized, such as the .22-250, .308, .30-06 and others; and Magnum bolt faces for cartridges like the 300 Win. Mag and larger.

In addition to the M12, Savage was kind enough to send me the detachable box hardware for a thumbhole laminated wood stock, and a fiberglass tactical stock with appropriate detachable magazine hardware. The Savage series of rifles are easy to bed since they have a cylindrical action, which makes for a very consistent bedding surface, unlike rifles of Mauser type, which are squarer bottomed.

All rifles pose unique challenges when building and the Savage is no exception. It has its two receiver screws in somewhat different locations than other rifles. The rear action screw is located midway to the receiver, not at the back of the tang. The rear of the tang is floating off of the stock.

To begin, remove the barreled action and internal magazine from the stock by removing the two action screws. Set the stock to the side. The trigger assembly is removed very easily. First, remove the bolt latch and spring by removing the cross pin. Then carefully remove the c-clip holding the Accu-Trigger, and push out the retaining pin. Be very careful and do not lose this c-clip, it's very easy to accidently launch it during removal. The safety bears against an internal spring, which you compress with a punch, and pull out with a pair of needle-nosed pliers. One point about the Accu-Trigger: Do not try to use it without the safety lever. Some shooters do not like the safety lever, just like some shooters don't like the trigger safety on the Glock. But if you remove the safety lever, you run the

The Timney trigger is a great addition to the Savage rifle.

LEFT: The old barrel is removed with the barrel clamp and the Savage head on the barrel wrench. RIGHT: The factory barrel nut is installed onto the Shilen match barrel.

real risk of an accidental discharge. If you want to use a trigger without the safety lever, install the Timney (which we'll do for this project rifle).

In the first phase of this conversion, we'll use Savage's excellent laminated thumbhole stock with a detachable flush-mounted box magazine. And we'll install Shilen's pre-threaded match-grade barrel in .308 Winchester. Savage employs a notched lock nut at the receiver to secure the barrel to the receiver. Use the same barrel vise and wrench you did for the previous project guns, with the exception of the wrench head, which on the Savage has a notch to fit into the barrel nut. Clamp the barrel into the barrel vise. You can even use the same

epoxy barrel inserts as you did for the Remington barrel. Operate the action wrench to loosen the barrel nut from the action and unscrew it from the barrel. You do not have to unscrew the barrel nut very far to break the bond in order to unscrew the action from the barrel.

BARREL INSTALLATION

Installing the new barrel is a snap. The rear bolt plug is removed using a 6mm Allen head. Remove the bolt handle and baffle assembly, pull out the cocking piece pin, and take off the cocking piece sleeve followed by the firing pin assembly. You could actually install the

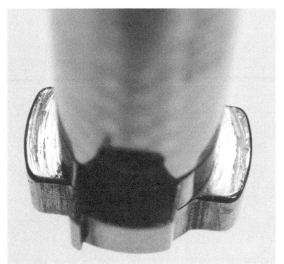
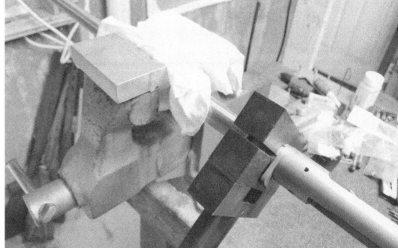

LEFT: The bolt locking lugs are making good contact with the receiver. RIGHT: The action is installed onto the barrel and with the head-space gauges minimum headspace is set.

barrel without disassembling the bolt, but I would recommend against it. Clamp the barrel in your bench vise with a set of AR-15 aluminum barrel blocks, or you can use the barrel vise you used to remove the original factory barrel. Screw the barrel nut onto the barrel, and get out the two .308 Win. GO and NO-GO headspace gauges. Remove the ejector for all rifle bolts in order to get a true reading when using headspace gauges — the ejector can push forward on the gauge and give a false reading. The ejector is removed simply by driving out the retaining pin with a 1/16th-inch punch, and carefully easing out the ejector and ejector spring. Screw on the action, with the recoil lug located onto the barrel about a half inch or so. Reassemble the bolt without the firing pin or ejector in place. Place the GO headspace gauge under the extractor and slide the bolt into the action, continuing to screw the action onto the barrel until it stops. This is minimum headspace. Now tighten the barrel nut onto the action, noting that this will cause the action to slightly unscrew, increasing the headspace.

Make sure the action stays tight against the barrel and does not move, while using the barrel wrench to tighten the barrel nut down on the action. You can also put the action into the vise and tighten the barrel nut down, but make sure the barrel doesn't move or otherwise come off the action as that will increase the headspace. You should now be able to open and close the action with the GO gauge without stickiness or any difficulty.

Keep the bolt slightly sticky against the GO gauge just when the bolt is fully closed. This is the point of minimum headspace, and will give the most accuracy, but may be a little too tight for a tactical rifle — one exposed to the elements — as dirt or debris could cause the rifle not to close on a cartridge. Now try to close the bolt with the NO-GO gauge. The bolt handle should not start to drop down. If it does, you have excessive headspace and need to start the process over again. Again, if you are unsure of your work, have the rifle checked by a qualified and competent gunsmith that is thoroughly familiar with rebarreling centerfire

The barrel is installed
and headspaced.

ABOVE: The polyurethane layer is scraped off with inletting tools.

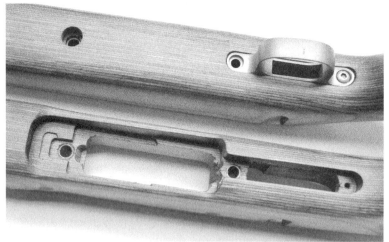

LEFT: The blind magazine rifle stock being replaced with the drop magazine version.

rifles. If you only have a GO gauge but do not have a NO-GO, you can place a piece of Scotch tape on the rear of the GO headspace gauge and try it again. The bolt should NOT close on the GO gauge with this piece of tape in place.

BEDDING THE SAVAGE ACTION: LAMINATED THUMBHOLE STOCK

Now that you have the rifle rebarreled, you can bed the barreled action into the new thumbhole stock (later in this chapter we'll use a different bedding technique to set the barrel and action into a Savage synthetic tactical stock for phase two). Keep in mind that the bedding procedure I'm going to outline could be performed prior to rebarreling the rifle with the factory barrel in place. First, since this is a laminated stock, use scrapers and chisels to scrape off the epoxy finish and get down to the bare wood so the epoxy sticks. The bedding procedure I use is commonly referred to as pillar bedding, and in this case, the engineers at Savage already know this technique and have installed steel pillars into the thumbhole stock, saving you considerable time and effort.

Place a small layer of electrical tape onto the bottom of the recoil lug to make sure the lug does not bottom out when you screw the rifle back together. Place your bedding modeling clay into all of the recess of

The rifle is bedded, and the epoxy flows out well around the stock.

the trigger assembly. Do not try to bed the rifle with the trigger in place. This rifle will get bedded with the barrel completely free floating, so run a single layer of bedding tape around the barrel nut just forward of the recoil lug. Also place a strip of clear tape under the barrel nut and over the stock. This will allow you to lift off the excess epoxy that will flow under this area when it's bedded. Finally, place a roll of electrical tape around the front of the barrel at the forend tip in order to keep the barrel and action sitting square and level, as well as to get the proper spacing of the barrel into the barrel channel. It may take a few turns of tape to get the right spacing, but you'll see how this works when you do it. Place modeling clay into the recess of the trigger area and around the magazine latch of the bottom metal, anywhere you don't want the epoxy to flow.

Before mixing up the epoxy, screw the rifle together to make sure everything fits and functions correctly, including the magazine box. Cycle a few dummy rounds through it again to make sure the rifle's magazine box is positioned properly in the stock and not sitting too high or too low, which will affect feeding and functioning. Cycle the bolt to make sure it's not binding or contacting the stock in the bolt handle notch.

Once satisfied that everything is ready to go, disassemble the rifle, lightly scraping to make sure all of the wood is thoroughly degreased. Coat the guard screws and into the receiver and action threads in paste wax. Spray the action and bottom metal thoroughly with Brownells release agent. Mix the steel epoxy to the 2.5:1 ratio and, starting from the bottom recoil lug recess in the stock, apply epoxy in the receiver area all the way back to the rear guard screw. Remember, you want the rear tang floating, and if the epoxy flows under this area it can be scraped out later. Alternatively, you can place cellophane packing tape under this area to lift it off when you break the rifle out of the stock after the epoxy cures. Once the epoxy has been placed in the upper receiver area, turn the stock over and place four dabs of epoxy into the four corners of the magazine bottom metal, and one spot of epoxy under the rear of the trigger guard, just to make sure the bottom metal is locked in place, and doesn't move around when firing. Use the stockmakers' screws to screw everything together. Use Shooter's Choice and several rags to clean any excess epoxy from around the stock area. Let the rifle set up overnight. This is key, as some people like to break the rifle apart too soon in order to see what their bedding job looks like. Resist this temptation and let the epoxy fully cure overnight, or a little longer if it's cold. My garage at the time I bedded this Savage was in the low 40s, and I let the rifle cure for two days, just to make sure.

Once certain that the epoxy has cured, unscrew the rifle and break the barreled action away from the stock. Use the cutoff tool with the Foredom to cut away the epoxy forward of the recoil lug and lift it from the stock using the cellophane tape. This procedure may leave a small strip of epoxy when you lift out the tape; simply scrape it out with the stockmakers' scrapers or grind it off with a structured tooth carbide bit. Use a small file to take down the epoxy that rises up around the edges of the action flush to the top of the wood. Drill out the holes for the front and rear guard screws using a drill just a shade larger than the guard screws. In this case, the screw shanks are .227, so a .250-inch drill is about right to gain the needed clearance. Remove the modeling clay from the trigger area, and check the locking recess of the barrel for a blob of epoxy that usually gets pushed up in there. Typically, there is enough grease/oil to keep the epoxy from sticking, although sometimes you may have to tap it out with a brass punch. This is not unique to the Savage; it happens with the Remington rifles as well. You can spray release agent into the chamber area prior to bedding, but always degrease any release agent from the barrel/chamber area as lubricant in the chamber can and will increase pressure, possibly to unsafe levels.

At this point, you can reassemble the rifle with the old trigger assembly, function test the gun with dummy ammunition. It's now chambered in .308 Win, and with the thumbhole stock in that caliber, would be a good candidate as a long-range predator rifle, especially for coyotes.

BEDDING THE SAVAGE ACTION: SAVAGE TACTICAL STOCK

During this next phase we are going to convert this rifle to a tactical model with a synthetic stock. First disassemble the rifle, and go through the procedure again, this time with the Savage tactical synthetic stock. This stock is patterned after a McMillan A5, but without the adjustable buttstock and cheekpiece. It does not come with pillars installed like the laminated stock did. We could fit aluminum pillars into it but for this project I'll outline how to use a different technique using "poured" pillars — ones that we create using the epoxy bedding

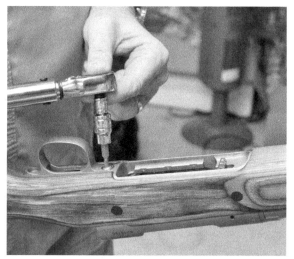

ABOVE: The front and rear guard screws are torqued to 65 in.-lbs. for best results.

BELOW: The rifle with the new barrel bedded into the stock, and the Nightforce scope installed.

ABOVE: The stock is prepped as before, and the epoxy applied to the entire action area. Make sure there is a good amount of epoxy in all the correct areas.

RIGHT: The thin gray line shows where the epoxy bedding has been applied.

material during the bedding process.

Screw the barreled action and bottom metal into the bare stock using the stockmakers' screws. Make sure the bolt can actuate, and the magazine box goes fully up into the magazine well, snapping in place. Cycle dummy cartridges through the gun to make sure everything works as it should. Just to be certain, you can screw everything together with the regular front and rear guard screws instead of the stockmakers' screws, ensuring everything goes together properly. The stock does not have any type of coating that needs to be removed like the laminated stock did, so you can proceed. Check again to make sure the barreled action is sitting square and level to the stock, and make any adjustments needed.

The process is the same: Remove the barreled action and use the modeling clay to plug any areas around the trigger recesses where you don't want epoxy. Place a strip of electrical tape on the bottom of the recoil lug, and tape off the barrel at the barrel nut and forend to achieve proper spacing. Apply release agent in thin, even coats to the barreled action, guard screws and bottom metal. Don't forget to apply the release agent down into the rear of the trigger guard screw threads. Ensure the trigger mechanism is removed at this point.

Mix up the epoxy in the now familiar 2.5:1 ratio and start applying it to the stock, beginning with the guard screw holes. Use a thin section of Popsicle stick to really get the steel putty down and around and into the guard holes. Don't be afraid to put too much down in there as any excess will get squeezed out. Apply to the bottom of the recoil lug area, and work your way around the action. Turn the stock over and apply four dabs at the corners of the magazine box holder, and a small dab at the rear of the trigger guard.

Screw everything together with the stockmakers'

screws and wipe off the excess with rags and Shooter's Choice solvent. Let cure overnight. Once cured, break apart and clean up with the Foredom tool and the carbide bits. Drill out the guard screw holes with the ¼-inch bit you used on the wood stock, and remove the tape from the stock and barreled action. Remove the modeling clay from the action and clean all release agent off the metal parts. Now you can install the trigger parts.

INSTALLING A TIMNEY TRIGGER IN THE SAVAGE M12

As good as the Savage Accu-Trigger is, the project rifle will be upgraded with the Timney adjustable trigger, which is made for the Savage series of rifles. First, install the two-piece safety lever button and spring. The new Timney trigger is installed with the trigger spring and c-clip, then install the bolt release with the bolt release spring and retaining pin. Adjust the new Timney trigger for engagement and weight of pull. Since this is a tactical rifle, you don't really want the trigger to go below 2 pounds, and 3 is even better. Test the trigger with the barreled action out of the stock using the NRA weights for a true reading.

Clean up the excess epoxy from around the stock and the magazine well top and bottom. Install the barreled action into the stock, and secure it with the bottom metal, the two guard screws, and the rear trigger guard screw, which doesn't really do anything other than keep the back of the trigger guard secured to the stock. Torque the front and rear action screws down to 65 in.-lbs. and test the rifle with dummy rounds. It should feed and function perfectly.

To squeeze a bit more range out of this rifle, I've installed the Nightforce 20 MOA tapered one-piece base. Time precluded me from taking the rifle to the range, but I have no doubt it will shoot with the Shilen match barrel, Timney trigger and the bedding job.

RIGHT: The Nightforce scope and the 20 MOA tapered base makes a good combination in .308 Win.

BELOW: The rifle ready to go to the range.

Chapter 13

CUSTOMIZING THE AR-15

The AR platform has proved to be one of the most successful ever designed. Within the last 10 to 15 years or so, the growth of the black rifle has exploded as more and more shooters have discovered how versatile it can be. Since this is just a small chapter of the book, and there have been many written on customizing the AR-15 for a variety of uses, I'll demonstrate a few simple custom modifications that are easily performed to make the AR shoot more accurately, and to improve the ergonomics. Make no mistake, there are literally thousands of potential combinations of ways to set up an AR-15, and the following is but a small sample.

Basically, modifying an AR platform really comes down to improving the accuracy, trigger pull quality, and ergonomics, or the way the rifle interfaces with the shooter. For this project, DPMS was kind enough to supply me with a basic flat top. The DPMS has a Picatinny rail on top of the upper receiver for mounting a variety of optics, and is a good base gun with which to start. There are many manufacturers of AR platforms, including Colt, Bravo Company, Daniel Defense, Noveske Arms, and many, many others.

Since our project gun is to be used for 3-Gun competition and not tactical use, per se, we want the most accuracy we can get — to handle the tough shots out to 500 yards or so. A quick call to Brownells and I was able to secure a match-grade stainless barrel chambered in .223 Wylde, which allows you to fire both .223 and 5.56 ammunition in the same gun. I also received a muzzle brake, Magpul forend, pistol grip and buttstock, JP Enterprises adjustable trigger, and two sights — a C-More red dot and the Ultra Dot. Both optics are extremely popular in competitive shooting circles. I also acquired a Blackhawk! single-point sling and Magpul mounting hardware. Finally, a Surefire tactical light rounded out the mods for this gun.

MODDING THE AR-15

First, the handguard is removed by pulling back on the retaining ring and lifting up and out. Sometimes, especially with a new rifle, the retaining spring under the retaining ring is quite stiff and may require brute force to remove. A helper tool like a tape-covered flat screwdriver blade can help. (When I was a Small Arms Tech in the 82nd Airborne Division, we would work on dozens and dozens of M16s each week and many handguards could be a real bear to remove if the rifles were new. Older ones did not have this issue as the spring had much less tension.) Next, the pistol grip is removed using the screw inside the grip, but be careful: the pistol grip houses the spring and detent that provide tension to the safety selector. Always have a drawer full of various small parts for the AR-15 rifle, since it's easy to lose them, and they wear out as well. Springs and detents are cheap, and replacement ensures the gun works as it's supposed to without delay. On the same note, the AR, as well as other firearms, uses roll pins. These are OK for one-time use, but once removed they should be tossed and replaced. When driven into a hole, the cold-rolled steel pin fits via spring tension. Once removed, however, it will never have the same gripping power as when new. So, always toss roll pins and replace them with a new one every time you drive one out of a firearm.

To remove the buttstock, loosen the latch and pull down to slide the buttstock off the buttstock extension. Remove the bolt and bolt carrier by pushing the rear receiver hinge pin from left to right, unlatch the carrier handle and pull the bolt carrier and bolt handle out. Set them off to the side. You'll take the bolt out

The Magpul forend, muzzle brake, gas block with Picatinny rail, and Surefire tactical light on a cantilevered rail is one way to configure the AR platform for many types of shooting.

ABOVE: The barrel wrench is used to install the new barrel.

RIGHT: The old barrel is removed and the new one installed and tightened with the barrel nut wrench.

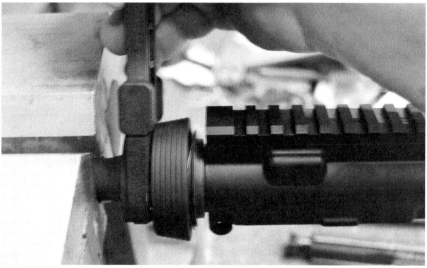

later. The test rifle didn't have a front sight, so, with the handguard off, remove the gas tube and gas block by driving out the retaining roll pin with a 1/16th-inch punch. Always start driving out pins with a short stubby starter punch, then use the longer pin punch to drive out completely. This keeps the punch from needing when encountering a stubborn pin, which will happen at some point. Clamp the gas tube in the padded vise and slide it forward and off the rifle.

AR-15 BARREL REMOVAL

To remove the barrel, you'll need a couple of special tools. The barrel block will hold the barrel securely, and the barrel nut tool will allow you to unscrew the barrel nut holding the barrel on. You may have to use a little bit of rosin on the vise blocks to keep the barrel from turning. Once the barrel nut starts to turn, unscrew it all the way off and remove the upper receiver. Since for this project we are using the same handguard mounting system as the original, and not installing a free floating barrel, keep the nut, spring and retainer and place them off to the side. Slide the upper receiver off of the barrel and set it off to the side as well.

TRIGGER WORK

For the hammer and trigger, drive out the retaining pins for these two parts from either direction. Make sure you capture the disconnector that sits on the trigger as

The JP Enterprises hammer installed with the hammer retaining pin.

well. It's spring loaded, although the spring should be captured by the trigger. The JP Enterprises trigger is fully adjustable for engagement and overtravel, and is an easy drop-in fit. It comes with an extended Allen wrench to make the adjustments, and will yield a clean, crisp trigger pull of about 3.5 lbs. Install the trigger with the disconnector by placing it under the safety selector, and driving the pin in from either direction. Replace the hammer with the hammer spring oriented correctly. The top loop goes behind the hammer, not in front. Push it down into the receiver and drive the retaining pin into place. Always adjust the engagement first to make sure the rifle is safe, and then tweak the overtravel screw. JP Enterprises provides excellent instructions for installation. Once the trigger parts have been installed and adjusted, put a tiny amount of blue Loctite on the threads to keep the adjustments from moving during firing.

Once you have the trigger installed, check the engagement by holding the hammer back past the point where it engages the trigger; squeeze the trigger and release it, it should be captured by the disconnector. If not, you don't have sufficient engagement. Once the engagement is set, adjust the overtravel screw to provide a firm stop just past the point at which the hammer is released by the trigger. For a competition or tactical rifle (or any firearms for that matter with an overtravel stop) do not set the stop too close, as dirt can get into the mechanism, preventing the firearm from firing. The trend now is to install modular trigger systems that have the hammer and trigger integrated into a single, drop-in unit, and there are several on the market from which to choose.

INSTALLING THE MATCH BARREL

The next step is to install the match barrel. Since we are keeping the original barrel nut and handguard retainer, simply install the barrel nut assembly onto the barrel, and slide the upper receiver on using the barrel nut wrench to tighten the barrel nut until the teeth line up so the gas tube will slip through the upper receiver and barrel nut assembly. Install the forend retainer cap and the gas block. This rifle is using a barrel that requires a mid-length gas tube and handguard assembly, so make sure you order the correct parts when building your rifle. There are three lengths; short, mid-length and extended. The barrel we used has fixed headspace, but you should always check for proper headspace in any new barrel with a correct GO gauge and the rifle bolt, with the ejector removed.

Once the barrel is installed, secure the gas tube with the set screws using blue Loctite to ensure the gas block stays secure. Now, install the muzzle brake, again with blue Loctite. The pistol grip is installed, along with the

LEFT: Once the old barrel is removed and the new one installed and tightened, the gas tube is reinserted through the receiver and back into the gas block. RIGHT: The new handguard is installed with the snap ring in place.

safety spring and plunger. The Magpul buttstock has a latch and a lock installed on it. The latch is pulled down, allowing the buttstock to slide onto the buttstock extension. When the buttstock is at the length you desire, the locking latch is squeezed, which locks it in place.

OPTICS

As mentioned at the outset, I opted for the C-More tactical railway model with an aluminum body and a click switch. I took the rifle to the range and put the rifle through its paces. Then, I brought the rifle home and switched to the Ultradot Match Dot. There are other sights out there that would be appropriate for 3-Gun from Leupold and Nightforce. Dot sights are superior for shorter range, while the Leupold rifle-type scopes work well at extended distances. I took the rifle back to the range and put about 300 rounds through it without issues. The AR platform is a great system because you can configure it in many different ways.

The C-More sight and Ultradot were taken to the range with the rebarreled rifle.

TOP: The best part about working on custom guns is the range time! BOTTOM: The AR platform, even in this legal short-barreled version, is a good candidate for customizing.

Chapter 14

SCOPE MOUNTING

Mounting an optical sight on a rifle is one of those things that can seem fairly straightforward on the surface, but once you actually start doing it, can go sideways very quickly. When mounting a scope you must make sure it's securely mounted and installed on the rifle straight and level. It needs to be securely mounted because, obviously, you don't want it coming off the rifle while shooting. Catching a scope in your lap, when it's supposed to be on the rifle, is not conducive to good accuracy. Also, even slight looseness in the scope can cause huge shifts in the point of impact, especially when shooting past 100 yards. It may seem like you have the scope on tight, but looks can be deceiving — especially with sharp recoiling firearms. You must follow proper torque settings for each part of the mounting system to ensure rock-solid optics. Straight and level are critical because you want to have available the maximum click adjustments in all directions. If you mount a scope and have to use up almost all of your windage or elevation just to get the rifle zeroed, you'll have little to no adjustment left to account for point of impact variations in different ammunition. The scope reticle must be as mechanically centered as possible to give you the widest range of adjustment.

So for this book I'm going to focus on two types of mounting systems for a centerfire rifle, and the correct way to get the scope securely mounted so it can do its job when needed.

TWO-PIECE BASE AND RINGS

The first application I'll talk about is the standard, steel two-piece base with scope rings that utilize a dovetail mount. The dovetail ring fits into the base very snugly by rotating 90 degrees. Many manufacturers use this type of system because it's strong. I prefer two-piece steel bases over one-piece, because with the latter, if the receiver's mounting holes are not lined up with the screw holes machined into the base, tightening the base screws can induce stress into the scope mounting system. Granted, it won't be much, but any stress is to be avoided for maximum accuracy. With the two-piece base, if the front set of screw holes are not aligned with the rear, you can correct that offset somewhat.

To get started, make sure the receiver threads are cleaned of any oil, grease or residue. If rebarreling the rifle, and you have the barrel off the receiver, go ahead and chase out the scope base mounting threads with a good, sharp thread tap. Often the threads have been damaged by attempts from other people to install a scope. Cross threading is a fairly common occurrence with people

The front and rear scope rings need to be centered with each other. The alignment tool is very useful to see if the rings are misaligned.

who are unfamiliar with firearm tools and techniques.

If you are removing an old scope and can't get the original screws out, they may have been screwed on too tight, or the wrong thread locking compound was used, probably the latter. Loctite makes various grades of thread adhesive. Blue is for small/fine threads that you want to be removable, red is for threads that you want to be permanent. Green is for larger threads like 1911 compensators that you don't want to remove later. Always use blue Loctite for base screws, and never use any adhesive on the ring screws. If you can't get the base screws off and you suspect someone used the wrong adhesive, remove the scope, and take the barreled action out of the stock. Place a wet towel around the receiver and you can carefully apply heat to the screws with a propane torch to break the bond of the adhesive.

The next step is to degrease the screws and the threads in the receiver. One of the best degreasers I've found is Acetone, but it is highly flammable. Automotive brake cleaner works well, too, and has an additional benefit of being in aerosol form. Compressed air is very useful when mounting scopes, or anytime working on firearms around the home workshop. I have a small air compressor from Sears that I bought new for about $120.00 that works very well around the shop.

Once the base screws are degreased, mount the front and rear bases without thread locker. Remove the front base screw and look down into the threads of the receiver and the tip of the screws to see if the screw has bottomed out on the barrel threads. If it has, shorten the screw on a bench grinder to make sure there is no contact between the front screws and the barrel extension. Don't use a file on the screws — they are too hard and you will end up damaging the file. Screw the bases down onto the receiver and attach the rings to the base.

With the Mark 4 mounting system explained later, always attach the rings with the large, keeper nuts to the left of the receiver, rather than on the right, as you don't want anything interfering with the proper ejection of cases. However, with the dovetail mounting system, attach the top half of the ring of the front set and rotate the ring into the dovetail with a 1-inch piece of wooden dowel rod; a hammer handle works as well. Leupold makes a handy ring wrench for this purpose. The dovetail system causes the most frequent misalignment issues with regards to the front and rear rings, although you also want to check misalignment with the Mark 4 mounting system. The rear ring is adjustable for windage and you want to get that as centered as possible.

When selecting the rings for your particular rifle, always try to get the correct height for your gun. Most scope manufacturers offer low, medium and high rings

The dovetail system is very strong, but the front and rear ring need to be matched up and aligned for stress-free scope mounting.

ABOVE: The scope needs to be mounted as close as possible to the barrel, without touching.

RIGHT: The lapping tool, with a small amount of lapping compound, will make the rings round and concentric.

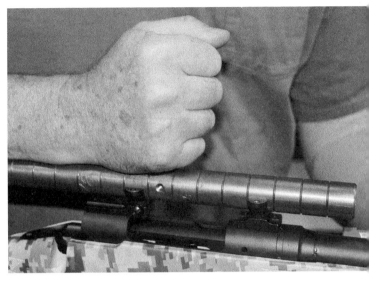

to accommodate various mounting situations. Choose the combination that mounts the rings at the lowest possible height.

With both rings mounted on the bases, check front to rear ring alignment. Brownells makes a nifty scope ring alignment tool for this task that checks for angular misalignment. With today's modern mounting systems, you will not likely have to shim the bases to get the rings aligned for elevation, but with side to side or angular misalignment you will need to correct with a lapping tool. Install the scope alignment tool onto the rings and lap them with the lapping compound and plenty of oil until you get about 90 percent contact with the bottom ring. When lapping the rings in, rotate the tool side to side as you run it front to back. Use a figure-eight motion. This will put even pressure all the way around the

base of the ring. Check your work as you go, keep good contact. Eventually, you will remove the finish from the bottom of the ring and you will see what kind of contact you are getting.

Once you have the rings lapped in, remove them and the bases and clean all lapping compound and oil before reinstalling the bases. This time, apply blue Loctite on the base screws only. I usually clean everything with a good solvent, then degrease using acetone or brake cleaner.

Mark the bottom rings so you don't get them mixed up. Put the mark on the left side of the rings for orientation — a single stake mark on the rear ring and double stake mark on the front ring. This ensures proper orientation after lapping in the rings. Install the bases. Tighten the base screws down using a torque wrench, the 6-48 screws to about 22 in.-lbs., the larger 8-40 screws torqued to 26 in.-lbs.

The scope ring keeper nuts are torqued with a torque wrench.

LEUPOLD MARK 4 MOUNTS AND RING SYSTEM

The other type of system I'll cover is the Mark 4 mount and ring system from Leupold, which uses a Picatinny rail for the base. These all-steel ring and base systems are very tough.

When installing the Mark 4 rings and bases, the large ½-inch keeper screws on the rings should be torqued to 65 in.-lbs. Install the rings and use the scope ring alignment tool to line everything up. Make sure you have equal gap between the top and bottom

The lapping process will reveal where contact is being made, and where it isn't.

rings, this maintain even pressure when you tighten the top ring screws. And it looks much more professional.

SCOPE LEVELING AND BORE SIGHTING

With the rifle leveled, place a target on the wall using a level. Align the vertical crosshair with the vertical lines on the target and you're good to go. You can also do this in your garage by setting the scope on its lowest power and marking a plumb line on a wall across the garage, for instance.

Now that the rifle is leveled and the scope is mounted and tightened, bore sight it at home to save time when at the range. This process ensures you have the crosshairs aligned with the probable point of impact. Again, Brownells carries a neat little laser bore sighter that makes quick work of getting the rifle on paper at 100 yards. The Site-Lite Level is a laser bore sighter that mounts into the barrel with a spud. The bore is protected with O-rings on the spud, and the laser target is placed about 25 ft. away. Turn the laser on and point it at the target provided. Then place the crosshairs just above the red dot, and you will be on paper at 100

yards. The Site-Lite also has a crosshair alignment grid with a built-in level that makes quick work of aligning the crosshairs vertical and horizontal.

Once you have the scope mounted and bore sighted, take the rifle to the range for zeroing. If you run out of time to bore sight at the bench, it's really easy to bore sight a bolt-action rifle at the range. It's also really easy to get the rifle zeroed with one shot. This one shot method will save you much time, ammunition and frustration when zeroing a rifle. How many times have you been to a range and watched a shooter trying to zero a rifle with a friend as they take a shot and call out, "Three clicks left." They then take another shot, "Four clicks up," and so on. The "One-Shot Zero" method I'll outline has been around for decades, and I'm surprised more shooters don't know about it. I first read about it in Jim Carmichaels' The Book of the Rifle.

Zero the rifle from a solid bench, using a front pedestal rest and a rear sandbag. This technique can be used off of a front bipod, but it's much less effective. Set the rifle on the front and rear rests, making sure the rifle will recoil in a straight line without impediment. That is, make sure the front swivel stud will not crash against

Zeroing and testing the McMillan tactical rifle after mounting the Leupold Mk 4.

the front rest when the rifle is fired. Remove the scope caps and the turret caps, if the scope has them. Remove the bolt, and while holding the rifle as steady as possible, look down the center of the bore. Place a zero target at 100 yards. Look through the bore and center the target, while moving the scope crosshairs to the same point on the target. You want the intersection of the center of the bore to coincide with the crosshairs at the same point on the target. You should be able to look through the bore, and the scope, going back and forth between the two, superimposing each at the exact same spot in the center target. Congratulations, you've successfully bore sighted the rifle!

Carefully replace the bolt and load the rifle. Sit at the bench behind the rifle and carefully place the crosshairs back on the original aiming point you used to bore sight the rifle. Now, using your best bench shooting technique, fire a single, well-aimed shot. You should have a bullet hole somewhere on the paper. Careful-

ly place the crosshairs back onto the target using the original aiming point used to fire the first shot. While you are looking through the scope, and holding the rifle as carefully and as steady as possible, have a shooting buddy turn the windage and elevation turrets so the crosshairs "walk" down to, and ultimately intersect, the bullet hole from that first shot you fired. Once the crosshairs and the bullet hole coincide you've zeroed the rifle with one shot! You may need to sometimes fire another shot or two, since it's very difficult to hold the rifle absolutely steady while your shooting buddy turns the windage and elevation knobs on the scope. But you should be within about an inch or so of being zeroed. This technique is very effective and will save you quite a bit of time, ammunition and.

Properly mounting a scope doesn't have to be intimidating. Once you have the proper tools and install a few, it becomes easier and you'll have the confidence to tackle other projects.

Chapter 15

RIFLE CLEANING BASICS

For many people, cleaning firearms after a fun day at the range is about as exciting as a trip to the dentist. But just like a good teeth cleaning, maintaining your firearms is important to proper function and longevity. Certain classes of firearms require more cleaning and maintenance than others. Fully automatic firearms require regular cleaning because of the volume of rounds put through them. Handguns are different. I've shot literally hundreds of rounds of factory ammunition through my Glock 17 with little to no cleaning. Not that I recommend doing that, I was just seeing how susceptible the gun was to malfunctioning when I first purchased it. That being said, neglecting your firearms will definitely increase wear and tear as the powder fouling builds up, acting like an abrasive when parts rub together.

Reloading your own ammunition can affect how often you need to clean your firearms. Certain reloading powders are known to be "dirtier" than others. Semi-automatics are prone to malfunctions due to lack of cleaning. This chapter I'm going to focus on cleaning and maintenance tips for the bolt-action rifle. Most of these tips are not specific to any particular brand.

There are two ways to clean a rifle, the quick way and the thorough way. The quick method involves focusing on cleaning all of the powder and copper fouling from the bore, and a quick wipe on the bolt with a small amount of oil in strategic places. A more thorough method is to disassemble the rifle from the stock, remove the trigger from the action and disassemble the bolt.

QUICK CLEANING METHOD

I'll start off with the quick method for cleaning a rifle after a trip to the range. If you're shooting a precision rifle for best accuracy, clean the bore after every 20 shots or so, ideally after 10 rounds. That means taking your cleaning gear to the range. Clean the bore when testing ammunition and switching from one type or brand to another, or when changing bullet weights even within the same brand. That'll keep your test and evaluation beginning from a clean rifle for each variable, so it does not skew your data.

To begin, let's assume that you didn't clean the rifle at the range and have brought the rifle home after firing about 20-30 rounds. Make sure it's unloaded, then

There are dozens of cleaning products on the market and these are just two.

place it in a rifle cradle. This makes it easy to clean and inspect. There are several on the market but I really like the Lyman cradle. The rifle I'm using for this chapter is the Savage Precision Carbine in .223, so some aspects will be different for your particular gun regarding disassembly and reassembly.

Open the bolt, and press the trigger while depressing the bolt removal latch. Remove the bolt and set it off to the side. Since this is a quick clean, you're not going to remove the scope or the barreled action from the stock, but you will when doing a more extensive cleaning.

Since the scope and barreled action will stay attached, you need to protect them from the cleaning solvents. This rifle has the Leupold Mk 6 tactical scope already mounted, it comes from the factory with scope covers so make sure they are closed when cleaning. This is especially important when on the range trying to clean the rifle when the wind is blowing. Cleaning solvents can damage the coatings on any optics, so be careful to protect them.

There are a couple of tools that are crucial to proper rifle cleaning. One is a bore guide. This is a tool that does a couple of important jobs. Probably the most important is to protect the bore of the rifle from the cleaning rod itself. Dirt, grit and powder fouling can become embedded in the cleaning rod, and if the rod contacts the interior of the bore it can damage the

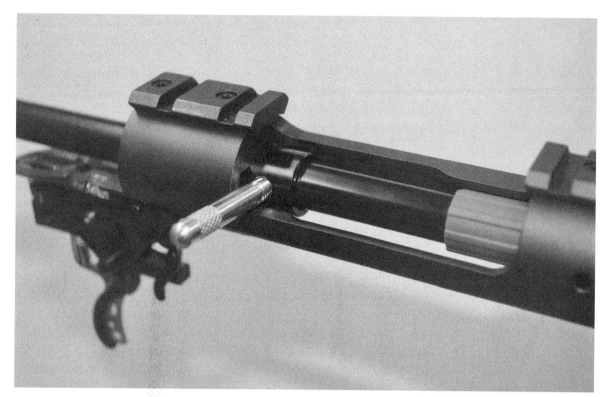

ABOVE: The bore guide is extremely important to properly clean the precision rifle.

RIGHT: The bore guide offers a cleaning port to allow you to apply cleaning solvents conveniently.

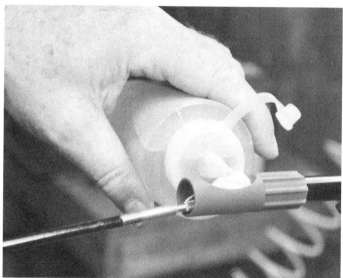

lands and grooves, degrading accuracy over time. The bore guide and the coated cleaning rod both originated from the benchrest shooting community — shooters obsessed with accuracy. The bore guide keeps the cleaning rod centered in the bore and away from the rifling. Its other function is to keep cleaning solvents from entering the stock when pushing solvent soaked patches through the bore. It does this by sealing off the chamber area so the excess solvent doesn't run back into the action area. This is especially important with a wood-stocked rifle. Solvent can soak the wood, causing the stock to get spongy under the front and rear guard screws causing the accuracy to go south really fast.

You also need a coated, one-piece cleaning rod. For years, the gold standard has been the Dewey rod. Make sure you use the correct type of jag, one which grabs pieces of patch and not the loop type — run the patch through the bore and then let it fall off when it exits the muzzle. Never drag a dirty patch back through the bore.

And don't use a jointed cleaning rod in a precision rifle. Be diligent to always wipe off the rod between passes.

There are two types of chemical solvents to use for cleaning a rifle. One removes powder fouling and the other takes out copper fouling. Both need to be utilized in order to get the barrel clean. For powder fouling, I use Shooter's Choice. For copper fouling, Sweet's 7.62 does the trick.

The ways to remove fouling and copper residue can be categorized as either removing it chemically with

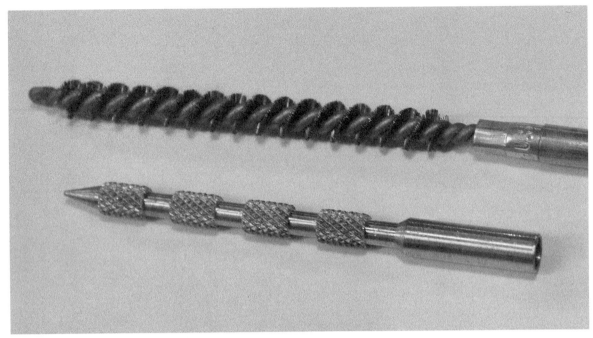

ABOVE: Use brushes and pointed jags on your cleaning rods for best results.

LEFT: Push the patch through the rifle and let it fall off the bore.

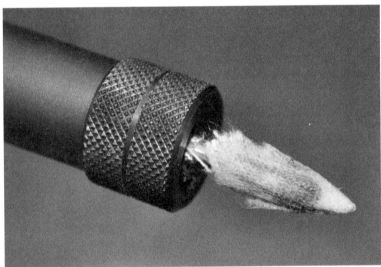

in still in the bore. Also, when you pull the brush back through the bore, ease it back into the barrel to protect the critical muzzle crown from any possible damage. I usually push a new solvent-soaked patch after about every five strokes or so. This cleaning regime takes care of the powder fouling, but you also have to remove the copper fouling. Push a patch with a neutral solvent or a couple of dry patches to re-move the Shooter's Choice before using Sweet's sol-vent, so you don't create a chemical reaction. Some say this chemical reaction can etch the bore. When using Sweet's Copper remover, never use a brush, just keep pushing wet patches through the bore until they come out clean. Patches will come out with a blue residue, indicating that the solvent is working as it should to remove copper. Never leave Sweets in the bore. Push dry patches through until the bore is completely dry. Once the patches come out clean, your barrel has been cleaned. It doesn't take long and is vital to keeping a precision rifle shooting at peak accuracy.

solvents or mechanically with mildly abrasive com-pounds. Chemical solvents like Shooter's Choice and Sweets do a great job. Some people like to use various abrasive pastes like JB bore compound, which doesn't use chemicals, but an extremely mild abrasive paste to remove powder and copper fouling.

The gun cleaning process is to remove the bolt and install the bore guide. Find a patch of the appropriate size. Wet the patch and push it once through the bore and let if fall off when it comes out of the muzzle. Install a bronze brush on your rod, and push the brush back and forth through the bore — once for each shot fired. Make sure you completely exit the bore before you pull it back through. Never reverse direction while the brush

Spray-type cleaner is a great way to clean out the trigger mechanism of any rifle.

DEEP CLEANING THE BOLT-ACTION

If you are performing a deep clean on the rifle, all of the above applies, but you need to remove the barreled action from the stock. If the rifle has been exposed to the elements, rust can form very quickly between the action and the stock. Remove the scope, and turn out the stock screws. Lift the barreled action from the stock. Place the barreled action in a padded vise and perform the cleaning steps as outlined above.

Since you have the barreled action out of the stock, wipe down all of the exterior surfaces with an oily rag, and clean out the trigger mechanism. One good way to clean out the trigger without removing it is to spray it out with brake cleaner. This will clean the interior trigger surfaces, remove water, dry fast and won't leave any residue. I usually don't put any oil in the trigger mechanism since this will just attract dirt.

When reassembling any precision rifle, you'll need a torque wrench that measures in a range of 20-100 in.-lbs. The Leupold tactical scope rings need to be torqued to a specific setting, as do the nuts that secure the mounts. Also, the front and rear stock screws need to be torqued. Remember, this cleaning regimen does not just apply to tactical rifles, but to any rifle that you want to keep shooting as accurately as possible, be it a varmint, competition, or custom hunting rifle. And when it comes right down to it, when we are talking about rifles, isn't accuracy what it's all about?

Chapter 16

CUSTOM REMINGTON 870

The two shotguns featured in this book represent the opposite ends of the spectrum. The Remington 870 pump action has been used as a standard police model for decades. And the 11/87 autoloader is one of the most popular waterfowl and upland game shotguns on the market. But as good as these guns are, they can always be improved by the application of aftermarket parts and the ingenuity of a custom gunsmith.

Setting up a Remington 870 shotgun for defense is easier than you may think. Keep in mind that this gun can also be used in 3-Gun competition in the Heavy Metal Division, where the only firearms allowed are 12-gauge pump shotguns, .308 rifles, and .45 ACP handguns.

For the project shotgun, I selected the Scattergun Technologies ghost ring sights with tritium inserts, a sidesaddle shell carrier, Timney sear, Vang systems oversized safety button, Magpul buttstock with spacer system and raised cheekpiece, and a Surefire 6V tactical forend light. I also selected a Trulock tactical breacher combination muzzle brake and stand-off, an extended magazine tube, Kick-Eez recoil pad, and opted to Magna-port the barrel and add a Blackhawk! sling.

Since the rear sight on this gun has to be precisely located, I sent the gun off to Accurate Plating to have them drill and tap the rear sight holes on their milling machine. This could be performed on a drill press, but it can get a little tricky, especially with a small bench drill press. Once the receiver came back, I turned to the trigger group. I wanted to install the excellent Timney sear unit, which comes with three sear springs to set the trigger pull to the weight desired. I chose the mid-weight spring for a trigger pull of about 3 lbs.

The sidesaddle shell carrier, ghost ring rear sight, and Magpul sling attachment are essential Model 870 upgrades.

To install the trigger, drive out the two trigger group retaining pins, and lift out the trigger group. Compress and lift out the sear spring, and remove the shell lifter by disengaging the c-clip and pushing out the lifter retaining pin. Be careful to retain the carrier dog and spring. Then drive out the sear retaining pin. Replace the sear with the Timney unit, and press in the sear retaining pin. Then, using the Silver Bullet, press in the large carrier retaining pin, and replace the c-clip. Replacing the safety is a simple matter of pushing out the retaining pin and safety, inserting the new safety and replacing the retaining pin. Be careful not to lose the spring and detent. Note that the Timney sear has a set screw that allows for small adjustment in the trigger pull weight once installed.

To modify the barrel, I opted to lengthen the forcing cone, and install a Rem Choke system so I could install the breacher muzzle brake. I first installed the Scattergun Technologies front sight, which is accomplished by mixing the included epoxy, degreasing the front sight and front sight base on the barrel after removing the front sight bead. Apply the epoxy, wipe off the excess, and secure with a rubber band. Let it set overnight and you're done.

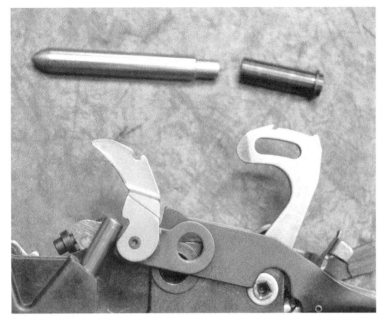

TOP: The Timney sear is a great addition. The Silver Bullet is used to replace the carrier retaining pin. Don't lose the c-clips or the carrier dog spring. BOTTOM: The Scattergun Technologies front sight is epoxied on and secured with a rubber band until cured overnight.

Next ream the choke for the choke tube, and lengthen the forcing cone. Lengthening the forcing cone is a very common modification among shotgun competitors to reduce recoil. Factory forcing cones have a fairly sharp angle from the chamber to the bore, which makes the shot column slam into the forcing cone when the gun is fired. The shot column slows down when it hits this sharp angle, increasing recoil force against the shooter. Lengthening the forcing cone allows the shot column to transition from the chamber to the bore gradually. This operation can be performed by hand with a spiral flute forcing cone reamer and a tap handle, with a little cutting oil. The job should only take about 30 minutes. Flush out the chips and oil and you're done.

Installing the Rem Choke is a little more difficult. This operation should really be done with a lathe or a floor-mounted drill press. Since this book is about projects for the home hobbyist, I reamed the choke by hand and it took about 13 hours, whereas if I would have reamed it on a lathe, it should only take about an hour. Ream the barrel until the rear shoulder of the reamer butts up against the face of the barrel. There are calculations that need to be performed in older barrels or barrels of questionable thickness prior to any choke reaming. Be absolutely certain the barrel has sufficient wall thickness before you do any type of choke work.

When performing an installation of screw-in choke tubes on shotguns, and machining the barrel to accept screw-in chokes, measure the outside diameter (O.D.) with a micrometer to determine if there will be sufficient wall thickness after machining. Measure the O.D. of the barrel and the O.D. of the tap for the particular gauge. Subtract the O.D. of the tap from that of the barrel, divide by 2, and this will give the wall thickness after machining, providing the O.D. of the barrel is concentric with the inside diameter (I.D.). A sample calculation appears below.

Barrel O.D. (12 Gauge)
Tap O.D. (12 Gauge) Win-Choke™
.850-.814=.036 / 2 = .018 Wall Thickness – Anything thinner than .015 wall thickness is not a candidate for screw-in chokes.

Since this is a new Remington shotgun barrel, I knew it was of sufficient thickness for screw-in Rem chokes, but always measure just to be sure before proceeding. Without sufficient wall thickness the end of the barrel could blow out when the gun is fired, causing injury or death.

The choke reamer is used by hand, with some extra muscle from the author's son. This job should really be done in a lathe, but can be done by hand. Once properly reamed, the tap is used to cut the threads.

Before you start to ream the barrel, install the pilot onto the reamer. There are different sizes of pilots, so pick the one that gives the best fit. Ream the muzzle until the rear shoulder of the reamer just touches the face of the barrel, then — using the same pilot — tap the threads for the breacher. The reamer has two steps, so make sure you understand that the shoulder of the reamer is the rear, or second shoulder, and ream all the way to the rear of the reamer. Carefully follow the instructions provided by the reamer manufacturer. If performed incorrectly, the barrel muzzle can burst on the

first shot due to the choke serving as an obstruction in the bore. Again, if you are unsure of how to do this, take your gun to a qualified gunsmith and have them install your choke tube. The breacher, also known as a stand-off, allows you to breach doors — you can press the end of the breacher against the door lock or door hinge, or both, and blow them off using a special breaching round. Fun stuff. The teeth keep the breacher from slipping off the door, and the cutouts serve as a muzzle brake to safely vent the gas sideways.

One caveat with the use of the breacher; Right now,

The breacher, Scattergun Technologies sights, Mag-na-porting, elongated forcing cone, long mag tube, and the Surefire light are all installed.

The Kick-Eez recoil pad is installed just like any other pad.

the shotgun has an extended magazine tube that reaches almost to the end of the muzzle. This will make it a little difficult to effectively use the breacher the way it's supposed to be used. Since this gun is my house gun, I can leave it like that since I won't be blowing off locks and hinges in my house anytime soon, and I want the extra rounds that the longer magazine extension provides, but if it were a dedicated breaching shotgun, I would install the shorter, two-shot magazine extension to make sure there was clearance for the breacher to make contact with door hinges without the magazine tube also hitting the door.

After installing the front sight and breacher, turn your attention to the buttstock and forend. There is a special tool to remove the forend retaining ring. Once that's removed, you can install the Surefire tactical light onto the forend hanger and screw the ring nut down. Put a small amount of blue Loctite to make sure the forend retaining ring doesn't loosen up with firing. A steady diet of slugs and buckshot through the gun will generate a significant amount of recoil, and the Loctite will keep the retaining ring in place, but will also allow it to be removed later if needed.

The Magpul buttstock is very simple to install. It and the cheekpiece work very well with the Scattergun Technologies ghost ring rear sight.

ABOVE: The shell latches can be tightened if needed, with the shell latch tool from Brownells.

RIGHT: The breacher and Mag-na-porting work well to redirect gas, reducing recoil.

In order to install the extended magazine tube, remove the stop pressed into the tube by the factory. This stop limits the number of shells that can be loaded into the tube. Brownells sells two tools that can remove this detent: a dent raiser, and a magazine tube swage that both work great. I used the swage to remove the limiter in my firearm. Be sure that the limiter is completely removed, and that by using the swage, it doesn't raise material on the outside of the tube and cause the forend to bind when cycling the action. Usually, the swage will raise a small amount of material on the outside of the magazine tube; always check for this. I had to file the outside of the tube, and used my Foredom with a 120-grit sanding drum on the inside of the tube to eliminate the stop completely from both the outside and inside of the magazine tube. Once removed, install the shell follower, and check to see if it binds around the area of the magazine limiter you just removed. Consider using the fluorescent shell followers that have bright visibility, telling you if the gun is empty.

Next up is installing the buttstock and fitting the Kick-Eez recoil pad. Remove the old recoil pad, which will expose the buttstock mounting bolt. Remove the buttstock, and install the Magpul sling attachment, then the Magpul buttstock. This model has a separate raised cheekpiece that can be added. It's an important detail since the Scattergun ghost ring sight forces the head a little higher, and the cheekpiece comes in handy to get a good cheek weld when firing the gun, especially with harder kicking rounds. The buttstock also has a

Firing the 870 shows how the porting and muzzle brake and lengthening the forcing cone is really effective for controlling recoil.

spacer system to adjust the length of pull. Since I'm taller than six foot, with fairly long arms, I installed a couple of the spacers. The Kick-Eez pad is ground and fitted as covered in the rifle section of the book. Once mounted, the buttstock installation is complete. Install the bolt assembly and forend back into the gun, along with the barrel. Reinstall the trigger group, and with the cross bolts provided, install the sidesaddle shell carrier onto the side of the receiver. Install the extended magazine spring into the magazine tube, and screw on the extended mag tube. I used a clamp by Blackhawk Industries that secures the extended tube to the barrel, and also provides a sling mounting point on one side, and a Picatinny rail on the other. I opted to install a two-point Blackhawk sling. Cycle the gun with dummy rounds about a dozen times, and then it's time to go to the range.

The combination of muzzle brake, Mag-na-porting, long forcing cones, and the Kick-Eez recoil pad makes

for the softest recoiling 870 shotgun I've ever shot. My son and I shot the gun with a variety of loads, from #7 1/2 birdshot, to #4 buckshot, to 00 buckshot and Federal slugs in 3-inch shells. All of them were easy to shoot and the combination of the light, crisp trigger, Scattergun Tech ghost ring sights, and the Magpul stock made for a quick-pointing, fast shooting gun.

TESTING THE M870

I waited for dusk to see if I could see some flame escaping from the barrel ports and the muzzle brake of the upgraded Model 870. I was not disappointed. The Mag-na-porting and the muzzle brake work to redirect the gas, softening and controlling recoil. The Surefire light was very effective in lighting up targets at dusk. The light has a momentary pressure switch and a permanent on-off switch as well. This shotgun is now ready for tactical, home defense, or 3-Gun competition.

TOP: This shotgun was fun to shoot with its noticeably low recoil. BOTTOM: The two-point sling helps the shooter control the recoil of the shotgun.

Chapter 17

CUSTOM REMINGTON 11-87

3-Gun competition is one of the fastest-growing forms of competitive shooting in the U.S. Setting up a Remington 11-87 for competition is not difficult, and not too different from the Model 870 as customized for tactical use. Many of the same tools and techniques are used. You do not need to ream and tap the barrel for choke tubes, because the barrel is already fitted with them, but you can install the Carlson 3-Gun tubes, which extend out the end of the barrel about an inch, and are marked IC, MOD and FULL.

Like the Model 870, I did have the barrel Mag-na-ported, and lengthened the forcing cone. I also installed the same Timney match sear and medium sear spring, along with the Vang Systems oversized safety button used on the 870. Finally, I used my orbital sander to rough up the buttstock and forend, and then degreased and applied Brownells Spray grit to them for additional grip. A Kick-Eez recoil pad was likewise installed. Finally, since there are, at times, some really long shots for the shotgun stage of a 3-Gun match, including some out to 70 or 80 yards, you should install a set of Tru-Glo fiber optic turkey hunting sights. These are attached to the ventilated rib with screws, and offer a more precise way of aiming when firing slugs at long distance.

You'll have to iron out the shell limiter in the magazine tube, just like you did on the 870, and file down the exterior of the magazine tube as well as polish the interior to make sure the gun feeds shells flawlessly. Later, you can install a Picatinny rail onto the receiver in order to mount some type of optical sight, but for now, the set of iron sights are very quick and solidly mounted.

HOW THE 11-87 SHOOTS

Being a semi-auto, the 11-87 is a soft-shooting shotgun as it is, but adding in the Mag-na-porting, extended forcing cone, and Kick-Eez pad, it becomes a very, very easy-to-shoot autoloading shotgun. It would be a comfortable gun to get you through a long day of 3-Gun practice. In my experience, shotguns tend to get practiced with the least, since they do have rather stout recoil.

Patterning the shotgun with the Carlson's choke tubes was performed with a small variety of loads at 20 yards. At that distance, the diameter of the patterns were pretty much equal with the IC, MOD and FULL chokes, and only when the distance grew did the shot patterns start to open up and the difference in pattern diameter become apparent.

TOP: The Remington 11-87 comes stock with the Rem Choke system, so it's easy to substitute the stock choke with a set of 3-Gun choke tubes from Carlson's. The Carlson's tubes are marked for easy recognition, and come in a handy case. They provide ready references to which choke is installed. BOTTOM: The Mag-na-port barrel porting works well for semi-auto shotguns without affecting functioning.

Tru-Glo sights offer a more precise aiming system for long shots presented in some 3-Gun matches.

Chapter 18

FIREARM FINISHES

Once you've completed work on a firearm, the next step is to apply some type of protective finish to the gun. Working on the firearm involves filing, grinding or machining bare metal. However, once you're done making chips, the metal needs a protective coating. That's true even if the metal is stainless steel or aluminum, since both of these metals — while very corrosion-resistant — can still corrode. So, this chapter will provide an overview of the various finishes available to the custom gunsmith.

BLUING

Bluing is one of the oldest finishes, and is applied to carbon steel parts. It's a very beautiful finish, but is also one of the most fragile. Bluing is actually a controlled oxidation process, and does not provide much in the way of corrosion resistance. Nonetheless, it's still a popular finish, especially for high-end rifles and shotguns. The key to a good bluing job is in the metal preparation, as any surface imperfections will be magnified when the bluing is applied. For this reason, sanding and polishing are more important than the actual bluing process. Since bluing is accomplished with caustic salts at very high temperature, the finish is best left to the professional. You can do all of the metal prep work, then send the firearm off to a pro to have the finish applied. A variation of this is known as rust bluing.

PARKERIZING

A phosphate coating applied to carbon steel that has been bead or sand blasted is known as Parkerizing. It's a common finish for military firearms and can be either a zinc or manganese phosphate finish. The downside to Parkerizing is, it cannot be applied to non-ferrous metals. But it's a good looking and fairly durable finish when applied. It can also be applied by the home hobbyist, since the temperature the chemicals operate at are much lower than in the bluing process. You will need a sandblasting cabinet with fine glass beads, as sand can be too aggressive and will change the dimensions of small parts.

ELECTROLYTIC NICKEL

This finish has been used on firearms for a very long time, and was popular in the 1980s. It's a plating process and, while not as durable as hard chrome, is still very tough and water-resistant. It has a slightly gold hue to it, and is very pleasing to the eye on two-tone guns, with a nickel frame and blued slide.

HARD CHROME

This is not automotive bumper chrome. Hard chrome is a very hard, industrial plating that gives the gun a "stainless steel" look. Hard chrome is a plating process that builds up on the part when applied. So the gun cannot be too tight before the plating process or parts can become overly tight. It's been a very popular finish in the firearms industry for many years. Hard chrome can be finished with either a "brushed" 400-grit finish, or a matte, non-reflective finish. The STI pistol I built for this book was finished by Accurate Plating and Weaponry in brushed chrome, and came out beautifully.

BLACK-T

A proprietary finish offered by W. Birdsong and Associates, Black-T is a multi-step process that involves Parkerizing the parts, and then applying a Teflon coating. It can be used over a variety of metals, including aluminum, brass, stainless steel and others. It has a very low coefficient of friction, and all parts, once coated, need no lubrication. It's a beautiful, extremely durable industrial finish that's used by agencies such as the FBI and U.S. Navy. Black-T is also available in green, known as Green-T.

ROBAR

Robar offers several finishes for the firearms aficionado, including NP3 and NP3 Plus. NP3 is an electroless nickel finish popular with many shooters, with an added element of Teflon. It's very durable and attractive. Also offered is their Roguard finish. This is also a Teflon-based black finish that meets the U.S. Military Machine Gun Dry Firing Requirements after 60 days sea water immersion or 1,000 hours salt spray MIL-STD-TEST. I paired Roguard with the NP3 Plus finish for an old-school two-tone finish on my little Officer's Model 1911 built for this book and it's one of the most attractive finishes of any firearms I have. The nice aspect of Roguard is that it's a very thin finish, only about .0005 inches thick, but is still incredibly durable.

Robar also offers Poly-T2, one of the most durable finishes available, which conforms to the industry's corrosion protection necessary to exceed 1,000 hours salt spray exposure. It's available in various colors, including black, tan, and more. I had the tactical Remington .308 rifle built for this book coated in Poly-T2 Gunmetal Grey. It matches up really well with the Spectre finish of the McMillan stock. Robar also offers other finishes as well, including traditional bluing and blackened stainless steel.

CERAKOTE

Cerakote is the latest coating available for firearms. Instead of Teflon-based, Cerakote is an oven-cured ceramic that is applied in a very thin coating. It's available in a wide variety of colors and patterns and, as a licensed process, certified Cerakote finishers are widely available, making the turnaround time for having the finish applied very short, usually just a few days. It has very high corrosion resistance and is super durable.

Chapter 19

HOW THE
PROS
DO IT

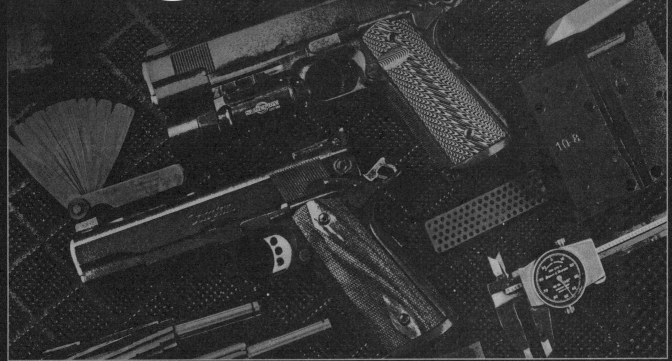

The United States Army Marksmanship Unit (USAMU) was established March 1, 1956 at the direction of President Dwight D. Eisenhower to raise the standards of marksmanship throughout the U.S. Army. USAMU is composed of six competitive shooting sections utilizing world-class facilities for both training and competition. The team's primary mission is to win at all levels of competition. Facilities consist of 260 acres with 8 ranges and 18 buildings. Service Rifle, Action Shooting, International Rifle, Cross Functional Team Pistol, Shotgun and the Paralympic team comprise the shooting sections. The unit makes or customizes its own small arms and much of its own ammunition through the Custom Firearms Shop. That shop, headed up by Steven Young, employs gunsmiths, machinists, range technicians and ammunition loaders as the "backbone" of the unit.

One of the benefits of this expertise is that much of the firearms and ammunition knowledge and technology spills over from the competition side to the individual soldier. As a result, the combat readiness of the Army is greatly enhanced. During my time as a summer pickup shooter with the Army's Marksmanship Unit #1, I was able to visit the gunsmithing shop on several occasions in the mid-1980s when I stayed at Ft. Benning during the shooting season, and talked with many of the pistolsmiths at the time. For this book, Mr. Young was gracious enough to grant me an extensive interview about the Unit. We discussed the professional men and women that make up the Custom Shop and the custom gunsmithing they perform in order to put quality firearms into the hands of champion shooters, day in and day out.

Civilian gunsmiths work alongside military gunsmiths with the common goal of making the finest firearms and ammunition in the world.

LEFT: USAMU civilian gunsmiths working on the match .22 rifles of the unit. RIGHT: The shooters and custom gunsmiths of USAMU work together to support each other and collaborate on solutions to constantly improve.

The pistolsmiths at USAMU work on a variety of handguns for different types of competitions, including Bullseye, Action Pistol and USPSA.

BAR-STO PRECISION MACHINE

Bar-Sto Precision Machine has been making autopistol barrels since 1967. Bar-Sto barrels have been used by the U.S. Marine Corps Marksmanship Unit since 1977, as well as for the Army Marksmanship Unit, National Guard, Air Force, and the Special Operations community. They have also been used to win every major pistol tournament worldwide, including Camp Perry, the U.S.P.S.A. Nationals, Steel Challenge, the Masters, and many more. Irv Stone III currently owns and operates the company founded by his father. They do custom work on a wide variety of firearms, and also offer custom work beyond simply fitting their own products, including customization of the 1911, Glock, STI, Sig, Springfield XD and Browning Hi-Power. They also offer complete guns for sale, including a Limited Class STI in .40 S&W designed for USPSA competition.

Pistolsmith of the Year. Irv Stone III.

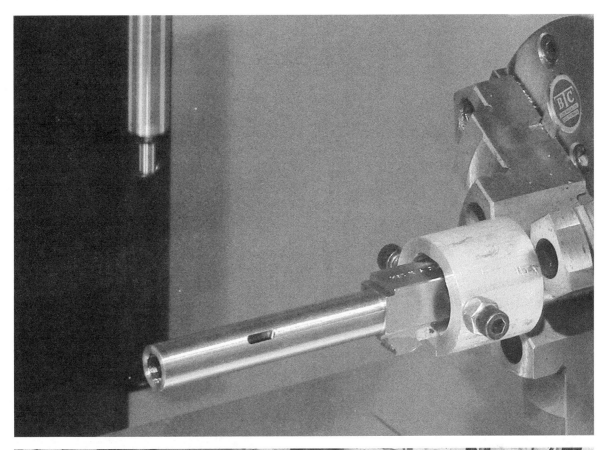

TOP: The barrel making process includes fluting the barrels at Bar-Sto Precision. BOTTOM: Controlled chaos of the custom gunsmith. Irv Stone III at work.

Bob Cogan of Accurate Plating and Weaponry milling the slide for a dovetail front sight.

ACCURATE PLATING AND WEAPONRY

Accurate Plating and Weaponry (APW) opened its doors in 1977 and has been in operation ever since. They recently moved from Florida to Alabama, and continue operations from there. They are a full-service gunsmithing shop specializing in some of the finest finishes in the industry, including hard chrome, nickel, and Cerakote. APW also offers metal refinishing to the firearms industry, and some of the biggest manufacturers send their guns to them to be finished. Yet, if you simply need a rear sight screw drilled and tapped, they are not too big to accommodate individual small jobs. The STI I built for this book was coated in hard chrome by them, and they also finished the Government Model and the tactical model I built for this book in black and Sniper Gray Cerakote, respectively. In addition, they drilled and tapped the receiver for the rear sight on the 870 shotgun.

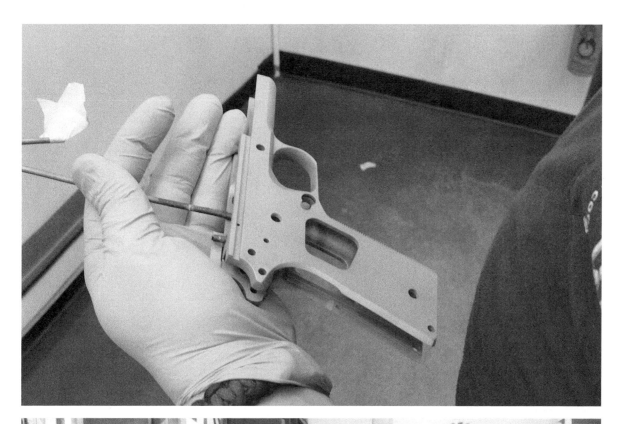

TOP: The author's 1911 frame getting a Cerakote finish. BOTTOM: Bob Cogan, President of Accurate Plating and Weaponry at work.

8 CYCLES OF FIREARM OPERATION

FEEDING	The cartridge begins its journey toward the chamber. The cartridge is stripped from the magazine, or introduced by hand, (single-shot rifle, break-open shotgun) and begins to go up the feed ramp.
CHAMBERING	The cartridge is held by the extractor (if controlled round feed, or CRF) or otherwise pushed into the chamber by the bolt, and seated into the chamber.
LOCKING	The breechbolt/cylinder/slide/breechblock is locked into position with the receiver/barrel. This part is critical in that the two parts — breech and barrel/receiver — must be locked together in order to contain the expansion of the propellant gas that is burning in the cartridge case.
FIRING	The trigger mechanism is released and the primer struck, detonating the primer and igniting the gunpowder held in the cartridge case. This burning powder then propels the projectile/shot column down the bore.
UNLOCKING	After the projectile leaves the barrel, unlocking occurs. The breechblock/bolt is disengaged from the barrel/receiver assembly.
EXTRACTION	The spent cartridge case, still being held by the extractor, is removed from the firing chamber.
EJECTION	The cartridge case is fully removed from the chamber and is forcibly expelled from the firearm.
COCKING	The firing mechanism is reset, ready to go through the cycle again.

THE 5 MODES OF FIREARM OPERATION

BLOWBACK	The pistol's breechblock — in the case of small handguns, the slide — is locked to the barrel by tension of the recoil spring and the weight of the slide. When the firearm is fired, gas pressure overcomes the spring pressure and the mass of the slide, causing the slide to move rearward, hence the term "blowback." The slide is literally blown back by the force of the expanding gas. This is common in firearms shooting low-powered pistol cartridges such as the .22LR and some submachine guns.
RECOIL OPERATION	The slide/breechblock is locked together with the barrel/receiver for a short distance, and moves rearward as a unit during recoil until unlocked — usually by camming action or some other means. You can view this in the 1911 pistol by carefully pulling the slide to the rear, and observing how the barrel and slide move as a unit for a short distance, until the barrel drops down and the slide continues to the rear. This type of operation is also common in a variety of firearms from handguns and shotguns to the venerable Browning .50-caliber machine gun.
GAS OPERATION	A small amount of the expanding propellant gas is siphoned off when the bullet, traveling down the bore, passes a small gas port drilled into the barrel, usually close to the muzzle end of the barrel. This expanding gas is used to actuate the operating system, typically some type of operating rod attached to the breechbolt. Gas operation is a very common mode of operation and widely used in a variety of firearms from shotguns and rifles to some medium belt-fed machine guns.
RECOIL OPERATION WITH GAS ASSIST	A fairly obscure mode of operation that was used in coaxial machine guns like the M219. Here, the main mode is recoil operation, but the barrel has a jacket shroud and an internal tapered section in which the expanding gas, escaping from the muzzle, impinges to "push" the barrel rearward.
DELAYED ROLLER LOCKED	Proprietary to the HK family of small arms. The bolt is locked to the barrel by spring pressure and a set of steel rollers that are cammed into recesses in the barrel/receiver that keep the two locked together until pressure drops to a safe level so the two can unlock.

SUPPLIERS

Brownells, Inc.
200 South Front St.
Montezuma, IA 50171

www.brownells.com

Clymer Tools
1605 West Hamlin Rd.
Rochester Hills, MI 48309

www.clymertool.com

Nightforce Optics, Inc.
336 Hazen Lane
Orofino, ID 83544

www.nightforceoptics.com

STI International, Inc.
114 Halmar Cove
Georgetown, TX 78628

www.stiguns.com

Caspian Arms Ltd.
75 Cal Foster Dr.
Wolcott, VT 05680

www.caspianarmsltd.com

ABM Ammunition
4275 N Palm Street
Fullerton, CA. 92835

www.buyabmammo.com

Savage Arms, Inc.
100 Springdale Road
Westfield, MA 01085

www.savagearms.com

Hornady Mfg.
3625 West Old Potash Hwy
Grand Island, NE 68803

www.hornady.com

Leupold, Inc.
14400 NW Greenbrier Parkway
Beaverton, OR 97006-5790

www.leupold.com

Oehler, Inc.
P.O. Box 9135
Austin, Texas 78766

www.oehler-research.com

National Rifle Association of America
11250 Waples Mill Road
Fairfax, VA 22030

www.nra.org

Black Hills Ammunition
PO Box 3090
Rapid City, SD 57709

www.black-hills.com

Federal Premium Ammunition
900 Ehlen
Anoka, MN 55303

www.federalpremium.com

Blue Grass Sportsmen's League
2500 Handy's Bend Road
Wilmore, KY 40390-8029

www.bgslinc.com

Sturm, Ruger & Co.
411 Sunapee Street
Newport, NH 03773

www.ruger.com

Ransom International Corporation
P.O. Box 25519
Prescott Valley, AZ 86312

www.ransomrest.com

Smith and Wesson
2100 Roosevelt Avenue
Springfield, MA 01104

www.smith-wesson.com

Bar-Sto Precision Machine
3571 Hansen Ave.
Sturgis, SD 57785

www.barsto.com

Glock, Inc.
6000 Highlands Parkway
Smyrna, GA 30082

www.glock.com

Nosler
115 SW Columbia St
Bend, Oregon, USA 97702

www.nosler.com

Sig Sauer, Inc.
72 Pease Boulevard
Newington, NH 03801

www.sigsauer.com

SureFire
18300 Mount Baldy Circle
Fountain Valley, CA 92708

www.surefire.com

Remington Arms Company, LLC
870 Remington Drive
Madison, NC 27025-0700

www.remington.com

C-MORE Systems
680-D Industrial Road
Warrenton, Virginia 20186

www.cmore.com

Ultra Dot
6304 Riverside Drive
Yankeetown, FL 34498-362

www.ultradotusa.com

Accurate Plating and Weaponry
5229 County Road 99
Newville, AL 36353

www.apwcogan.com

Mag-na-port
41302 Executive Drive
Harrison Township, Michigan 48045-1306
www.magnaport.com

The Robar Companies, Inc.
21438 N. 7th Ave, Suite B
Phoenix, AZ. 85027

www.robarguns.com

McMillan
1638 W. Knudsen Dr., Suite 101
Phoenix, AZ 85027 USA

www.mcmillanusa.com

H-S Precision
1301 Turbine Dr.
Rapid City, SD 57703

www.hsprecision.com

Shilen Rifles, Inc.
P.O. Box 1300
Ennis, TX 75120

www.shilen.com

Wenig Custom Stocks
103 North Market St
Lincoln, MO 65338

www.wenig.com

Sporting Arms and Ammunition Manufacturers Institute (SAAMI)

www.saami.org

GUNSMITHING SCHOOLS

Colorado School of Trades
1575 Hoyt St.
Lakewood, CO 80215

www.schooloftrades.edu

Iowa Valley Community College
3700 S Center St.
Marshalltown, IA 50158

www.iavalley.cc.ia.us/grinnell

Lassen Community College
478-200 Hwy 139
Susanville, CA 96130

www.lassen.cc.ca.us

Montgomery Community College
1011 Page Street
Troy, NC 27371

www.montgomery.edu

Murray State College
One Murray Campus
Tishomingo, OK 73460

www.mscok.edu

Pennsylvania Gunsmith School
812 Ohio River Blvd.
Pittsburgh, PA 15202

www.pagunsmith.com

Piedmont Community College
Person County Campus
1715 College Drive
Roxboro, North Carolina

www.piedmontcc.edu

Pine Technical and Community College
900 Fourth St. SE
Pine City, MN 55063

www.pine.edu

Trinidad State Junior College
600 Prospect Street
Trinidad, CO 81082

www.trinidadstate.edu

Yavapai College
1100 E. Sheldon St.
Prescott, AZ 86301

www.yc.edu

Wabash Valley College
233 East Chestnut
Olney, IL 62450

www.iecc.edu.wvc

NRA Summer Gunsmithing Program
https://gunsmithing.nra.org/

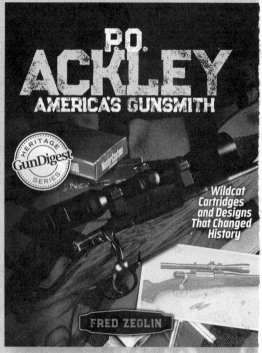